THE
BUSINESS OF
SUSTAINABLE
WINE

HOW TO BUILD BRAND EQUITY IN A
21ST CENTURY WINE INDUSTRY

SANDRA E. TAYLOR

To: Linda

Enjoy!

Sandra

WINE APPRECIATION GUILD

Business of Sustainable Wine
How to build brand equity in a 21st Century Wine Industry

Managing Editor: Bryan Imelli
Book designer: Publishers' Design and Production Services, Inc.
Cover designer: Chris Matulich

ISBN: 978-1-935879-30-5

Catalog in publication data on file with the Library of Congress

Wine Appreciation Guild
is an imprint of
Board and Bench Publishing
www.boardandbench.com

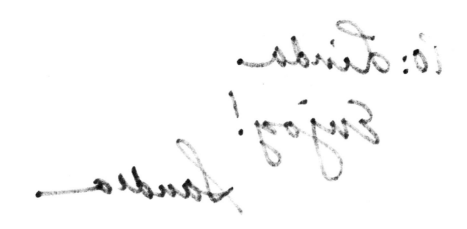

CONTENTS

iii

INTRODUCTION

HUMANKIND needs a clear way forward to a sustainable future, and agriculture can be a key driver. Of all human activity, modern agriculture is the largest single contributor to global greenhouse gas (GHG) production, to deforestation, and to water consumption. Protecting and improving the natural environment are fundamental, and issues like biodiversity, climate change, energy, soil degradation, and water scarcity need to be addressed.

Scientists and professionals are far from having clear and irrefutable recommendations. Every decision in agriculture today has myriad rippling consequences. Even when we take "obviously green" or sustainable approaches, such as continuous applications of organically approved applications of copper to soil, the result will often lead to counterproductive consequences.

The key to an effective and sustainable response, it seems to me, is to accept that there is not one perfect earth-supporting choice or end-state. Rather, to be realistic and successful, we have to direct our everyday behaviors strongly toward more sustainable outcomes without dogmatism. It is my belief that human-caused climate change is bringing extraordinary and likely catastrophic changes to life on earth, unless we work collectively and quickly to reverse our damaging practices and behaviors in order to pursue a more sustainable future. To reverse our many damaging practices, we must become informed about the practices and how they can be monitored and measured and then shifted toward greater sustainability.

As awareness is growing among businesses, sustainable sourcing is becoming a point of differentiation in the marketplace. Moreover, customers are increasingly concerned about where their food comes from and pay greater attention to whether it is produced in a responsible way, but often without a clear understanding of how best to determine the provenance of the foods and beverages they consume. Public interest in this type of product is on the rise, judging by the commercial success of many food products that guarantee protection of the environment and respect for ethical and social principles.

The necessity of industry collaboration is clear as we consider the inherent complexity of managing biology-based production systems. With improved information and understanding, our choices as consumers, producers, or distributors can then reflect more pro-climate and pro-earth preferences.

If almost all of us shift our everyday behaviors in the direction of informed sustainable consumption and production, we have a chance to collectively impact our earth's future.

My goal in writing this book is to use the world of sustainable wine to help all of us gain important insight into the complicated world of agricultural sustainability and what it is for a wine to be a sustainable food product. Drinking and learning about wine is fun. Moreover, among agricultural products, wine is uniquely positioned to open the door to the world of sustainable agriculture.

WHY WINE IS UNIQUELY POSITIONED TO HELP ADVANCE SUSTAINABILITY IN AGRICULTURE

First, wine is a broadly consumed agricultural product that consumers regularly engage in and enjoy gathering knowledge about their purchases. This is unlike nearly any other common agricultural product. Think of corn, zucchini, bread, cheese, or other products. It is highly unlikely when purchasing these products that buyers know or pursue the location of the product's origin or the details about its processing. Yet with wine, both the consumer and the producer will often focus on the wine grape's place of origin and the details of the wine's making. Wine is the only major agricultural product where consumers and retailers can visit websites of growers and winery producers to learn about the specific origin of the product, the growing conditions and practices encountered in that growing year, and the prescribed approaches used during the crush, fermentation, racking, and aging.

Second, wine growers and producers and even some retailers are now making available to the public information about product sustainability. Today, unlike other agricultural products, consumers can fairly easily learn about many growers' pursuit of biodynamic or organic farming or about a winery's drive to make their wine sustainably. The information is available from self-reported comments in marketing materials and websites and from third-party certification programs.

Third, since wine is a fully international agricultural product that, as a bottled good, always retains its identity of origin, we can easily compare the sustainability practices of various wine regions around the world and factor the burden of transportation into an overall assessment of environmental and climate impacts.

Fourth, because many wine buyers are informed consumers and because the information about a wine's sustainability (or not) is becoming readily available, whether the product originated locally or internationally, consumers and their proxies—the retailers and distributors—can now factor in the value of sustainability in their purchase decisions. Today in the United States, there is a strong and growing consumer contingent that prefers to purchase organically grown and unprocessed food. As (and if) sustainability (which is quite different than organic, as this book will reveal) becomes better understood, informed consumers will be able to direct their purchasing power toward the specific wines and other products that are identified as being sustainably produced.

For these four reasons, I write this book to share a new view of the role that the world of wine plays in creating a sustainable future for our planet—environmentally, socially, and economically. In wine regions worldwide, vineyard managers, farmers, and winery owners are implementing better growing practices, preserving biodiversity, and conserving energy. In some regions, there is an increasing emphasis on social responsibility due to community circumstances and economic conditions of farm labor. Consumers will be introduced to the various systems and certification programs that have developed globally to ensure sustainability for the wines they drink. I will differentiate them according to the varying level of standards to be achieved, their value, and authenticity toward improving the natural environment and will point out where those in the wine value chain—producers and distributors—are failing and could do much better.

WHAT THE READER WILL LEARN FROM THIS BOOK

Sustainability certification programs have been fairly well embraced by many (but not all) winegrowing regions around the world. These programs naturally vary from country to country, and even within regions, as climatic conditions differ. Yet sometimes they even differ within a single state; in the United States, multiple certification programs abound with little standardization. Compounding these differences are abundant misconceptions, even among the highly informed, about what it is to farm sustainably or organically or to operate a winery sustainably. (Hopefully, this book will help clear up these many misconceptions.)

Understandably, consumers are confused, and the certification seals and claims affixed to bottles of wine can exacerbate this confusion. Those in the trade—retailers, hotels, restaurants, sommeliers, event planners—have become curators in a sense for their customers regarding sustainable food and beverage products, yet they too lack a real understanding of the differences between, and relative effectiveness of, sustainability certifications and assertions in wine.

Producers will receive tools so they can make better choices going forward— tools and frameworks for how to go about integrating sustainability into their winegrowing. This will be done through presenting case studies.

Consumers will be able to make sense of certification and sustainability labels. I will clear up confusion and explain a complex topic that is of interest, both consumption interests and environmental interests, and provide easy "thumbnail" takeaways to assist consumers in making purchase decisions.

The wine trade will find support for their decisions to offer sustainable products to customers across many product lines and to satisfy the customer who is socially and environmentally conscious. This book will assist retail chain procurement managers in assessing sustainable attributes of wines on offer.

A number of books have been written on this topic—sustainable, organic, biodynamic, natural wines—several of which have treated the subject lightly or incompletely. Some simply describe the history and motivations of selected winemakers. Others, while informative, are limited to specific regions. In addition, there are many well-researched and statistically documented academic papers that have studied a specific aspect of consumer behavior, supply chain theories, or environmental practices in the wine value chain.

What is offered here is a book, international in scope, that appeals to the educated consumer and the producer alike; to the wine collector who seeks to expand her knowledge about specific wines and winemaking; the retailer and sommelier who want to be knowledgeable about the sustainability trend as it applies to grape growing and wine consumption; and the environmentalist who is becoming more interested in sustainable practices of wine production and how the wine industry can push the agricultural world toward increased accountability for climate change.

Based on government data, economic analysis, available research papers, relevant industry data, original research, and interviews, this book will offer a new view of wine as an important factor in sustainable agriculture, leading the way for a more responsible approach to our common future. Besides, can you think of a more fun product to help consumers and producers understand their role in pushing the agricultural world toward increased sustainability? I can't!

The focus will revolve around the U.S. consumer. The United States in 2010 became the largest wine-consuming nation in the world, surpassing France for the first time. The U.S. wine industry is benefiting from a domestic population of almost 311 million people—five times the size of France's—and a surge of young people becoming interested in wine.

California's wine output accounts for 61 percent of the consumption volume in the US. With the U.S. as the largest consuming nation, wine producers from around the world want to sell in the US market. On the East Coast of the United States, 50 percent of wine consumption is composed of imports, whereas west of Chicago it is mostly consumption of California and other U.S.-made wines. For these reasons, the geographic focus of this book will be on wine consumption in the United States and will examine the sustainability programs of the top wine producing nations, and regions, that are suppliers to the U.S. market.

Today, wine is taking on a new, unique attribute as industry participants throughout the winemaking world are working voluntarily and cooperatively to establish broad sustainability certification programs. Previously, the coffee, cocoa, and tea industries adopted a limited sustainability program when they endorsed the Fair Trade program in response to the urgings of social activists. By its internal motivation and its broad sustainability programs, the wine industry is helping to lead the growing global movement toward increasing sustainability in farming and food processing.

Before this discussion enters into the world of sustainable wine, the first chapter provides useful background on sustainability in general: the definition and evolution of sustainability as a concept and practice, including a review of sustainability trends in consumer domains and an introduction to sustainable agriculture.

CHAPTER 1

SUSTAINABILITY DEFINED

Agriculture, Consumption, and the Triple Bottom Line

As a champion of sustainability, I am often asked, "What does the term 'sustainability' really mean?" People wonder whether environmental sustainability is simply a passing trend, much as they wonder about social responsibility and sustainable development.

There can be no denying the academic debate regarding rapidly rising populations and the negative impacts of industrialization since the 18th century, when Thomas Malthus wrote *An Essay on the Principle of Population*. But the sustainability movement as it exists today is mostly a modern movement that gathered significant momentum in the post–World War II period.

The post-war consumer boom, along with rapid technological innovation, brought about a dramatic increase in the consumption of resources. Agriculture, too, changed dramatically after the end of World War II. Productivity soared due to farming industrialization; new technologies; mechanization; increased use of chemical pesticides and fertilizers; specialization; and government policies that favored maximizing production. These changes raised concerns about key resources being consumed too rapidly and the overall impact of human activity on the environment.

In the 1960s, environmental awareness grew considerably in the economically developed Northern Hemisphere. As this momentum grew, ecological thinking moved from academia to the mainstream. Rachel Carson's book *Silent Spring*, published in the United States in 1962, argued that the use of pesticides was killing off wildlife and inflicting damage on humans. An instant top seller, the book did much to alert the public to environmental concerns and is widely credited with kick-starting the environmental movement due to her criticism of the indiscriminate use of chemically based fertilizers, insecticides, and weed killers.

Silent Spring alludes to the impending disappearance of songbirds because of the long-term effects of the chemical pesticide DDT. Carson reported that birds ingesting

1

DDT tended to lay thin-shelled eggs, which would break prematurely in the nest, killing the next generation of chicks. This drove bald eagles, peregrine falcons, and other bird populations to the brink of extinction—populations plummeted more than 80 percent in just one generation. Carson also highlighted the dangers of excessive pesticide use for our food supply, making organic agriculture attractive, as it eschewed the use of most synthetic pesticides.

By the late 1960s, headlines were filled with the efforts of various new organizations as they sought to raise awareness regarding global environmental concerns. Friends of the Earth, founded in 1969, became an international network in 1971 with support in the United States, Sweden, the UK, and France. Greenpeace grew out of the peace movement in the early 1970s Vancouver, and by the late 1970s had spread from Canada to become international in scope.

Throughout the 1970s, environmental science began to find its way into academic curricula, and environmental organizations were being formed locally, nationally, and internationally. In 1972, the Club of Rome, an international think tank, published *The Limits to Growth*, a highly influential book that modeled the consequences of a growing population on finite resources. It used computer simulations to predict the impact of changes and interaction among key variables, including population growth, pollution, food production, and resource depletion.

In 1987, the United Nations convened the World Commission on Environment and Development, headed by Gro Harlem Brundtland, a former Prime Minister of Norway. The Commission presented their report, *Our Common Future* (commonly known as *The Brundtland Report*), which offered the now-famous definition of sustainable development: "meeting the needs of the present without compromising the ability of future generations to meet their own needs." This definition is widely used today to describe what sustainability means.

BUSINESS AND SUSTAINABILITY: THE TRIPLE BOTTOM LINE

As books like *Silent Spring* and intergovernmental reports like *Our Common Future* were having their impact on our understanding of ecology and the effects of human activity, businesses began to look for a new way to measure success beyond shareholder value.

The confluence of environmental, social, and commercial concerns gave rise to the concept of the "triple bottom line" method of measuring sustainable business performance. John Elkington, a leading authority on sustainability and corporate social responsibility, championed the triple bottom line to advance sustainability in business practices. Referring to a company's environmental, social, and economic performance, and the impacts of the company on its internal and external stakeholders, triple bottom line has become the basic matrix for gauging a company's sustainability efforts, measuring:

- Profit: economic value created by the company, or the economic benefit to the surrounding community and society.
- People: fair and favorable business practices regarding labor and the community in which the company conducts its business.
- Planet: use of sustainable environmental practices and the reduction of environmental impact.

SUSTAINABILITY:
The "Triple Bottom Line"

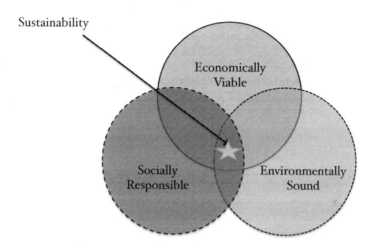

Ensuring viability over time... benefitting current and future generations.

Since he coined the term "triple bottom line," Elkington has been in the vanguard of sustainable business. But even prior to this, in 1987, he cofounded SustainAbility—part activist, part think tank, and part consultancy operation located in London, which has, over the years, advised businesses like Dow Europe, Novo Nordisk, Procter & Gamble, Starbucks, and Unilever. SustainAbility brokers consensus, agreement, and détente between nongovernment organizations (NGOs) and leading-edge companies, because both sides have trust and confidence in SustainAbility's credibility and sincerity. They drove the evolution of the corporate reporting agenda and built a connection to financial reporting and higher regard within the financial community for corporate social responsibility (CSR) reporting. Greenpeace called them "campaigners in pin stripes."

Today Elkington wants most of all—and urgently—to drive transformative change. In his book *The Zeronauts: Breaking the Sustainability Barrier*, he posits that in order to move from incremental to transformative change, we must embrace wider framings, deeper insights, higher targets, and longer time-scales. This latest book investigates some ways in which leading Zeronauts—a new breed of innovator, entrepreneur, and investor—are determined to drive problems such as carbon, waste, toxics, and poverty to zero.

He believes that what has been an NGO activist agenda is starting to come into the mainstream. "Business is now waking up to the reality that if we carry on using the natural resources of the world unsustainably, they'll quite simply run out," he said in a 2014 interview. "With a burgeoning population, more people are living in poverty than ever before, inequalities are increasing in many parts of the world and unemployment rates are at frightening levels.

> "Civil Society alone cannot solve the tasks at hand, while many governments are unwilling or unable to act. While there are myriad reasons we've arrived at this juncture, much of the blame rests with the principles and practices of 'business as usual.'"[1]

Companies must move to initiate breakthrough innovations in their business strategies in response to demographic, environmental, and resource pressures. They must redefine the bottom line to account for true long-term costs throughout the supply chain. In *The Breakthrough Challenge: 10 Ways to Connect Today's Profits with Tomorrow's Bottom Line*, a book by Elkington and Jochen Zeitz, the authors advocate for chief executive officers (CEOs) to do just that, while highlighting their successes.

Indeed, many corporate CEOs have accepted the premise that sustainability issues are material to the long-term success of their business, and many mainstream investors are also embracing the sustainability agenda. Key drivers of sustainability that are not only reshaping the way businesses and governments operate, but also redefining the value they deliver, include consumer demand for sustainable products and services; stakeholder influence; resource depletion; employee engagement; capital market scrutiny; and regulatory requirements. A sustainable business seeks to combine environmental stewardship and social improvements with financial success. Making commitments on issues such as climate change, resource usage, ethical sourcing, human rights, labor, and community relations has become part of the cost of doing business. Reporting progress on these issues can only improve the company's reputation.

Environmental Sustainability

Environmental sustainability refers to the perpetual maintenance of vital human ecological support systems. This includes the planet's climatic system, systems of agriculture, industry, forestry, and fisheries and human communities. Furthermore, it is meeting human needs without compromising the health of natural, physical ecosystems.[2] It involves making decisions and taking actions that are in the interests of protecting the natural world, with particular emphasis on preserving the capability of the environment to support all life. For businesses, environmental sustainability is about making responsible decisions that will reduce their negative impact on the environment. It is not simply about reducing the amount of waste produced or using less energy, but is concerned with developing processes that will lead to businesses becoming completely sustainable—becoming Zeronauts—in the future.

In an effort to meet the demands of their customers, businesses can and do deplete resources and cause damage to a great many areas of the environment. Some of the common environmental impacts include:

- removing rainforests and woodlands through logging and agricultural clearing to provide for humanity's shelter, food, and warmth,
- polluting waterways with industrial pollutants,
- over-fishing of oceans, rivers, and lakes to satisfy the demand for fish,
- polluting the atmosphere through the burning of fossil fuels to provide for transportation and energy needs, and
- damaging prime agricultural and cultivated land through the use of unsustainable farming practices that feed populations through aggressive agriculture.

Social Sustainability

Social sustainability, often referred to in the business context as CSR, has been defined as ". . . the continuing commitment by business to behave ethically and contribute to economic development while improving the quality of life of the workforce and their families, as well as the local community and society at large."[3] CSR has become a "catch-all" term for good business behavior, a process to embrace responsibility for a company's actions and encourage a positive impact on the environment, consumers, employees, and communities, including corporate giving and philanthropy. Sometimes called corporate citizenship, social performance, corporate responsibility (CR), sustainable business practices, or ethical and responsible business, this activity is essentially a form of corporate self-regulation.

Economic Sustainability

The third element of the triple bottom line, economic sustainability, sometimes referred to as commercial viability, is a more complex picture, the nature of which cannot be fully understood without looking at both the internal and external setting in which an organization operates.

Why is economic sustainability important? For social and environmental purists, the only companies worth having around are the good guys—those who manage the environment responsibly and provide positive socio-economic benefits to the communities in which they're operating. In a sustainable economy, only the best should and will survive. They're the companies that put social and environmental sustainability at the center of their business strategies, while still remaining profitable.

These companies understand the business case for corporate responsibility, and by adopting sustainable practices they attract and retain employees; increase customer loyalty; reduce operating costs (e.g., energy, water); strengthen their supply chain(s); enable license to operate; and fulfill social commitments to communities and to the planet.

Some companies adopt sustainable practices to atone for past environmental mistakes; others are guided by personal convictions of the company's founder or senior executive. Both motivations have created strong CR leaders throughout the business community. These leaders have now established sustainability as a firm business strategy and a key pillar of their brand. And they have addressed the supply chain to ensure their suppliers also adopt the priorities of social and environmental responsibility and philanthropy.

These leaders have a priority to reduce their environmental footprint. They do so by measuring climate impacts while setting specific goals to reduce emissions. In addition, they determine which environmental challenges are the most material for their products and sector—water conservation, waste management, and packaging. They engage in dialogue and partnership with key stakeholders such as local government, community leaders, NGOs, and neighbors. They provide a great work environment for employees and engage them and their customers in CR programs.

INTEGRATING SUSTAINABILITY INTO CORE BUSINESS

How can an organization incorporate sustainability into their core business strategy to become a sustainability leader, attain the same level of value and influence as other key elements of business performance, and use it to drive profitability, innovation, and engagement? Of all the strategies, integrating sustainability into the supply chain may be the most critical, especially for the agricultural industry.

Start at the Top

Ensuring environmental and social responsibility must rest at the top of the organization, with the CEO or business owner assigning clear responsibilities, resources, and leadership roles to address these issues on a day-to-day basis.

There must be a clear definition of what sustainability means for the company, addressing key issues, stakeholders, and spheres of influence relevant to corporate citizenship in the company and the industry. This is a process of materiality assessment based on products, lines of business, and geography, and determining the most important issues facing the business and leveraging them.

This concept comes from materiality in a company's financial reporting, where information is deemed material if its omission or misstatement could influence the economic decisions of users taken on the basis of the financial statements. Materiality in that context relates to the significance of transactions, balances, and errors contained in the financial statements. Materiality defines the threshold or cutoff point after which financial information becomes relevant to the decision-making needs of the users and must be publicly disclosed. In the corporate responsibility realm, this concept relates to what stakeholders believe are the most critical issues for the company and what the firm itself believes are its most critical environmental and societal issues.

CASE IN POINT

Ethical Sourcing of Coffee Is Material to Starbucks

A great example in the agricultural sector is Starbucks Coffee Company, which has long identified sustainable and ethical sourcing as one of its most critical issues. In its 2007 CSR report, the company identified coffee purchasing practices as the most material issue in its materiality matrix, and since then, the company has expanded its work and communication on this topic. Starbucks has maintained a focus on ethically sourced coffee as one of its three most material issues and has worked to embed it as a priority across the business. (The other two are waste reduction—all those paper "To Go" cups—and energy impact.) The company set an ambitious goal of ensuring that 100 percent of its coffee would be ethically sourced by 2015* and developed its own sustainable coffee standards, known as Coffee and Farmer Equity (C.A.F.E.) Practices.

C.A.F.E. Practices is a comprehensive set of measurable standards focused on four areas—product quality, economic accountability and transparency, social responsibility, and environmental leadership.

By 2014, Starbucks verified 99% of their coffee as ethically sourced through C.A.F.E. Practices, Fair Trade, or Organic Certification. In addition, over a million coffee farmers in 22 countries on four continents have benefited from the program by improving their sustainability over time using a score-based system. Implementation of the program has prevented forest canopy loss, as 99 percent of participating farms have not converted forest for coffee production. Preventing tropical forest loss is an important means of fighting climate change, because the forest is a major carbon sink. Ensuring fair employment conditions has also been a success for the C.A.F.E. Practices program. Over 440,000 workers on coffee farms earned better than the local minimum wage, 89 percent of workers received paid sick leave during the analysis year, and all children living on coffee estates attended school. And the program has funded agronomy training and made training a major goal, so participating in the program means that farmers can learn and implement better practices in the future to improve both their yield and their sustainability, with reduced use of chemicals.

---

* Ethical sourcing means ensuring that the products being sourced are created in safe facilities or safe conditions for workers who are treated well and paid fair wages to work legal hours. It also means that the supplier is respecting the environment during the production and manufacture of the products.

Sustainability leaders focus on a narrow set of issues and goals for handling their concerns in a socially and environmentally responsible way—and they track progress. For most wine businesses, the likely material issues revolve around climate change, water reduction, sustainable packaging, and winery design and operations. But much also depends on the region, climatic conditions, the organization's culture, and external factors such as the economic circumstances of the surrounding community (and the community's expectations). Also, distance to market may be a material issue as it relates to energy use and emissions in transportation.

CASE IN POINT

Material Issues at Constellation Brands

In the wine and spirits business, Constellation Brands has identified water as one of its most material issues. Its Water Policy acknowledges that water is essential to the production of its brands and vital to markets, consumers, and local communities. As an agriculture-based company, Constellation Brands recognizes that changes in quantity and/or quality of water supply can have far-reaching and extended impacts. Accordingly, it has set specific goals to implement this policy:

- Establish specific targets for water usage reduction and water efficiency.
- Understand water use and discharge in relation to the local watershed.
- Regularly review all facilities' water systems and establish specific action plans.
- Prioritize water programs in areas of high risk.
- Establish contingency plans for incoming water sources and effluent discharge.

- Educate employees on water issues so that they can become effective water stewards for the company.
- Promote collective action on water issues in local communities.
- Engage with supply chain on relevant water measures.
- Reduce water usage without compromising safety or quality.
- Disclose targets for water reduction and efforts made to achieve these goals.
- Establish partnerships with relevant stakeholders to collectively address water issues.

Look at the Supply Chain

As with Starbucks and their focus on coffee growers, examining a company's supply chain offers the greatest opportunities for innovation and bottom-line impact. Start by assessing the supply chain's effect on surrounding communities and the environment in order to design, preferably at the outset, processes with sustainability. Take particular note of those points in the chain that the business can control or influence. This could include raw material sourcing, manufacturing, packaging, warehousing, logistics (transportation and distribution), retail consumption, and post consumption.

The complex nature of supply chains presents urgent sustainability challenges to businesses and the suppliers they work with. In order to protect their own company bottom lines, businesses must ensure that their suppliers are held to certain standards of sustainability and incentivized to exceed these standards.

Procurement is at the core for embedding sustainability practices, and it's time for wine companies to see it as more than just a conduit to savings and efficiencies, but as an important agent for change that is opening up an array of new opportunities for businesses, ultimately with consumers. Procurement functions are also starting to realize that they cannot improve their own sustainability performance without improving the practices of their supply chain partners.

In order to address the verification gap effectively, businesses must take responsibility for the performance of their agricultural supply chain. Partnering with growers and producers to help accelerate the adoption of better and more responsible practices is key to ensuring impact at the ground level. Approaches that provide technical and financial assistance, communicate clear timelines for progress, and help mitigate some of the risk to farmers, sending signals to growers that they have the support needed to pursue new methods. Some businesses are developing capacity-building programs for farmers, with efforts commonly focused along commodity-specific supply chains. They sometimes accomplish this by providing financial support to their suppliers to help them adopt sustainability priorities.

CASE IN POINT

Benziger Brings Along Its Supply Chain

In 2000, Benziger Family Winery became the first certified biodynamic winemaker in California's Napa and Sonoma counties. By 2007, Benziger had the distinction of having all 50 of its growers certified as sustainable, organic, or biodynamic. Benziger understood that their sustainability leadership started at the beginning of the supply chain and involved training and incentives for growers to undertake the steps to meet Benziger's goals. As part of this process Benziger created a certification program in 2005 called Farming for Flavors. This program is a unique and customized quality assurance program that seeks to challenge growers to create grapes with strong character and distinctive flavor through environmentally sound practices. The program uses a Distinct Quality Point Assessment to rate growers on an annual basis and is overseen by Demeter Association's Stellar Certification Services, a third-party certifying agency. Growers must improve both the health of their land and the quality of their grapes to continue to receive the certification, and the bar required for certification is continually being raised.

An important aspect to this supply chain strategy is rewarding suppliers for their efforts. When Starbucks first launched its coffee farmer sustainability program, initially called the Preferred Supplier Program, it paid a premium to those farmers who achieved high marks on its code of conduct scorecard; the higher the score, the higher premium paid per pound of coffee. Using this incentive in wineries, Sonoma County's Jackson Family Wines and Francis Ford Coppola Winery—two of the county's largest wine producers—pay premiums for sustainably grown grapes from their vineyard suppliers.

Be Innovative

Rather than approving projects and then asking how the product, feature, or service can be developed and delivered more sustainably, add a sustainability lens (through scorecards, life cycle analysis, and indices), at decision-making points, ensuring sustainability is factored in before any go/no-go decision. This not only reduces risk and saves money by averting expensive course corrections later in the development process, but also drives more sustainable product design from the beginning.

CASE IN POINT

Sustainability in Design Phase at Timberland

Boot manufacturer Timberland incorporates sustainability at the front end of product development decisions, in the design and development process of its materials as well as in manufacturing of its boots and shoes. Whether they use textile, leather, foam, or plastic in the product, Timberland researches it extensively to make sure it's the best available option from both a design and environmental perspective. The product line that best represents these values in action is the Earthkeepers Collection®, which uses the most environmentally responsible material options possible to substitute for virgin raw materials. One of those materials, recycled polyethylene terephthalate—commonly called PET—the plastic used to make water and soda bottles, is used in boot linings, laces, uppers and insulation, even faux shearling. Incorporating recycled PET into footwear design was not as simple as replacing another material. It required an environmental approach to designing the product from the ground up. Timberland has even developed guidelines, ensuring every material that goes into its products meets certain criteria at the design phase, long before it gets to the stage of manufacturing.

Also, Timberland makes transparency and communication with customers a priority. On every Timberland shoe box is a "Green Index® Label." Much like ingredient labels on packaged foods, this Green Index Rating System lists how much fossil fuel it took to create each pair of footwear, as well chemicals used and resource consumption (e.g., the percentage, by weight, of recycled, organic, and renewable materials). The lower the score, the smaller environmental footprint associated with a product, from raw materials to final product. This is intended to encourage consumers to make more informed choices by communicating the good and the bad associated with Timberland products.

Be the Impetus

Embed corporate responsibility and sustainability into every part of the business—planning, strategy, operations, marketing, and human resources—and make the company's approach to CSR a competitive differentiator for the brand. Of course, integration can be such a broad and deep concept that it runs the risk of meaning everything and nothing at the same time. It means incorporating sustainability into the business strategy so that the business model itself creates social and environmental value in addition to financial value. In other words, by the very act of succeeding as a business, a company creates greater value for society and the environment. A simple way to achieve this is to embed a designated sustainability manager into the operations team and also the procurement team, and involve that manager in all decision-making. Include a sustainability screen in marketing plans and creative choices. The mistake companies make is assuming that the sustainability manager's job is limited to selecting recipients of philanthropic donations, or drafting complimentary press releases and laudatory creative materials, rather than understanding that to be a truly sustainable brand, this manager should have involvement and interaction at every part of the decision-making process.

The need for integrated sustainability is urgent. In order to address today's pressing global issues such as resource scarcity, climate change, and inequality, the private sector must take into account environmental and social considerations regarding every business decision. This includes putting corporate citizenship and sustainability on the board agenda, encouraging innovation and creativity, and empowering the next generation of leaders.

Measure Outcomes

Establish internal performance, communication, incentive and measurement systems for all sustainability goals and conduct quarterly business reviews. Management systems must measure progress and provide assurances that the sourcing strategy a company pursues is delivering the intended results. Ideally, progress should be benchmarked against a set of time-bound, measurable goals laid out as part of the overarching strategy, *and* publicly disclosed. Third-party verification schemes, such as Fair Trade, UTZ, Organic, and Demeter (biodynamic), play an important role in providing credible information to customers on a product's (or company's) authenticity in terms of sustainability. The verification landscape is complicated, however, with stronger frameworks for some commodities than others. Coffee, for instance, has a fairly robust set of certifications that examine both environmental and social metrics. Wine sustainability schemes also must have third-party verification to be considered authentic and robust by retailers and consumers.

CASE IN POINT

Walmart's Sustainability Index Measures Product Sourcing

The scorecard used by the world's largest retailer, Walmart, is known as the Sustainability Index. It's a supplier tool first developed in the United States in 2009 by Walmart and continues to be applied to new product categories. By 2017 it is expected that 70 percent of the merchandise sold in Walmart's U.S. stores will have been sourced from suppliers who use the index, highlighting the degree to which sustainability principles are being integrated into purchasing by this leading retailer. To support further integration at the consumer level, Walmart launched a "Sustainability Leaders" portal on walmart.com in early 2015, where suppliers meeting the Sustainability Leader criteria in a product category are recognized as more sustainable and listed for online shoppers to peruse. While Walmart's approach is still somewhat limited, it highlights the opportunity to fully consider sustainability factors by applying a lens such as a scorecard from supply chain through point of sale.

Be Transparent

Transparency is about reliable indicators of sustainability progress and honest communication with various stakeholders about policies, practices, and progress, including formal external reporting. Whether an organization chooses a full-scale corporate responsibility report, following Global Reporting Initiative (GRI) guidelines, puts environmental performance data on product packaging, or simply communicates progress on its website, external communication is critical to gaining consumer trust.

CASE IN POINT

Treasury Wine Estates and Diageo Reveal Calorie Information

There are also examples of leading drinks companies voluntarily using their brand marketing and packaging to provide consumers with dietary information to make informed and responsible choices about alcohol purchases and their health. In a move claimed to be a first for the global wine industry, Treasury Wine Estates (TWE) committed to providing calorie information across its entire portfolio starting in 2015. Previously Diageo was the first drinks producer to commit to calorie labeling, confirming it would later also add nutritional information to all of its products—largely spirits. TWE, however, is the first wine producer to make a similar promise regarding calorie information (although Félix Solís Avantis was the first to put nutritional information on its domestic wines sold in Spain). TWE initially included calorie information on its wine brands in Europe, where there is "heightened consumer interest" in such information, and then planned a rollout to other regions around the world (their wines are sold in more than 70 countries). Calorie information will also be provided online, with a dedicated web address printed on wine labels.

Think Beyond Corporate Walls

Eventually, every company realizes that the biggest environmental and social challenges often require not just supply chain cooperation but also industry-wide collaboration. This is happening in the wine industry in several countries through the establishment of regional sustainability programs to educate, train, support, and encourage individual vineyards and wineries in adopting and implementing better growing practices and sustainable protocols. In several instances, third-party verification is a prerequisite to adding a bottle seal or label attesting to their certification. Opportunities exist at the industry and multistakeholder level to work collaboratively within the supply chain to influence growing practices. Farming businesses need to leverage these opportunities at the community and regional level and contribute meaningful expertise and investment to these efforts.

SUSTAINABLE CONSUMPTION

The responsibility to conserve natural resources and to reduce waste does not rest solely with business. As active participants in the global supply chain, consumers, too, must take responsible action for a more sustainable world.

The theories of Thomas Malthus in 1798 have become a reality in countries like China and India. A growing world population and expanding middle class make unlimited consumption unsustainable. The statistics are troubling. World population is expected to reach 9 billion by 2050, the global middle class is expected to triple by 2030, and natural resource consumption is expected to rise to 170 percent of the earth's bio-capacity by 2040.[4] The implications of these changes are dire.

Sixty percent of the Earth's ecosystem services "are being degraded or used unsustainably."[5] This is largely driven by the growing culture of "consumerism" among higher-income groups, which account for the greatest per capita share of global consumption.

The Organization for Economic Cooperation and Development (OECD) forecasted in 2011 that, "if current consumption patterns persist, 3.9 billion of the world's population will live in areas of high water stress by 2030, as opposed to 2.8 billion" in 2011."[6] Another 1 billion people's regions will be without sufficient water resources. Equally frightening, the OECD predicts world energy needs—and CO_2 emissions—will be 60 percent higher in 2030 than in 2011.[7]

> Water stress occurs when the demand for water exceeds the available amount during a certain period or when poor quality restricts its use. Water stress causes deterioration of fresh water resources in terms of quantity (aquifer over-exploitation, dry rivers, etc.) and quality (eutrophication, organic matter pollution, saline intrusion, etc.).

These statistics don't only apply to developing countries; we see water stress and health crises in poor neighborhoods of American cities as well, due to deteriorating infrastructure, aging water delivery systems, inefficiency, inequality, and neglect. Consumers in developed countries are becoming increasingly more concerned with environmental, social, and economic issues, and willing to act on those concerns.[8] Currently, over half of global consumers take "green" factors into account when making purchasing decisions.[9] One in four Americans report taking systematic "green" steps, such as recycling, home weatherproofing, using eco-friendly products, or driving energy-efficient vehicles.

Several research studies reach these same conclusions. A 2011 study identified a big consumer shift from mindless to mindful consumption, which author John Gerzema, president of Brand Asset Consulting, calls the "spend shift," the rise of a vibrant, values-driven post-recession economy, a movement in society where the majority of American consumers are embracing both value and values in their purchases. People who want to patronize businesses that reflect their values, so-called "spendshifters," make up 55 percent of the U.S. population, according to the study. Between 2005 and 2009, the key brand attributes that grew in importance for American consumers include kindness and empathy, which increased by 391 percent; friendliness up by 148 percent; high quality up by 124 percent; and social responsibility up by 63 percent.

This Spend Shift means taking care to purchase goods and services for themselves and their homes only from sellers who meet specific standards (e.g., spending with a purpose) even as consumers seek more value and better prices in their purchases.[10]

In September and October 2012, the Regeneration Consumer Study (developed by BBMG, GlobeScan and SustainAbility) surveyed 6,224 consumers in six major international markets (Brazil, China, Germany, India, the UK, and the United States) regarding their attitudes, motivations, and behaviors around and toward sustainable consumption. Nearly two-thirds of respondents across the six markets (66 percent) believe that "as a society, we need to consume a lot less to improve the environment for future generations," and 65 percent say they feel "a sense of responsibility to purchase products that are good for the environment and society."[11]

Consumers in developing markets (Brazil, China, India) are more than twice as likely as their counterparts in developed markets (Germany, the UK, the United States) to report that they purchase products because of environmental and social benefits (51 percent to 22 percent), are willing to pay more for sustainable products (60 percent to 26 percent) and encourage others to buy from companies that are socially and environmentally responsible (70 percent to 34 percent).[12]

On the issue of trust, consumers across all six markets look to certification seals, such as Fair Trade or Certified Organic or other labels on product packaging (40 percent) as the most trusted source of information about whether a product is environmentally and socially responsible, followed by media reports (31 percent);

consumer reviews and ratings (28 percent); friends, family, or coworkers (27 percent), and government information and reports (27 percent). Certifications are ranked highest by consumers in developed countries (43 percent), while those in developing markets list media reports (37 percent) as their most trusted source.[13]

Despite these encouraging findings, consumer concern does not automatically translate into changes in sustainable consumer behavior. This is due to a variety of factors—availability, affordability, convenience, product performance, conflicting priorities, skepticism, over-demanding schedules, and force of habit. Six out of 10 claim they "sometimes" take such action, and only a small minority says they never do so.[14]

The tension between the values consumers hold and the awareness that the actions they take in the marketplace run counter to those values leads to guilt about their unsustainable consumption. In mature consumer societies or affluent communities, consumers regularly receive information on dysfunctional or unethical businesses, learn of poor working conditions in developing countries, or receive scientific insights on the health drawbacks of their favorite food or beverage.

Corporate marketers argue that consumers will respond to specific and engaging actions that make their purchases more sustainable. Middle class consumers want to feel less guilty about their consumerism and the impact they are having on the environment. By presenting a green brand, a responsible brand, a human brand, a sustainable brand, an honest brand, or a transparent brand, corporate marketers and brand managers have an opportunity to fulfill consumers' desire for more aware, more ethical, and more sustainable consumerism.

In fact, business can play a major role in mainstreaming sustainable consumption. Business approaches to sustainable consumption can be grouped into three broad categories:[15]

- *Innovation:* Business processes for the development of new and improved products, services, and business are shifting to incorporate provisions for maximizing societal value and minimizing environmental cost.
- *Choice influencing:* The use of marketing and awareness-raising campaigns to enable and encourage consumers to choose and use products more efficiently and sustainably, while also enhancing positive brand positioning.
- *Choice editing:* The removal of "unsustainable" products and services from the marketplace in partnership with other actors in society.

ENGAGING CONSUMERS—STARBUCKS SHARED PLANET

With a recession brewing in the United States and consumer confidence low in 2008, consumers reexamined many of their regular purchases. Premium coffee began to look like a luxury item. Starbucks marketers needed to give consumers a compelling reason to pay those premium prices. And they had one. Starbucks displayed posters in-store that connected their ethical and responsible approach in coffee regions. The message:

"You.

You work with 1.2 million people to grow and harvest even better coffee that earns even better prices.

Everything we do, you do. You buy coffee at Starbucks. Which means we can work with farmers to help improve their coffee quality and their standard of living. We call it coffee that is responsibly grown and ethically traded. And thanks to you, we've grown big enough to be able to do this kind·of good on this kind of scale.

Good job, you."

The poster was part of the company's "Shared Planet" CSR campaign, with the tagline "You and Starbucks. It's bigger than coffee."

"Shared Planet" works by drawing a clear connection between consumption and the work Starbucks does with coffee farmers. It's a great business strategy for Starbucks—the more consumers buy, the more good Starbucks can do. It also justifies paying a higher price for a handcrafted coffee beverage at Starbucks. This messaging also educates customers about sustainability and corporate responsibility, specifically what is meant by "responsibly grown and ethically traded."

As a company for which social responsibility is a core part of its brand, spreading the word this effectively has led to measurable increases in customer loyalty. Since the Shared Planet program was launched, it has gone on to become more than a CSR effort; it's a key pillar of the Starbucks brand.[16]

But even as corporations develop practices that make use of efficiency gains, technological advances and more responsible procurement, business practices will not be sufficient to bring global consumption to a sustainable level. Changes will also be required to consumer lifestyles, including the ways in which consumers choose and use products and services.

THE EVOLUTION OF GREEN SHOPPERS

While business has innovated, increasing consumer awareness about the environmental imprint of consumption patterns has produced a category of "green shoppers." In 2009, accounting and consulting firm Deloitte estimated that as many as 54 percent of American shoppers were "leaning green," with 2 percent being classified as "committed," 18 percent classified as "proactive," and 24 percent classified as "influenced."[17]

To learn more about these green shoppers, the Grocery Manufacturers Association and Deloitte conducted a primary research study. They found that green shoppers are a large, high-value segment of importance to retailers and many manufacturers. They visit stores more frequently, buy more products on each trip, and demonstrate more brand and retailer loyalty. Demographically, the most typical green shopper is somewhat older, has more income than average, has fewer people in their household, and is better educated than the averages of the total sample population. These behaviors and qualities suggest that green shoppers will be particularly valuable to retailers.

The greenest shoppers are the baby boomers, born between 1946 and 1964. Notably, even though the most committed green shoppers pay more, most are price conscious. While younger generations are environmentally conscious, they are constrained by their weaker earning power. They are likely to develop "greener" consumption patterns as they grow older and their incomes rise.

Two leading categories for green purchases are everyday groceries and produce, constituting 33 percent and 31 percent, respectively, of all groceries and produce purchased. In comparison, green purchases of electronics constitute only 8 percent of all electronics purchased. These and other purchasing trends can be seen in the following chart.

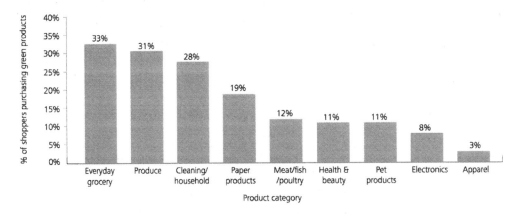

Green purchases are far larger in more consumable categories.
Source: 2009 GMA/Deloitte Green Shopper Study
Note: Sample size was 6,498 Shoppers interviewed. Percentage represents respondents purchasing a green product in that category on this shopping trip. Percentages don't equal 100% as respondents could select more than one category.

The Deloitte study found that green shoppers bought more than their planned purchases and shopped more frequently. These shoppers buy green to help reduce the social impact of their consumption and materialism. Importantly, green shoppers are considerably more loyal customers, since "once they made a switch to a green product, they were more likely to stick with it and buy regularly."[18]

The Natural Marketing Institute (NMI) has more formally described these tendencies using the rubric Lifestyles of Health and Sustainability (LOHAS), a huge U.S. marketplace of goods and services focused on health, the environment, social justice, personal development, and sustainable living. U.S. consumers spent almost $300 billion on LOHAS-related products and services in 2008, according to recent analysis by NMI. This is significant growth over the previous market size, from 2005, which showed spending at $219 billion.

Consumers active in the LOHAS market represent a sizable group in the United States. According to the LOHAS website, approximately 13 to19 percent of U.S. adults are currently considered LOHAS consumers—approximately 41 million people. These consumers will play a significant role in the future of business and also in the future of progressive social, environmental, and economic change in this country.

LOHAS market sectors and size include the following:

- *Alternative energy:* LOHAS consumers spent $1 billion in 2008 on alternative energy sources such as renewable energy credits and green pricing.
- *Alternative transportation:* LOHAS consumers spent $20 billion on hybrid and electric vehicles, car sharing, biodiesel fuel, and other green transportation methods.
- *Ecotourism:* LOHAS consumers spent over $42 billion on ecotourism[19] by participating in "responsible travel to natural areas that conserve the environment and improve the wellbeing of local people." A growing number of consumers also expect their travel providers (hotels, inns, bed and breakfasts) to be environmentally and socially responsible.
- *Green building:* In 2005, LOHAS consumers spent $10 billion on Energy Star appliances, certified homes, wood alternatives, and other green building materials; in 2012, they spent $85 billion, demonstrating strong and growing interest in this area of sustainable consumption.[20]

Did You Know?

According to the Solar Energy Industries Association, in 2004 the total market value of alternative energy was $380 million. Since then, the market has grown 87 percent. Additionally, in 2012 solar energy accounted for 10 percent of all new electricity generation capacity added. In 2013, it jumped to 29 percent.

And, according to Green Car Reports, from 2012 to 2013 the number of hybrid and electric cars sold in the United States almost doubled—increasing from 56,000 to 96,000.

- *Natural lifestyles:* According to a LOHAS survey, LOHAS consumers spent $10 billion in 2008 on organic cleaning products, apparel, and social change philanthropy. In 2011, they spent $640 million on green cleaning products alone,[21] and in 2009 they gave over $3.1 billion to social justice philanthropies.[22]
- *Organic Food and Personal Health:* The biggest category of purchases by LOHAS consumers is natural and organic food, which is perhaps the most relevant for the wine industry. LOHAS consumers spent $117 billion in 2008 on nutritional health products as well as natural/organic food.

American consumers spent more on health and wellness products in 2014 than ever before as more have become concerned about the quality of ingredients being used in processed foods. Estimates project that the global market for healthy foods and drinks will reach $1 trillion in sales by 2017.

U.S. consumer demand for organically produced goods has continuously increased since 1990 when the U.S. Congress passed the Organic Foods Production Act (OFPA), part of the Food, Agriculture, Conservation, and Trade Act of 1990, or Farm Bill. After the 2007–2009 economic recession, during which Americans economized food purchases, the growth in demand for organic products quickly rebounded.[23]

The purpose of OFPA was to establish national standards for the marketing of certain agricultural products as organic in order to assure consumers of a consistent organic standard and to facilitate interstate commerce in organically produced food. The act established standards for organic products and criteria for certifying a farm or part of a farm as organic.

The Organic Trade Association, a membership-based business association for the organic industry in North America, indicated in its 2013 industry survey that U.S. organic food sales reached $32.3 billion and accounted for roughly 92 percent of the total organic sales. Organic food sales worldwide amounted to $63 billion in 2013. Nonfood organic products like flowers, fiber, household products, and pet food were a smaller part of the total organic market, but sales of these items are steadily increasing. At almost $2.8 billion in 2013, nonfood organic items jumped nearly eight-fold since 2002, almost doubling in market share.[24]

The Organic Trade Association's 2013 industry survey also indicated that the fruit and vegetable category continues to lead the sector with $11.6 billion in sales, up 15 percent. With more than 10 percent of the fruits and vegetables sold in the United States now organic, the $1.5 billion in new sales of organic fruits and vegetables represented 46 percent of the organic sector's $3.3 billion in new dollars. (The relatively small organic condiments category posted the strongest growth, at 17 percent, to reach sales of $830 million.) Also showing double-digit growth was the organic snack food sector, up 15 percent to $1.7 billion; organic bread and grain sales up 12 percent to $3.8 billion; organic meat, poultry, and fish sales up 11 percent to $675 million, and the rapidly expanding organic packaged and prepared food sector up 10 percent to $4.8 billion.

A niche sector in the food industry just a decade ago, organic food now accounts for more than 4 percent of the $760 billion annual food sales in the United States. Interestingly, the growth rate of organic food sales (which has averaged almost 10 percent every year since 2010) has overshadowed the average annual growth of total food sales (just over 3 percent) during that same period.[25]

Today, many large corporate farms have an organic division, and there is no limit to organic farm sizes. Organic products often have their own sections within large-scale supermarkets, as consumers must rely on product labeling ("Certified Organic") and government regulation to be assured of their organic purchases. However, in the past decade organic food sales have increased by 17 percent, despite the fact that organic foods cost one to three times more than their nonorganic counterparts.

As demand for organic continues to grow and accessibility to organic products increases, the industry is facing critical challenges. Farmland in the United States is not being converted to organic at the pace needed to meet the growing demand. Additionally, supplies of organic feed and organic grain have been tight and costly, which could limit growth, especially in the organic dairy and meat sectors.[26]

SUSTAINABLE FOOD MOVEMENTS

How did this shift to sustainable food and such dramatic growth in the organics market occur?

It is worthwhile at this point to look back on how the sustainable food movement began and see how it progressed to this level. From farming methods to consumer buy-in to perceptions about the health benefits of sustainably farmed produce, the history of the sustainable food movement can be instructive for the wine industry as it moves into broader adoption of sustainable winemaking.

Until the 1920s, organic agriculture was the norm. Farmers used natural means to feed the soil and to control pests. This all changed after the two world wars: During World War I, chlorine and mustard gas (*a chlorine derivative*) were turned against enemy soldiers as chemical weapons. During World War II, both sides worked diligently to invent poisonous weapons far more pernicious than chlorine and mustard gas. WWII marked the rapid acceleration of experiments to combine gaseous chlorine with organic matter (*organic = combinations of carbon and hydrogen atoms that are the building blocks of all life on earth*). Many of these substances were tried out on insects, and when the war ended, they were turned with a vengeance against agricultural pests.

One prominent example was DDT (dichlorodiphenyltrichloroethane). Developed in 1939 by the Swiss chemist Paul Hermann Müller, DDT was the first in a new class of insecticides, called chlorinated hydrocarbons. It was a colorless, tasteless, and almost odorless organochloride known for its insecticidal properties. Originally, DDT was used in the second half of World War II to control malaria and typhus among civilians and troops. After the war, DDT was made available for use as an agricultural insecticide, which saw its production and use duly increased.[27]

For his discovery of the highly effective DDT, Müller was awarded the Nobel Prize in Physiology or Medicine in 1948. (As noted earlier in this chapter, biologist Rachel Carson's landmark book *Silent Spring* cataloged the environmental and health impacts of widespread DDT use. The book created public outcry against the pesticide and the eventual ban of its use in America.)

The danger of organochlorides rests in the fact that they can persist in the environment for long periods of time.

Nitrogen fertilizers originated after World War I when there was ample supply of nitrogen left over from the production of TNT and other explosives. When Fritz Haber, a German chemist, discovered how to stabilize nitrogen for use as modern explosives in World War I, he also discovered its use as a chemical fertilizer and won the 1918 Nobel Prize. Thus, agriculture changed dramatically after the end of World War II. U.S. agriculture became increasingly mechanized and reliant upon resource-intensive inputs like synthetic fertilizers and chemical pesticides.

Tremendous postwar increases in the productivity of American farmers, made possible by cheap fossil fuel—the key ingredient in both chemical fertilizers and pesticides—allowed for the provision of cheap food for Americans. With this increased productivity, farms became larger. They became more specialized and centralized and drove many small, family-owned farms out of business. Thus, the market became controlled by a handful of powerful farm "corporations."

This industrial farm system, with its reliance on monoculture (industrial crops produced on huge monocrop farms), mechanization, chemical pesticides, and synthetic fertilizers, made food abundant and affordable. Biotechnology, genetically modified crop varieties, specialization, and implementation of government policies that favor maximizing production all allowed fewer farmers with reduced labor to produce the majority of the food and fiber in the United States and led to the outright repudiation of traditional natural farming methods.

Although industrial agriculture now produces great quantities of food at low prices, the trade-offs pose great risks to our ecological and social health. Prominent among these are topsoil depletion, erosion, groundwater and soil contamination, depletion of water resources, and deforestation. Conventional farming is the largest nonpoint source of water pollution, contaminating food and water with pesticides and nitrates and lowering soil productivity.[28]

Other social and environmental costs of industrial agriculture include the loss of biodiversity; increasing costs of production; air and water pollutants that threaten the health of farm workers, neighbors, and consumers; worsening treatment of farm laborers; the disappearance of the family farm; and the disintegration of economic and social conditions in rural, agricultural communities.[29]

THE MODERN SUSTAINABLE FOOD MOVEMENT IN AMERICA

It was not until the 1980s that Americans began to seriously consider where their food comes from or what food production does to the planet, their bodies, and their society. This food movement emerged from a realization that industrial food production was in need of reform. The high social, environmental, public health, animal welfare and gastronomic costs caused many Americans to see their food and the farming economy as unsafe and "unsustainable." Food price inflation and the publication of books by Wendell Berry, Francis Moore Lappé, and Barry Commoner that criticized industrial agriculture brought a different perspective to readers regarding their everyday food choices.[30]

Frances Moore Lappé's groundbreaking book *Diet for a Small Planet*, published in 1971, showed the connections between our everyday food choices and the environmental crisis, as well as world hunger. Her premise was that the American way of growing and eating food is "unsustainable." Continuing to eat in a way that undermines health, soil, energy resources, and social justice cannot be sustained without eventually leading to a breakdown—either environmental or health.

Then, in the late 1980s, a series of food safety scandals opened people's eyes to the way their food was being produced, each one drawing the curtain back a little farther on a food system that had changed beyond recognition.

The Alar Scare

In 1989, an environmental nonprofit organization, the Natural Resources Defense Council (NRDC), publicized on television the dangers of Alar (chemical name: daminozide), which was then being sprayed on apples as a growth-deterrent and color-enhancer. NRDC claimed that Alar could eventually cause cancer in children who ate Alar-treated apples or drank juice made from them. This sparked panic across America. Within a short time, apple juice and applesauce were being thrown away. Apples were taken out of school lunches, and hysterical parents called the U.S. Environmental Protection Agency (EPA) about risks of cancer to their children. The publicity campaign was so effective that sales and prices of apples declined sharply and 20,000 U.S. apple growers suffered substantial financial harm—even the large number who never used Alar. Orchards across the country lost millions of dollars and farmers went bankrupt.

This was actually an overreaction to NRDC's report, as the public confused a long-term cumulative threat with imminent danger. Despite the overreaction, there was some truth to the report, and the EPA eventually banned Alar on the grounds that "long-term exposure" to this carcinogen posed "unacceptable risks to public health." However, before the EPA's preliminary decision to ban all food uses of Alar went into effect, Uniroyal, the sole manufacturer of Alar, agreed to voluntarily halt all domestic sales of Alar for food uses.[31]

Mad Cow Disease

Outbreaks of mad cow disease (bovine spongiform encephalopathy [BSE]) in England in 1986 made Americans and Europeans increasingly wary and critical about meat quality and food safety. In response to subsequent incidents of BSE in the United States, cattle associations went to great effort to assure consumers of the safety of the handling of their product. McDonald's Corporation, the largest beef purchaser in the fast-food industry, mounted public relations campaigns indicating that these incidents had nothing to do with its supply chain. McDonald's gained experience from the very first outbreak in the UK and assured customers that they had a tremendous depth of experience and best practice operating procedures learned from the mad cow problem in several countries.

McDonald's later joined the Center for Environmental Leadership in Business, a division of Conservation International, to implement sustainable agriculture and conservation practices and standards within McDonald's global food supply network, relating to both livestock and fisheries.

Consumers grew tired of hearing about food safety issues and how chemicals in various pesticides could make them sick. The result was a new, heightened awareness of the carcinogens that are present in many pesticides. These scares led to a period of renewed consumer interest in the "natural" way of living and "green" farming methods in the United States. The market responded. Farmers markets sprung up, and farmers, once again, took up more natural "sustainable" farming methods.

SUSTAINABLE FARMING METHODS

Industrial farming, in the case of crop production, is characterized by extensive use of off-farm inputs of fertilizers, use of "labor-saving" technologies such as pesticides instead of weeding, and heavy machinery for planting and harvesting. In the case of animal production, industrial farming typically involves a dense population of animals raised on limited land and requiring large amounts of food, water, and medical inputs.

In contrast, sustainable agriculture embraces a wide range of techniques, including organic, free-range, low-input, holistic, and biodynamic methods.

Free range

There are no government-regulated standards to determine what makes certain products (mostly poultry and poultry products) free range. Typically, free-range poultry are contained within cage-free barns and have access to the outdoors. However, since there is no government regulation for this term, there are no standards for the quality of outdoor space, length of time allowed outdoors, or other factors that could affect quality of life.[32]

Low input

Low input farming systems seek to optimize the management and use of internal production inputs (e.g., on-farm resources) and to minimize the use of production inputs (e.g., off-farm resources) such as purchased fertilizers and pesticides, whenever feasible and practicable. This approach is intended to lower production costs, avoid pollution of surface and groundwater, reduce pesticide residues in food, reduce a farmer's overall risk, and increase short- and long-term farm profitability.[33]

Holistic

Holistic farming (or management) is a method of agriculture that emphasizes whole-farm planning. The cornerstones of managing holistically are financial planning, grazing planning, land planning, and biological monitoring. Managers learn to monitor their progress and adjust plans as necessary to achieve the desired results.[34]

Biodynamic

Biodynamic farming is both a concept and a practice, derived from the work of Austrian scientist and philosopher Dr. Rudolf Steiner. Dr. Steiner emphasized how farmers could work within natural forces and parameters, specifically with regard to compost and fertilizers.[35] Sometimes referred to as an organic farming system, biodynamic farming treats soil fertility and health, plant growth, and livestock care as equally important and interrelated parts of the ecosystem. The practice also emphasizes spiritual and mystical properties of the universe.

As of 2016 biodynamic techniques were used on 161,074 hectares (398,000 acres) in 60 countries. Germany accounts for 45% of the global total; the remainder average 1750 hectares (4,324 acres) per country. [36]

To the general public, the term "biodynamic" is less familiar than organic, although it is most familiar in the area of wine. According to biodynamic viticulturists, the basic principle of biodynamic grape growing is that a good grape begins in the compost heap. In fact, a growing number of wineries in California, France, New Zealand, and Oregon have joined the international discipline—and they're producing critically acclaimed wines. You'll read more on organic and biodynamic winegrowing in the next chapter.

Biodynamic certification

Demeter International manages certification of biodynamic farms internationally. An umbrella organization, Demeter International provides uniform standards to member affiliates in individual countries where certification is carried out. As opposed to organic certification (where standards vary from country to country), biodynamic certification is globally more standardized because all certification falls under Demeter.

Organic

Unlike previously discussed sustainable farming methods, organic farming is unique in being regulated by government, both in the US and abroad. The U.S. Department of Agriculture (USDA) defines organic food as "agricultural products produced by cultural, biological, or mechanical methods while reusing resources, promoting ecological balance, and conserving biodiversity."

Organic farming does not permit the use of synthetic fertilizers, chemical pesticides, sewage sludge, irradiation, or genetic engineering.[37] Organic farming is a form of agriculture that avoids or largely excludes the use of plant growth regulators and livestock feed additives. As much as possible, organic farmers rely on methods such as crop rotation, animal manures, and mechanical cultivation to maintain plant and soil health and productivity and to control weeds, insects, and other pests.

Animals producing organic meat and dairy cannot be fed antibiotics or growth hormones. Organic farms replace the use of chemical pesticides and fertilizers with pesticides derived from natural sources (such as biological pesticides)[38] and rely on intensive labor and management of food production, which is more expensive.[39]

Organic certification

Currently, the European Union, the United States, Canada, Mexico, Japan, and many other countries require producers to obtain certification in order to label and market food as organic within their borders. In turn, organic food is produced in a way that complies with a variety of standards set by national governments and international organizations.

Organic farming is based on resource recycling, ecological balance, and biodiversity conservation by integrating cultural, biological, and mechanical practices. Regardless of where organic food is grown, it is grown without the use of synthetic chemicals such as pesticides, herbicides, fungicides, and fertilizers. Under limited conditions, certain naturally occurring pesticides may be used. Additionally, organic foods are not processed using irradiation, industrial solvents, or chemical food additives.

USDA regulations require that farmers with organic sales over $5000 in a given year must obtain independent certification. USDA currently provides accreditation to over 50 organic certifiers in the United States, both state and private organizations.[40]

INTERNATIONAL ORGANIC FOOD MOVEMENTS

United States

The organic food movement in the United States was more of a renaissance than a revolution. As consumers learned more about the health hazards associated with the use of chemicals in food and household products, they became motivated to demand alternatives. The organic food crusade began as a grassroots movement for small-scale, locally sourced, sustainable agriculture.

Small specialty health food stores and farmer cooperatives were responsible for bringing organic food to a wider consumer audience.[41] In turn, consumer demand for organic products increased, and high-volume sales through more mainstream supermarkets rapidly replaced the direct farmer connection. Products that were originally offered only through specialty stores in the 1970s and 1980s made their way to supermarket shelves in the 1990s.

The 1990s saw sustained growth in the organic food industry. Major chains such as Whole Foods Market and Wild Oats Markets grew rapidly and bought up smaller chains and independent organic grocery stores.[42] The buying power of these organic grocery chains somewhat offset factors that had made organics more expensive, such as increased production costs, smaller-scale production, and the fees associated with government certification. These large chains marketed organic food to consumers as a moral and enjoyable alternative to conventionally grown food products.

Yet according to the Organic Trade Association's (OTA) 2014 industry survey, consumers are still confused about what "organic" really means. How does "organic" compare to "natural" foods and what about the presence (or nonpresence) of genetically modified organisms (GMOs)? Despite the confusion, it's presumed that many consumers believe that eating organic is the healthy option—healthy for them and healthy for the planet.

Europe

Small-scale and family farming have historically been an important part of daily life in many parts of Europe. Industrialized corporate farming did not dominate as fully in Europe as it did in the United States, and farmers and consumers started seeking alternatives to industrialized agriculture as early as the 1920s. In 1924, Austrian scientist and philosopher Dr. Rudolf Steiner gave a course on biodynamic farming, and the first biodynamic farms converted in the late 1920s. In the 1940s, many countries founded their respective organic organizations, and private sector interest in organic farming has been the driving force for sustainability since then. In 1991, European Union (EU) regulations on organic farming were published, and so began the official interest in organic agriculture on the pan-European level.

Today, more than 70 percent of EU consumers say they trust organic products,[43] and areas farmed using organic methods in the EU have grown by 13 percent every year between 2002 and 2011, thanks to rising consumer demand.[44]

Despite this robust organic ethos, European agriculture has seen the fast-food industry and industrialized agriculture make inroads into some of the oldest cities in Europe as global trade and international tourism have increased. Those incursions have sparked pushback, most notably the Slow Food Movement, founded by Carlo Petrini in Italy in 1986.

The Slow Food Movement embraces small-scale, local agriculture that promotes biodiversity. It rejects the "fast-food" culture and farming methods that destroy biodiversity. Slow Food aims to reconnect food with a respective local culture, and help consumers be mindful about what they put in their bodies. It seeks to replace industrially farmed, highly processed products with carefully grown food that is healthier for people, animals, and the environment—and tastier, too.

Canada

While the organic food movement began with a few small-scale farmers in the 1950s, in Canada, it gained momentum in the late 1970s. At this time, farmers in various provinces formed organizations to govern their organic farming standards and methods. In the 1980s, the governments of each province increased their involvement in the development of their respective organic farming industry.

The various standards and guidelines across provinces caused the Standards Council of Canada to approve a National Standard for Organic Farming in 1999. However, since application of the standard is voluntary, there is little oversight and little uniformity as to what is designated as "organic" in Canada. Additionally, since 2000, the number of organic farmers in Canada has plateaued.[45] While annual organic agricultural sales exceed $2.6 billion, consumers are wary of what an "organic" label really means. One report from the Frontier Centre for Public Policy states, "organic crops and livestock are not tested in Canada before they are certified, thus making organic certification essentially meaningless."[46]

However, the majority of Canadian shoppers do assume that organic food contains significantly less pesticides and other additives, rendering it healthier than non-organically produced food.

Japan

The organic industry in Japan stems from what is known in Japanese as *teikei-saibai*, or a contract-based production and distribution arrangement. Through these arrangements, farmers agree to produce food organically or naturally and distribute it to the consumer. It's worth noting that the concept of *anshin-anzen* (peace of mind and safety) is very important in Japan, especially when it comes to food. Because of this, the *teikei-saibai* is a critical bond between producers and consumers.

However, these informal agreements led to confusion as to what "organic" and "natural" meant and how they were different. So, in 1999 the Japanese Ministry of Agriculture, Forest and Fisheries (MAFF) established an official organic grading system.

Despite this new system, Japanese consumers remain unclear about the distinction between organic and natural, what organic means to them, and why organic produce should command a premium. A recent survey indicates that the natural food market in Japan is estimated at around $6 billion, about five times the organic food market. The survey also indicates that there is enormous room for growth within the Japanese organic food market.[47]

This concludes our side trip into sustainable consumption in general and the introduction to sustainable agriculture. Now we move into the world of sustainable wine.

KEY TAKEAWAYS

- While the pace of change toward more sustainable behavior differs from region to region, today's consumers are increasingly aware of the environmental challenges that affect them. Interestingly, consumers have continued to value sustainability throughout the Great Recession, and more consumers are becoming active participants in the creation of a more sustainable economy.
- Consumers in developed countries are becoming increasingly more concerned with environmental, social, and economic issues and willing to act on those concerns. One in four Americans says he or she actively takes steps to make their home or lifestyle greener. However, factors like availability, affordability, and convenience of traditional products often override good intentions.
- The hopeful signs, however, are balanced by a competing reality. While consumers in the developed world are becoming increasingly sensitive to concepts of environmental harm and sustainability, consumption levels in these countries are already high, and behavior is still principally dictated by price, quality, and convenience rather than by origin of product and sustainable content.
- Sustainable food is the exception. The organic food movement of the 1990s changed how many consumers in the United States and elsewhere viewed food and broadly influenced agricultural production and marketing practices. The enormous success of American organic food chains like Whole Foods Market and Wild Oats Markets proved that organic food could be profitable to retailers and producers as well as appealing to the general public. Production and availability have grown substantially, and consumers are making the correlation between what they eat and their health, and the health of the planet.
- This has led to greater consumer interest in nonfood organic products. Increasingly, consumers are making purchase decisions based on their personal values and how their purchases will affect their health, the health of their environment, and the planet as a whole. The issue remains a niche one, however, and the disconnect between awareness and action is stark. Media attention and websites such as greenwashingindex.com have increased consumer awareness of this problem.
- But we are far from mainstreaming sustainable consumption. Despite their demand for organic goods, consumers are still confused about what the various terms (organic, natural, sustainable, biodynamic) really mean.

CHAPTER 1 REFERENCES

1. Makower, J. *John Ellington: "The Breakthrough Challenge" and Tomorrow's Bottom Line.* Available online: http://www.greenbiz.com/blog/2014/09/03/john-elkington-breakthrough -challenge-tomorrows-bottom-line (Accessed 21 August 2015.)

2. Morelli, J. "Environmental Sustainability: A Definition for Environmental Professionals." *Journal of Environmental Sustainability.* Volume 1. Issue 1 (2011). Available online: http:// scholarworks.rit.edu/cgi/viewcontent.cgi?article=1007&context=jes (Accessed 21 August 2015.)

3. Holme, L., Watts, R. *Making Good Business Sense.* The World Business Council for Sustainable Development. 2000. Available online: http://www.wbcsd.org/web/publications/csr2000 .pdf (Accessed 21 August 2015.)

4. World Business Council for Sustainable Development. *Sustainable Consumption Facts and Trends from a Business Perspective.* Available online: http://www.saiplatform.org/uploads/ Modules/Library/WBCSD_Sustainable_Consumption_web.pdf (Accessed 15 September 2014).

5. World Health Organization. *Ecosystems and Human Well-Being: Health Synthesis.* Available online: http://www.who.int/globalchange/ecosystems/ecosystems05/en/ (Accessed 15 September 2014.)

6. Deloitte. *Consumer 2020: Reading the Signs.* Available online: http://www2.deloitte.com/ru /en/pages/consumer-business/articles/consumer-2020.html (Accessed 15 September 2014.)

7. Birol, F. *International Energy Agency.* World Energy and Environmental Outlook to 2030. Available online: https://www.iea.org/publications/freepublications/publication/WEO2011 _WEB.pdf (Accessed 15 Sept 2014.)

8. World Business Council for Sustainable Development. *Sustainable Consumption Facts and Trends from a Business Perspective.* Available online: http://www.saiplatform.org/uploads/ Modules/Library/WBCSD_Sustainable_Consumption_web.pdf (Accessed 15 September 2014.)

9. Nielsen. *Doing Well by Doing Good.* Available online: http://www.nielsen.com/us/en /insights/reports/2014/doing-well-by-doing-good.html (Accessed 15 September 2014.)

10. Gerzema, J. *Understanding the Spend Shift.* Forbes. 29 November 2010. Available online: http://www.forbes.com/2010/11/29/recession-consumers-values-spend-shift-sentiment -shopping-sales-leadership.html (Accessed 24 August 2015.)

11. Globescan. *The Regeneration Roadmap.* Available online: http://www.globescan.com/news- and-analysis/press-releases/press-releases-2012/248-regeneration-consumer-study-finds -consumers-buying-less-and-buying-better.html (Accessed online 13 October 2014.)

12. Ibid.

13. Ibid.

14. Ipsos. *Sustainability Issues in the Retail Sector.* Available online: http://www.ipsosmorigrads .com/pdf/reputation_report_vl.pdf (Accessed 15 September 2014.)

15. World Business Council for Sustainable Development. *A Vision for Sustainable Consumption.* Available online: http://www.wbcsd.org/Pages/EDocument/EDocumentDetails.aspx? ID=13718&NoSearchContextKey=true (Accessed 15 September 2014.)

16. Starbucks. Starbucks Global Responsibility Report 2014. Available online: http://www .starbucks.com/responsibility (Accessed 8 February 2016.)

17. Deloitte. *Finding the Green in Today's Shoppers* 2009. Available online: http://www.gmaonline .org/downloads/research-and-reports/greenshopper09.pdf (Accessed 15 September 2014.)

18. Ibid.

19. The International Ecotourism Society. *2009 Annual Report*. Available online: https://www .ecotourism.org/annual-reports (Accessed 15 September 2014.)

20. Bernstein, H. *McGraw-Hill Construction: Green Outlook 2013 & ENR CICI*. Available online: http://www.worldgbc.org/files/8613/6295/6420/World_Green_Building_Trends_Smart Market_Report_2013.pdf (Accessed 15 Sept 2014.)

21. Packaged Facts. *Green Cleaning Products in the U.S.* Available online: http://www .packagedfacts.com/Tags/green-cleaning (Accessed online 15 September 2014.)

22. Foundation Center. "Diminishing Dollars for Social Justice Philanthropy." 17 November 2011. Available online: http://foundationcenter.org/media/news/20111117.html (Accessed 15 September 2014.)

23. Greene, C. United States Department of Agriculture. *Economic Research Service*, 24 Oct 2013. Available online: http://www.ers.usda.gov/data-products/organic-production /documentation.aspx (Accessed 2 September 2014.)

24. Haumann, B. "American Appetite for Organic Products Breaks Through $35 Billion Mark." Organic Trade Association, 15 May 2014. Available online: https://www.ota.com/news /press-releases/17165 (Accessed 2 September 2014.)

25. Ibid.

26. Ibid.

27. National Pesticide Information Center. *DDT Technical Fact Sheet*, 2000. Available online: http://npic.orst.edu/factsheets/ddttech.pdf (Accessed 29 August 2014.)

28. Gold, M. United States Departure of Agriculture. *Sustainable Agriculture: Definitions and Terms*. National Agricultural Library, August 2007. Available online: http://afsic.nal.usda. gov/sustainable-agriculture-definitions-and-terms-1 (Accessed 29 August 2014.)

29. Agricultural Sustainability Institute at University of California, Davis. *What is Sustainable Agriculture?* Available online: http://www.sarep.ucdavis.edu/ (Accessed 29 August 2014.)

30. Pollan, M. *How Change Is Going to Come in the Food System*. Michael Pollan. 11 September 2011. Available online: http://michaelpollan.com/articles-archive/how-change-is-going-to -come-in-the-food-system/ (Accessed 29 August 2014.)

31. Negin, E. *The Alar Scare Was Real*. Public Broadcasting Service. Available online: http:// www.pbs.org/tradesecrets/docs/alarscarenegin.html (Accessed 29 August 2014.)

32. The Humane Society. *How to Decipher Egg Carton Labels*. 3 July 2013. Available online: http://www.humanesociety.org/issues/confinement_farm/facts/guide_egg_labels .html?referrer=https://www.google.com/ (Accessed 29 Aug 2014.)

33. Gold, M. United States Departure of Agriculture. *Sustainable Agriculture: Definitions and Terms*. National Agricultural Library, August 2007. Available online: http://afsic.nal.usda .gov/sustainable-agriculture-definitions-and-terms-1 (Accessed 29 August 2014.)

34. Holistic Management. *What Is Holistic Management?* Available online: http://holistic management.org/wp-content/uploads/2011/12/HolisticManagement-1-22.pdf (Accessed 29 August 2014.)

35. Gold, M. United States Departure of Agriculture.

36. Paull, J. "Organics Olympiad 2011: Global Indices of Leadership in Organic Agriculture."

Journal of Social and Development Sciences. May 2011. Available online: http://orgprints .org/18860/1/Paull2011OlympiadJSDS.pdf (Accessed 15 September 2014.)

37. Agricultural Marketing Service. *What Is Organic Certification?* United States Department of Agriculture. Available online: http://www.ams.usda.gov/sites/default/files/media /Organic%20Certification%20Fact%20Sheet.pdf (Accessed 29 August 2014.)

38. Environmental Protection Agency. *Organic Farming.* Available online: http://www.epa.gov /agriculture/torg.html (Accessed 29 August 2014.)

39. Kutz, M. *Handbook of Farm, Dairy, and Food Machinery.* Delmar, NY: Myer Kutz Associates, Inc., 2007 p. 24.

40. Greene, C. United States Department of Agriculture. *Economic Research Service,* 24 Oct 2013. Available online: http://www.ers.usda.gov/data-products/organic-production /documentation.aspx (Accessed 2 September 2014.)

41. University of Santa Cruz. *Timeline: Cultivating a Movement, An Oral History Series on Organic Farming and Sustainable Agriculture on California's Central Coast.* University Library. Available online: http://library.ucsc.edu/reg-hist/cultiv/timeline (Accessed 2 September 2014.)

42. Whole Foods Market. *Whole Foods Market History.* Available online: http://www.whole-foodsmarket.com/company-info/whole-foods-market-history (Accessed 2 September 2014.)

43. European Commission. *Report on the Results of the Public Consultation on the Review of the EU Policy on Organic Agriculture.* 2013. Available online: http://ec.europa.eu/agriculture /organic/documents/eu-policy/of-publication-executive-summary_en.pdf (Accessed 3 September 2014.)

44. Bertini, I. *EU Organic Farming on the Rise Despite UK Government's GMOs Sympathy.* Organic Consumers Association. 28 July 2014. Available online: https://www.organic consumers.org/news/eu-organic-farming-rise-despite-uk-governments-gmos-sympathy (Accessed 3 September 2014.)

45. Forge, F. *Organic Farming in Canada: An Overview.* Parliament of Canada, 5 October 2004. Available online: http://www.parl.gc.ca/content/lop/researchpublications/prb0029-e.htm (Accessed 3 September 2014.)

46. Humphreys, A. *Canada's Organic Food Certification System "Little More Than an Extortion Racket," Report Says.* The National Post. 24 November 2012. Available online: http://news .nationalpost.com/news/canada/canadas-organic-food-certification-system-little-more -than-an-extortion-racket-report-says (Accessed 3 September 2014.)

47. Motomura, C. *Japanese Organic Market.* USDA Foreign Agricultural Service, 20 June 2013. Available online: http://gain.fas.usda.gov/Recent%20GAIN%20Publications/Japanese% 20Organic%20Market_Osaka%20ATO_Japan_6-20-2013.pdf (Accessed 3 September 2014.)

CHAPTER 2

SUSTAINABILITY IN WINE

*Organic, Biodynamic, Sustainable, and Conventional
Viticulture and Winemaking*

M Y WORK WITH SUSTAINABLE AGRICULTURE includes several years in the coffee industry, during a period of tremendous growth in high-quality coffee shops and retail categories around the world. As a senior executive at Starbucks Coffee Company, I led the company's global responsibility efforts focused on rigorous approaches to sustainable agriculture for coffee, tea, and cocoa, and fair and responsible relationships with farmers. Later, I joined the board of directors of DE Master Blenders 1753 of the Netherlands (formerly Douwe Egbert) and served on the board's Sustainability Committee. Being a wine enthusiast and student of wine at the same time that I worked in coffee cultivation, harvest, and the roasting process, I instinctively grasped the similarities between both agricultural commodities and naturally wanted to understand viticulture, winemaking, and the wine business. Along this journey, I pursued an MBA degree in wine management in Bordeaux, France, where my research concentrated on wine supply chain management and integrating sustainable supplier strategies.

Coffee occupies a place in the market and in our cultural life analogous to wine, and the experience of it can teach us a great deal when it comes to understanding the elements of a sustainable wine industry. Neither is a nutritional necessity, but both are integral to our food habits. They are both consumed for pleasure. And the aroma and flavors of both have the potential to connect those who imbibe with the lives and fates of people throughout the world, to their culture, their nation, their soil. What we enjoy is a direct result of their care of the plant, precision in processing, careful transportation and handling, and diligence in preparation. Consumer awareness of coffee cultivation and its sometimes-negative effect on people and the land foreshadows current expanding developments in the wine industry.

The industries that produce and bring these two drinkable commodities to market also share important similarities. Vintners confess that wine is made in the vineyard, and the same holds true for coffee. Both are agricultural products from specific regions that are grown according to exacting standards, and then prepared and sold to the consumer as a drinkable commodity. There are grades and flavor differences based upon where it was raised, how it was processed, and just flukes of nature that are recognized during evaluation, and priced accordingly. The soil, weather, orientation of the sun, altitude, and rainfall—in other words, terroir—affect the flavor of coffee beans and grapes.

Just like seasonal harvesters of grapes, coffee farm workers have to learn when and how to properly pick ripe fruit, sort the good from the bad, and care for the beans to prevent mold or desiccation. Pruning, spacing, pest management, and watering are among the many considerations for coffee farmers, just like grape growers, to control and optimize, and both are susceptible to flavor variability due to seasonality, as well as devastating weather that can wipe out their crops and livelihoods for the year.

But the similarities between coffee and wine don't end there. From the way we taste them to the words we use to describe them, it turns out that there's much more to two of the world's favorite drinks. But there are very clear differences. Wine and coffee operate along two very different supply chain structures.

For wine, growers of the fruit and producers of the beverage have traditionally supplied their own region of consumers, and the supply chain for wine is still largely immediate and fairly tight. If a winery does not literally own its own vineyard, for example, it is often within arm's reach of one as well as the other links in the value chain. This structure has saved costs and maximized profits in a way that coffee can't possibly begin to emulate.

Coffee, on the other hand, is produced quite far from its eventual market, and that is only the beginning of the differences between the coffee and wine supply chains. The coffee tree is a tropical evergreen shrub that only grows in a defined area above and below the equator, often called the "coffee belt." The coffee supply chain is often complex and varies in different countries but typically includes many layers, and the grower is often squeezed, receiving a small share of the value of production.

In addition to the coffee farmer, usually working on a very small plot of land of just one or two hectares, there are numerous intermediaries—perhaps as many as five intermediary links in the chain—who buy coffee at any stage between harvesting the coffee cherries and delivering green beans to the roaster. Some intermediaries do primary processing (drying or hulling) or collect together sufficient quantities of coffee cherries from many individual farmers to transport or sell to a processor. Processors are mill owners, or a farmers' co-operative that pools resources to buy the necessary equipment. In some countries, the government controls the coffee trade, perhaps by buying the coffee from processors at a fixed price and selling it in auctions for export. Then there are the exporters whose expert knowledge of the local area and producers generally enables them to guarantee the quality of the shipment. Next there are dealers and brokers who supply the coffee beans to the roasters in the right quantities, at the right time, at a price acceptable to buyer and seller. And finally, the roasters—firms such as Nestlé and Starbucks, whose expertise is to turn the green coffee beans into products people enjoy drinking, and retailers, which range from large supermarkets, to hotels and caterers, coffee shop chains to small independent retailers. Every intermediary gets a portion of the value in this chain, with the smallest amount typically going to the farmer.

Clearly from the perspective of environmental responsibility, the complex coffee supply chain is full of opportunities to pursue sustainable agriculture, and its social inequities and societal needs in these regions make the industry a priority for social activists. Coffee is the second most traded commodity in the world after oil, and market swings in the price can have a profound effect on incomes in coffee-producing countries. Small coffee farmers in developing countries are sometimes forced to sell their beans for less than they cost to produce.

Meanwhile, the largest coffee corporations continue to reap enormous profits from the growth in trendy coffee shops and consumer preference for high-quality Arabica-based beverages. Between 1997 and 2004 the price of coffee fell almost 70 percent to a 30-year low, in many cases forcing coffee farming families out of business. Some farmers cut down trees in rainforests to make room for planting more coffee trees, thereby destroying vital biodiversity. This was a period of escalating profits for branded coffee and not surprisingly coincided with a heightened level of activism by environmentalists, social justice campaigners, and fair trade advocates, all concerned with the negative impact of coffee growing on tropical rainforests and inequity in the coffee supply chain. Consumers were made aware of the destruction of biodiversity "hotspots" in coffee-growing regions and the social inequalities that have long plagued coffee farmers and seasonal labor in this complex supply chain. As a result, consumers in the United States and Europe opted for fair trade, organic, and shade grown coffee.

Coffee roasters, like Starbucks, Green Mountain Coffee, Nestlé, Illy, Douwe Egberts, and German giant Tchibo, all responded defensively to the criticism and campaigns organized by activists like Oxfam while working internally to develop codes of conduct and sustainable procurement policies that were more socially equitable and promoted greater environmental responsibility. These companies were not content to only procure certified organic and fair trade coffee, but rather to develop a holistic and comprehensive—water conservation, soil health, air quality, biodiversity, reduction of deforestation, and greenhouse gas emissions, and focus on improving coffee quality and taste, ensuring higher financial returns for farmer and the company—a true sustainable approach.

This includes negotiating long-term contracts with many farmers and coops, guaranteeing them a price per pound above the volatile commodity market price, in exchange for commitments to maintain high-quality Arabica coffee crop production, and to use greater care for the soil, protect biodiversity of the forests, and conserve and treat water used in coffee harvesting. The roasters codes typically include restrictions on the use of child labor, and the companies invest in social projects like schools, health clinics for seasonal labor, and access to clean drinking water.

Some companies have included policies for climate change adaptation, understanding the impact that climate change is having on Central America's and East Africa's coffee production (not unlike the impact of climate change on wine grape growing), which puts high-quality coffee supply at risk in 20 to 30 years. Climate change has meant that coffee farms are more susceptible to erosion and increased pest infestations. Shifts in rainfall and harvest patterns, especially for the Arabica bean grown at altitudes between 4,000 and 5,000 feet above sea level are shrinking the available usable land in coffee regions around the world, affecting not only supply but also the livelihoods of communities.

The sustainability performance of the wine industry has yet to receive the kind of media scrutiny and activist interest that other industries like coffee have in recent years. But such issues have started to gain prominence, as consumers want to learn the cultural and environmental stories behind the wines they drink. And a day of reckoning for the wine industry is fast approaching, judging by the increasing number of complaints over land use, objection to permits for new vineyards, water rights disputes, protests over pesticide spray drift, and legal actions that producers face as a result of the health impacts of chemical use in vineyards. The industry should heed the lessons from the coffee experience.

In Sonoma County, California, for example, more wineries face growing objections to the industry's expansion. Between 2000 and 2016, 300 new wineries and tasting rooms were approved—a nearly 360 percent increase over the previous three decades—and many of those wineries have decided in recent years to boost business by offering an array of events, from wine-tasting dinners to weddings and harvest parties.

Representatives of the county's multibillion-dollar wine industry say such events are vital for local vintners to sell their wines and stay competitive. But the industry's growth has sparked strong blowback from many rural residents, who say unruly crowds, loud noise, and traffic on narrow, winding roads is detracting from the peace and quiet of their neighborhoods. Critics say the industry's expansion has gone overboard, impacting daily life for winery neighbors while clogging area roads, attracting thousands of visitors to the most popular annual events. They object to the commercialization of agricultural lands and diminishing of the rural character of the county.

In France, pesticides awareness groups have sprung up in most viticulture regions, and anti-pesticide protests have been rife in 2016 with the Gironde administrative region and Bordeaux at its epicenter as the country's largest user of pesticides. Pressure groups in Burgundy and in the Mâconnais area have demanded that grape growers cut pesticide use. Alongside the protests, a former Bergerac vineyard worker successfully sued her ex-employer over pesticide-related illness—believed to be a first in France.

From here, this story builds on the uniqueness of wine and takes us into the emerging world of sustainable wines. This is a new world where growers and vintners alike are connecting to sustainability as an attitude that encompasses all of their work. Many practices used in producing wine have long been sustainable, even when they weren't labeled as such; others have not. Multiple choices exist about how the work can be done in the vineyard and in the winery.

The idea of sustainability allows us to think through our options with a broader understanding of the impact our choices have on the environment, on others, and on ourselves. Around the world, entire regions of growers and producers are adopting thoughtful and rigorous sustainability programs. For some, the goal is to continue to produce great wines while lessening their environmental footprint. For others, the goal is to preserve market share or gain a marketing angle. And still, for others, the goal is simply to not get left behind. From the industry as a whole, the goal should be to stay ahead of consumer and community concerns and avoid widespread pushback.

Some producers are even adjusting their work to specifically offset their greenhouse gas (GHG) production, as you will see later in Chapter 7, Measuring Sustainability and Life Cycle Analysis. Countries that export a large percentage of their total wine production are motivated to examine the transport burden and attempt to minimize it or offset it with other sustainability practices in the vineyard and in the winery that will create a net reduction in GHG, or reduce their overall environmental footprint. Australia, Chile, and New Zealand, for example, export to far away markets in the UK, Sweden, and the United States and are acutely aware of their emissions.

Viognier, Bell Vineyard, Gisborne NZ.
Credit: Doug Bell

But sustainability is not only about reducing the environmental footprint of the wine industry. The industry also recognizes social and ethical challenges in their midst—worker training and worker conditions, community needs outside the cellar door, and demands for ethics and authenticity amid an atmosphere of counterfeiting.

Adopting and incorporating sustainability into the work of wine growing and wine making is not trivial. These twin goals add substantial burdens to many who already work long hours, and additional costs sometimes where the margins are thin. In the beginning of this pursuit, there must be education and self-assessment. Then, with official certification comes increased paper work, inspection, and on-site audits. In the best-case scenarios, there are also real and significant changes in existing practices that will actually lead to a more sustainable future as a result of certification.

The sustainability performance of the wine industry has yet to receive the kind of media scrutiny and general interest that other industries have in recent years. But such issues have started to gain prominence, as consumers want to learn the cultural and environmental stories behind the wines they drink.

The industry is being shaped by rigorous, compulsory environmental regulations, voluntary assessment, and certification, as well as by more environmentally conscious consumers who want to be sure they are purchasing products that respect the environment. The management of the wine production process and its effects on the environment must be considered a critical performance factor for the industry.

The wine production process affects the natural environment that surrounds the vineyards and can negatively impact the quality of water, soil, and air. Pollution from the use of chemical products, such as insecticides, fungicides, or herbicides, can be as diverse in effect as the products that cause the pollution. Pesticides and other chemical fertilizers can remain in the soil, the clay, and the organic matter within the soil for years, causing a loss of fertility in the land intended for cultivation. Degradation of the quality of the soil also exhausts nutrients and allows erosion. Furthermore, if the soil is polluted, rainfall will cause the subterranean waters to be contaminated as well.

In response to these challenges, natural (organic or biodynamic) wines have developed a notable presence on the global wine scene over the last few years. Marketing sustainable winegrowing and promoting environmental issues have become a driving power on the world wine market. The New World producers have led the sustainable trend, with New Zealand cultivating its "green" image, Australia moving rapidly toward organic viticulture, and Chile passing a country-wide environmentally sustainable code of conduct, which also addresses social responsibility in a significant way. In Europe in 2011, 5.6 percent of all grape-growing areas were dedicated to organic grapes.[1] According to the USDA, the United States had 3.1 million acres of certified organic cropland in 2011.[2] In South Africa, over 500 acres of wine grapes were estimated to be under fully organic farming standards in 2002.[3]

WHAT MOTIVATES A WINE OPERATION TO ADOPT SUSTAINABLE PRACTICES?

Some wineries adopt these practices to avoid regulatory fines and market pressures, while others are more proactive in their efforts because of management's values, employee welfare, or competitive pressures. Successful winery regions are often part of economic clusters that include hospitality and tourism. Environmental stewardship in this unique agricultural environment intersects with wineries and tourism. The high visibility of wine regions encourages vineyards to adopt sustainable growing practices.

Wineries I have visited while researching this book have come to the decision to embark on a sustainability strategy for their own unique reasons. In some instances, industry mandates—like the New Zealand goal to be 100 percent sustainable by 2012 and the Sonoma County Wine Grape Commission voluntary commitment to be 100 percent sustainable by 2019—put pressure on producers to adopt sustainability. (New Zealand reached 99 percent compliance by 2012.) While most support their industry and association efforts, some are successfully implementing their own sustainability strategy and practices. An industry sustainability program provides them with structure, a self-assessment process, and exposure to best practices, certification, and, in most regions, a seal for their bottled wine.

While visiting New Zealand in 2014, I was impressed by how many producers opted for more rigorous organic or biodynamic certifications, believing that Sustainable Wine New Zealand (SWNZ) environmental standards were too low for their personal commitments. In Chile, the Sustainability Code of the Chilean Wine Industry is a voluntary program that encourages sustainable wine production in three areas: vineyards, wineries, and social commitment.

Their reasons for adopting these philosophies, systems, and practices are several: reputation, family succession, certification and bottle seal, a good marketing story, and the following issues:

Peer pressure: In the case of New Zealand sustainability, participation in the industry sustainability program was a prerequisite to receiving the marketing support of the association. Wines of Chile, the industry association, has an expectation that the vast majority of wineries there will participate in their sustainability code for wine.

The retailer hurdle: Concerned about their "sustainable" reputation, or while implementing their own CSR policy, retailers frequently play the role of "curator" for consumer purchases. A decade ago, it was rare for consumers to take notice of terms such as organic, biodynamic, sustainability, carbon-neutral, or "wine miles," but their concern in this regard is increasing. Retail chains are increasingly demanding purpose-made plans to show wineries' commitment to environmentally friendly approaches. Retailers present a sustainability "hurdle" that must be crossed by suppliers, sometimes without specific criteria. Other organizations, such as The Sustainability Consortium, Systembolaget of Sweden, and retail liquor monopolies in Canada—LCBO in Ontario and SAQ in Quebec—have very specific sustainability requirements as part of their procurement process.

Family ownership: These wineries are motivated toward sustainability because they have received an inheritance from prior generations and want to maintain the land and the productivity of the business for future generations. Regardless of age or size, many wineries are proceeding with sustainable practices, even if no differentiation advantage is manifest. The Lodi Winegrape Commission states that the top motivation for grape growers to participate in sustainable efforts is "to preserve the family's agricultural legacy and to pass that legacy along to future generations."[4] Sustainability practices are part and parcel of how cultural capital is passed from one generation to the next.

The business case: Research has been mixed on whether consumers are willing to pay more for eco-labeled wines, and yet the number of wineries adopting certified sustainable, organic, or biodynamic practices continues to rise. Certain demographic groups, such as millennials and LOHAS consumers, seek sustainably produced wines when they shop.

In a number of countries, winery owners have found that adopting sustainable strategies actually allowed them to focus on cost reduction. They reported reducing waste and improving operational efficiencies. Many winemakers also believe that their wine tastes better.

Personal values: Some viticulturists express a deep personal connection with the land and a feeling of personal obligation to take care of the vine, to protect it from disease and to ensure its long-term health. Others have a profound respect for natural habitats and the role such natural spaces play in preserving biodiversity and air quality.[5]

Some in the industry believe that sustainable farming can result in a more complex and interesting wine—that better grape quality can be achieved through a more holistic and deeper understanding of the vineyard agro-ecosystem.[6]

Community and land use: These concerns are among the most serious of the wine industry's issues, when neighbors and communities worry about the impact of a vineyard's operations on the local habitats and species, water supply, and water quality and the reduction of organic waste.

The wine industry in the United States has been the target of local communities who complain about overuse of available tracts of land, use of chemical pesticides, herbicides and fertilizers, tapping scarce water resources, and nonsustainable packaging materials. In August 2014, Los Angeles County supervisors approved a land use plan that prohibited the transition of more land in the Santa Monica mountains to vineyards, fearing similar developments as in other parts of the state where hundreds of trees were razed in order to make way for planting of vines. The sponsor of the plan indicated that the plan "would prohibit new commercial vineyards because of their serious impact on water quality in our streams, beaches and the Santa Monica Bay. The policy prohibiting new vineyards would also prevent the loss of sensitive habitat and avoid concerns over the industrial spraying of pesticides."

In February 2015, Joe Wagner (of the Wagner family that owns Caymus Vineyards, amongst other brands) began laying plans to expand his current vineyard acreage to include a pastoral stretch of Highway 12 between Santa Rosa and Sebastopol for a new Dairyman Winery. The facility would be capable of producing up to 500,000 cases of wine and 250,000 gallons of distilled spirits a year. Community members quickly mobilized against the project as soon as it was announced and long before public hearings were scheduled. They worried it would be too big a facility for the old dairy farm and would cause even more traffic and congestion problems on the already-busy Highway 12. Additionally, they expressed concern about environmental impact—including demands on the groundwater basin, given ongoing drought conditions.[7]

The wine industry's complex sustainability issues extend beyond the natural environment in the vineyard. Firms must also address environmental stewardship throughout the production and distribution of the wine, as well as maintain social responsibility in their community to be considered as truly "sustainable." Increasingly, both wine producers and consumers are looking beyond environmental practices to the broader concept of overall sustainability (the "triple bottom line" approach), and working to integrate three main goals: environmental health, economic profitability, and social and economic equity.

Social equity means taking care of people—increasing safety and developmental training, adding pay system bonuses and incentives such as housing and health insurance for seasonal workers, and taking care to focus on people issues as well as environmental issues. In fact, the wine industry has had its share of "people" challenges over the years, often focused on the treatment of seasonal labor and lack of advancement opportunities. In 1973, grape workers in California's Coachella and San Joaquin valleys went on strike for several months, protesting unfair working conditions and lack of protection by the government. More recently, a documentary from producer and actress Eva Longoria called *Food Chains* exposed the human costs involved in our industrial food supply chain. While not focused on the wine industry, the documentary takes on the fast-food and supermarket industries—citing how important they are to making change in the fields for seasonal and year-round agricultural labor.

Other external factors motivating sustainability in the wine sector include effects of the changing environment on the winemaking process. Problems derived from weather conditions are frequent sources of difficulty in all kinds of agriculture, and there is growing concern about the effects that climate change can have on crops.

Changes in average temperatures can affect important aspects of wine production, such as the varieties of grape that can be produced in a specific geographical region. The different varieties of grapes used for winemaking must be grown within certain average temperature margins in order for them to achieve adequate maturity. Problems such as deforestation, soil erosion, drought, and variability in rainfall affect the decision-making processes in winemaking businesses.

A 2013 study by Conservation International found that areas suitable for wine production could shrink by as much as 73 percent by 2050. Additionally, climate change could potentially lead to the creation of new vineyards in areas that are currently unusable due to their harsh climates. Equally, changes in the vegetative cycle of the grapevine could affect how the grapes taste and smell.[8]

Finally, other (and perhaps more tangible) motivations are seen as threats or opportunities for the future prospects for the wine industry:

Alternative packaging: Packaging formats present both pitfalls and opportunities, while offering huge potential for reducing costs, increasing profit margins, and creating loyal audiences. The drive to reduce distribution and breakage costs while addressing environmental concerns will force wineries to go the extra mile in terms of packaging innovation.[9]

Health concerns: The global obesity epidemic and rising levels of health awareness are giving rise to low-calorie variants. Female audiences and young urbanites provide a potential driver for new health conscious categories. Low-calorie, low-alcohol by volume (ABV) and organic variants will be the main tools in the alcoholic drinks industry's efforts to appeal to health-aware urbanites and meet the concerns of health advocacy groups. In fact, low ABV/low-caloric alcoholic beverages have become the main CSR initiative in some markets (e.g., Quebec, Australia).[10]

Now that we understand why grape growers and wine makers adopt sustainable practices, let's delve into their choices for sustainable farming. What are the differences between conventional wine growing, organic, biodynamic, and sustainable?

The term sustainability is often used quite loosely, and it is a term that has been abused by wineries and marketers alike. In the absence of a legal definition for sustainable wine, regional associations are establishing certification systems and codes of conduct for sustainable practice. Even so, consumers are confused by the myriad certifications that exist to assure the consumer of the "green" authenticity of the wine. There are overlaps among all the "green" practices associated with wine: How does one define organic, certified sustainable, and biodynamic?

Let's start with the basic foundation of winemaking: wine is made in the vineyard. All good wine producers know that you can't make good wine from bad grapes (though it is possible to take good grapes and make bad wine!). The most important part of the winemaking process happens long before the grapes get to the winery. Winemaking starts outside, in the fields when the grower is planting, pruning, picking, making decisions about what to plant where, when to prune, how to manage numerous pests and diseases, and when to harvest.

This is where the distinctions between these growing techniques are critical.

CONVENTIONAL WINEMAKING

In conventional grape growing, the viticulturist uses chemical pesticides and insecticides to control diseases and pests. Grapes often have very thin skins, and yet they are some of the most heavily sprayed farm items—meaning chemical pesticides can easily permeate the skin, and residues can "live" within the fruit and the skin. Often, we think of wine as something natural—straight from the soil and vines—more natural than soda or sugary juice. But it's surprising to learn how many chemicals can be a part of the winemaking process.

A conventional vineyard is a monoculture. Monoculture means that the vineyard has only one crop (the vine), and the grower does what he can to kill or remove almost every other living thing that could be harmful to the vine. Farmers use pesticides, fungicides, and other chemical sprays to prevent diseases and pests from attacking the vine, leaves, and grapes.

Unlike a natural and more biodiverse ecosystem—where the vine lives alongside other plants as well as insects, birds, and other small animals—conventional wine grape growing entails putting the vine first and eliminating any and all threats to the vine.

In a monoculture, where you only have a single crop, it is very easy for the crop to be completely (and quickly) destroyed by a single pest or disease. With a more diverse ecosystem surrounding the vine, it's only natural that some insects, birds, or animals may compete with or prey on the vine, but they will also compete with and prey on each other. This situation is beneficial (and more stable) for the ecosystem as a whole.

While conventional farming (and the overuse of chemical pesticides and fungicides) is still "the norm" in many places, vineyards are increasingly making use of a process called integrated pest management (IPM). Thus, there is recognition among many conventional vineyards that they must be more prudent in their pesticide use. IPM helps farmers and viticulturists set standards for when they will use chemical products and how much (i.e., when the pest activity reaches a certain threshold), what pests they will control (as not all pests require a chemical response), and how they will prevent pests from appearing in the first place. IPM is an effective and environmentally sensitive approach to pest control.

Currently, France has one of the highest levels of pesticide use in Europe. The French government enacted an "EcoPhyto" plan in 2008 with the goal of cutting pesticide use in half by 2018. Part of the problem with grapes (in general) is that they are more prone to disease than other crops and they require more regular pesticide spraying. Plus, many French farmers spray pesticides with air atomizers that allow the pesticides to drift into neighboring communities. Farmers are reluctant to upgrade their technology—partly from force of habit and partly from the increased cost associated with newer/safer pesticide applicators.

France has also decided to tighten laws on spraying practices. France's Senate approved a proposal in August 2014 that would prevent farmers from using spraying practices that pose a health risk to people. If that is not workable, local authorities would have the freedom to set a "minimum distance" between pesticide spraying and a particular public building or village boundary.

The move comes after 23 children and their teacher were taken ill in the Bordeaux region as a result of vineyard spraying near their school. Similarly, in April 2014, a winery in the Dordogne was convicted of "gross negligence" when an employee, Sylvie Sorneau, was hospitalized with nausea, headaches, and debilitating vertigo as a result of overexposure to pesticides.

The proposed law, which, at the time of publication of this book, must still be passed by France's National Assembly, would allow local governments to require farmers to limit spraying of pesticides during certain times of the day. It would also require farmers to take special precautions when spraying near heavily inhabited areas.[11] Environmental campaign groups, such as *Generations Futures*, have also called for a ban on pesticide use near villages and towns.

Pesticide use in France is increasingly in the public spotlight. A two-hour documentary aired on French television in February 2016 that claimed that 65,000 tons of dangerous pesticides are sprayed on French vineyards, which, the program indicated, are a real health hazard to the local population. Focused mostly on the health risks posed to children by pesticide use in agriculture, it put the spotlight on the Bordeaux region. More than 3 million people tuned in to watch the program, with the provocative title, "Pesticides, Our Children at Risk." It highlighted that 132 schools were situated close to Bordeaux vineyards, picking up on a debate around so-called "sensitive sites" that emerged after pesticide drift was blamed for several school children falling ill in Bordeaux's Blaye area in 2014.

Community residents and activists in the Bordeaux region continue to raise an alarm. In February 2016, about 600 activists took to the streets in Bordeaux to protest against the use of pesticides by the region's winegrowers. Wearing sanitation masks and suits, and holding placards with messages such as "Protect our children." And in June 2016, protesters staged a "lie-in" in Bordeaux close to where French president Francois Hollande opened the 80 million-euro Cité du Vin wine theme park.

A 2013 report by France's national science and medical research institute, Inserm, found that "exposure to pesticides," including those used on vineyards, during early childhood could "pose a particularly high risk for a child's development," and drew links to child leukemia.

Similarly, a study from local health agency ASR claimed that the rate of childhood cancer in Preignac, the central village in Sauternes, was five times the national average in France. The study said it could not exclude possible link between child cancer rates, five times the national average, and pesticides sprayed just yards from the local school. The response of the industry association, Conseil Interprofessionnel du Vin de Bordeaux (CIVB), was that wine growers abide by agreed standards and regulations, and that it's up to the state to change the rules. The protestors believe that this attitude ignores the responsibility of wineries to their local communities and to use alternative, less harmful products.

Even worse, some local government actions in France are forcing farmers to spray pesticides. In the spring of 2013, all wine producers in Burgundy were ordered to spray pesticides on their vines to combat a deadly bacterial disease. One vineyard owner, Emmanuel Giboulot, refused to spray—citing that there was no sign of infection in his vines or in vines in the greater Côte d'Or region. He was charged with defying a government order, and faced six months in prison and fines of up to 30,000€. In April 2014, he was convicted and charged a fine of 1000€ by an appeals court.[12]

For the government, Mr. Giboulot is an easy target, but for the organic and biodynamic food and wine community, he is a hero—with over 500,000 people signing a petition in favor of his actions. An appellate court eventually ruled in his favor, stating that the senior national administrator in the region had acted illegally by ordering all of the vineyards in Burgundy to be sprayed when there was no immediate threat. Later, the court ruled that both the administrator and the local agricultural board had acted without seeking proper approval from the Ministry of Agriculture.

Sustainable Becomes Normal Practice

Some practices, which started as "sustainable" or outside the norms of conventional practice, are now considered best practices in conventional wine growing. In my interview with Chris Savage, Head of Sustainability for Gallo, he said, "Best practices exist for a reason because they ensure that you are growing grapes in a way to get the most out of your wine. You maximize not only yield but also quality. And positive impact from an environmental standpoint, too. And all of those grow out of the program. There are a lot of things that are now accepted just as standard practice for good grape growing—like cover cropping and other things—that have led to better yield and better grapes, that have environmental benefit, which grew out of the sustainability efforts. Cover cropping is a simple one. The amount of top soil you lose and the amount of added chemical you have to use in your vineyard both drop dramatically if you cover crop properly. And typically the small growers do not have the resources to research these options. But now the sustainability program in California—CSWA—provides the guidance and the info."

An example of cover crops
Credit: Wine Institute

Additionally, hand pruning and leaf removal, while time consuming and labor intensive, are often more effective in controlling fungal infections than fungicide application.[13]

Water Usage

Irrigation practices in the vineyard are either regulated or controversial the world over. Generally speaking, more water (whether naturally—via rain, or artificially—via irrigation) in the vineyard leads to higher yields. But, too much water can cause grapes to swell and lose vital sugars, so the resulting wine is flabby or flat. On the other hand, little to no water can cause the vines to become stressed and produce too little fruit (with too little juice). Winemakers must strike a fine balance between too much water and too little water to create the "ideal" wine grape for their production needs.

Historically, countries of the EU have banned the use of irrigation, although Spain has begun loosening the reins on the irrigation ban,[14] as the fewer acres under vine there strive to produce higher volumes of wine. By contrast, some New World wineries and vineyards in Australia and California must use irrigation, as their lack of natural rainfall would prevent most types of agriculture from thriving. Yet producers in these countries have become accustomed to and perhaps overly dependent upon frequent and sometimes excessive irrigation rather than natural rainfall, to the point of diminishing available water resources.

The California drought, which began in 2013, has sorely tested and frustrated these farmers and the communities where they cultivate. The drought, which set water usage limitations for many residents of the Central Coast of California, has frayed relationships between longtime residents and area vineyards. Residents, environmentalists, and even fishermen have taken up issue with the wineries' water consumption and their desire to tap new groundwater wells.[15]

In those countries that allow irrigation, there are several options for farmers to consider:

- Surface irrigation—By using the gravity of a slope in the vineyard, the vines are "flooded" with water. This option offers the least amount of control and can often cause overwatering.
- Sprinkler irrigation—Farmers install sprinklers throughout the vineyards and can control the amount and duration of water the vines receive.
- Drip irrigation—The most expensive to install, drip irrigation allows the most control. Long rows of tubes are installed throughout the vineyard at the base of the vines, and farmers can control the amount of water released, down to the drop.

The most critical time for grape vines to receive ample water is during the budding and flowering period. After that, it is customary for farmers to induce "water stress" by reducing water application during the ripening period, so that all the energy (and water) that the vine can access is devoted to ripening the fruit—not growing excess vine leaves.

A particularly instructive example of over-irrigation is taken from Australian winemaking operations. The Murray and Darling Rivers (which are crucial to Australian farming in general) are at their lowest levels in over a century—having been overworked by farmers for irrigation.

Conventional Winemaking in the Winery

Consumers often expect their favorite wine to taste the same no matter when they buy it or the year it was made. Additives are the key to make mass-produced wines deliver a consistent taste or just drinkable.

Sulfur Dioxide—The most widely used wine additive. It kills microbes and prevents oxidation.

Ammonium Salts—A touch of diammonium phosphate revives dying yeast and keeps it from producing too much sulfur.

Water—Not surprisingly, adding water can reduce the alcohol level of a batch of wine.

Oak Flavoring—Adding oak chips—to give the flavor of oak tannins and vanilla—has become a very popular and cheaper way to give the taste of oak barrel fermentation or storage without the cost of buying expensive French oak barrels. Some winemakers also add sawdust, or "essence"—a liquefied wood product that can be added directly to a vat before bottling.

Tartaric Acid—Wines with low acidity can get a boost of tartness from powdered tartaric acid, a naturally occurring acid found in grapes.

Powdered Tannin—Tannins in wine come from the grape skins, the seeds, and oak barrels. Somewhat like oak chips, powdered tannin, made from a growth on oak trees called a nutgall, can add missing texture and bite to a mass-produced wine.

Sugar—If grapes aren't ripe enough when picked, adding cane or beet sugar to the must can help them ferment. This is a process called chaptalization, and it is forbidden in California, Italy, and Australia, though legal in prescribed amounts in New Zealand, Oregon, and parts of France.

Pectic Enzymes—Complex proteins that can be used to alter color, improve clarity, release aromatic compounds, and speed up aging.

Gum Arabic—Made from the sap of the acacia tree, gum Arabic softens tannins to reduce astringency and make the wine's body silkier. This can make a tough and somewhat bitter red wine ready to drink immediately.

Velcorin (dimethyl dicarbonate)—A microbial control agent that can kill certain bacteria and yeasts and is also used in fruit juices.

MegaPurple—Made from the concentrated syrup of Rubired grapes, MegaPurple is thick goo that winemakers rely on to correct color issues and to make a wine look consistent from batch to batch and also to deepen the color and make the wine look richer. MegaPurple is manufactured by Constellation Brands from the Rubired grape, which is dark purple in color and produces a dark red blending wine, with little character or body, and is used only to increase the color of generic or varietal table and dessert wines. But Mega-Purple isn't just used on mass-produced wines; some high-end wineries rely on it as well to produce wines that impress wine critics and to command higher prices in the marketplace. More and more Rubired is being grown in California's vineyards—in fact, 5.5 percent of all grapes crushed in California in 2013 were Rubired.[16]

There are also several high-technology processes for boosting a wine's flavor, including the following:

Micro-Oxygenation—This is used when wine isn't maturing fast enough. Tiny oxygen bubbles are piped into a holding tank.

Reverse Osmosis—Here water and ethanol are removed from the wine, allowing the winemaker to adjust the concentrations and add back some of each in the finished product to determine alcohol levels.[17]

It is clear from this discussion that wine production is largely industrial and relies on scientific research, additives developed in laboratories, and high technology. This runs counter to the image that average consumers have of grapes being picked in a bucolic setting, stomped by workers, naturally fermented in barrels, and then bottled, before landing on their store shelves.

There are many entry points on the path to sustainability, and many different reasons why vineyards and wineries choose to introduce organic, biodynamic, or sustainable practices. This next section provides a description of natural wine and then discusses the requirements for certification under organic regulations and biodynamic standards and introduces regional sustainability systems.

NATURAL WINES

There exists no official or legal definition of natural wine; neither has any legislation been passed to date by any regional, national, or supra-natural authority, and there are no organizations that can certify that a wine is natural. However, there are many unofficial definitions or codes of practice published by the different associations of natural wine producers in France, Italy, Germany, and Spain.

What we call natural wines are wines made with the least possible use of chemicals, additives, and overly technological procedures. That includes chemicals in the field, such as pesticides, as well as things like sulfur or any of the many various chemicals, additives, cleansers, and fining agents used in conventional winemaking that are legally permitted to protect the wine from spoilage or premature browning, overcome a deficiency, or promote a healthier fermentation. And there are many technological manipulations of wine that would not be used to make a natural wine.

There is some confusion regarding whether natural wine includes organic or biodynamic wine, largely because there is no official definition or certification for what is a natural wine. The rules or guidelines for natural wines are set by regional or national associations such as L'Association des Vins Naturels in France or the Italian natural wine associations—ViniVeri and Vin Natur. All prefer compliance with EU organic rules. The grapes must be picked by hand and fermented with natural yeast. All additives are to be avoided except for a small amount of sulfur. ViniVeri requires growers to plant only local cultivars, harvest by hand, and only use cuttings form the vineyard when planting new vines. No purchased vines are allowed, and no additives allowed in the winery, and temperature controlled fermentation is forbidden.

Isabelle Legeron MW, founder of RAW WINE, the annual natural wine fair in London and author of the book *Natural Wine: An Introduction to Organic and*

Biodynamic Wines Made Naturally, has written that "When wine was first made 8,000 years ago, it was not made using packets of yeasts, vitamins, enzymes, Mega Purple, reverse osmosis, cryoextraction or powdered tannins—some of the many additives and processes used in winemaking worldwide. The wines of these bygone days were natural: they were made from crushed grapes that fermented into wine." RAW WINE was created to promote small, artisan wine producers who make fine wine using natural farming techniques (including organic and biodynamic practices) and low-intervention vinification processes.

Legeron offers this definition: "Natural wine is made from grapes that are, at a very minimum, farmed organically or biodynamically, harvested manually and then made without adding / or removing anything during the vinification process. Ideally nothing is added at all but—at most—there might be a dash of SO2 at bottling. A handful of farmers manage to produce great wines without adding any SO2 whatsoever. It's basically good old grape juice fermented into wine. As nature intended. The cellar is simply the place to guide what is fundamentally a naturally occurring phenomenon rather than a high-tech lab, full of gadgets and sacks of sugar, tartaric acid and powdered tannins."*

So, what distinguishes natural wines from organic and biodynamic wines? Organic and biodynamic certification rules are primarily concerned with regulating the use of synthetic chemicals in the vineyard, rather than additives in the winery. For example, Demeter allows commercial yeast strains to be added to wines to kick-start fermentation in the winery. This is not acceptable to natural winemakers who believe that all the components necessary to start and complete fermentation and give balance and complexity to a wine must come from the vineyard alone.

When I have tasted natural wine, the wine looks cloudy and sometimes tastes oxidized, which is not a surprise to natural wine enthusiasts. My first impression is often that I cannot distinguish its origins, which can be disappointing since natural wine is purported to be a perfect reflection of its place, its terroir, wines that are true to where they are from—that have an authenticity of taste that supposedly most wines today have lost.

ORGANIC WINEGROWING

What Does It Mean to be Organic?

Many producers in the wine industry are trying to figure out how to enhance quality and production of wines while being more cognizant of their impact on their immediate and global environments. For some, this means reducing the use of certain chemicals. For others, it means making daily operations greener by reducing the waste stream and using more renewable energy sources.

---

* "It's Only Natural," *Decanter Magazine,* September 2011 edition, pp. 38–43.

The key question for many producers is whether or not the adoption of organic practices or ingredients adds value to their products, markets, and community.

According to the California Department of Food and Agriculture, there were 7,940 acres of certified organic wine grapes in California in 2003. In 2012, there were over 10,000 organic acres dedicated to wine grapes in California.[18] Although organic wine is still a niche market, the growth potential is strong.

Over the past decade, wine labels containing the phrase "made with organically grown grapes" seems to be increasing as the certified acreage increases, and the inclusion of this information on labels is used by some as a marketing distinction along with appellation or variety.

In organic farming, the use of chemicals is strictly controlled by law. Pesticides and chemical fungicides that are made available to the conventional farmer are prohibited from use by the organic farmer. The organic growers concentrate their efforts not on reacting to pests but on growing a healthy vine that is able to withstand pests and feed itself naturally. First and foremost, this means developing a healthy soil and a balanced ecosystem within the vineyard. The producer must implement cultivation practices that minimize soil erosion, including crop rotation that provides erosion control.

Soil is a living, breathing, and ever-changing part of the vineyard. A healthy soil is vital to the organic grower because it supplies the vine with nutrients. Organic farmers must adopt practices that maintain biologically active soil. The uses of beneficial insects, cover crops, natural fertilizers, and the planting of companion crops (such as Echinacea to attract natural predators) are common. In addition, weed management is integrative, allowing a cycle of growth, mowing, and composting, wherein the biomass is used as fertilizer instead of traditional chemical fertilizer sprays.

In organic viticulture, cover crops are secondary crops planted between the rows of vines. They can help the vines by:

- serving as food sources for pests that might prey on the vine,
- acting as decoys for pests that might prey on the vine, and
- naturally converting nitrogen from the atmosphere into nitrogen that the vines can use.

At the end of the season, cover crops are generally plowed back into the earth to enrich the soil for the next growing season.

Organic viticulture doesn't come easily, and to become certified is quite a process, taking up to three years. Converting conventional farm acreage to organic processes can take even longer, as it can take many years to get rid of all the chemical residues in the soil, and initial yields are likely to be small. Additionally, growers often have to spend 5 to 10 percent more on various production costs during their three-year certification transition, but after that, costs are similar to (if not less than) traditional farming.[19]

Insects on cover crops, from left Phacelia and Buckwheat
Credit: Doug Bell, President of Gisborne Winegrowers

In the United States, organic products are regulated by the U.S. Department of Agriculture (USDA), in accordance with the Organic Food and Production Act (OFPA). The USDA defines organic food as "agricultural products produced by cultural, biological, or mechanical methods while reusing resources, promoting ecological balance, and conserving biodiversity." Organic farming does not permit the use of synthetic fertilizers, chemical pesticides, sewage sludge, irradiation, or genetic engineering.[20]

Weed problems may be controlled through mulching, mowing, grazing, hand weeding, and mechanical cultivation, flame, heat or electrical means. When other practices are insufficient to control crop pests, weeds, and diseases, a substance included on the National List of synthetic substances may be applied.

In order for products to carry the organic seal on their packaging, they (and their ingredients) must be approved by the National Organic Standards Board (NOSB) and the National Organic Program (NOP). The NOSB defines organic agriculture as "an ecological production management system that promotes and enhances biodiversity, biological cycles and soil biological activity. It is based on minimal use of off-farm inputs and on management practices that restore, maintain and enhance ecological harmony. Organic Production . . . responds to site-specific conditions by integrating cultural, biological, and mechanical practices that foster cycling of resources, promote ecological balance, and conserve biodiversity."

In Europe, the EU defines organic farming as "an overall system of farm management and food production that combines best environmental practices, a high level of biodiversity, the preservation of natural resources, the application of high animal welfare standards and a production method in line with the preference of certain consumers for goods produced using natural substances and processes."

The EU is very specific and prescriptive about what products can and cannot be used in organic farming.

EU Organic Farming Standards Prohibit:

- artificial (synthetic) fertilizers
- chemical weed killers (herbicides)
- synthetic chemical insecticides and pesticides
- genetically modified products

EU Organic Farming Standards Permit:

- Organic fertilizer, comprised of:
- Animal compost
- Vegetable compost
- Animal dung
- Guano (bat dung)
- Algae
- Natural calcium and magnesium carbonates
- Natural potassium, calcium and magnesium sulfates
- Wine lees (leftover yeast)
- Grape compost
- Spraying with copper or sulfur

Natural Remedies for Disease

Since organic farmers don't use traditional pesticides and fungicides to protect their crops, they must adopt a "prevention rather than cure" approach in order to survive. In dealing with pests and diseases, there are no magic organic sprays capable of removing pests and diseases after they have taken hold. Organic growers must therefore rely on preventive procedures to enrich the soil. Otherwise, they only have sulfur and copper in their arsenal to deal with pests and disease, and these must be applied in advance and repeatedly since they get washed away with each rain. Additionally, rainfall causes moisture and humidity in the vineyard, which can lead to the development of mildew—so organic growers must be very watchful of weather forecasts.

Copper is the remedy for downy mildew, a type of mildew that delays ripening and makes the vine more vulnerable to other pests. Another fungal disease of the vine is powdery mildew, prevalent in hot, dry climates. Powdery mildew causes leaves to fall prematurely, and often prevents buds from opening. The organic remedy for powdery mildew is sulfur, and both sulfur and copper also serve as an organic remedy for botrytis, a fungus that causes grapes to shrivel and decay.

Despite being natural remedies for mildew, large amounts and/or repeated applications of sulfur and copper can be harmful to the soil and to the vine. Too much sulfur can be harmful to plants, causing nutrient uptake issues. Meanwhile, too much copper can be toxic to the soil, as it is a heavy metal. Copper, however, unlike chemical pesticides, presents no danger to the person who does the spraying. Organic growers recognize that extensive use of copper and sulfur are not consistent with good environmental stewardship and are vigilant about reducing the amounts used when possible.

Recently, an all-natural remedy for botrytis and pests was licensed in the EU. Called 3AEY, it is made from tea tree oil and lemon juice and is harmless to the honeybee (a frequent inhabitant of vineyards, whose population is under threat). 3AEY takes advantage of natural plant by-products called terpenes, which help the natural pesticide last longer in the vineyard.

Several other natural treatments are being used (experimentally) to treat the diseases above: ground limestone, citrus extract, Tricoderma (a fungus that accelerates composting), and fenugreek (a legume plant that can serve as green manure), but their effectiveness is still uncertain.[21]

Unwanted pests include grasshoppers, which spread flavescence dorée, a bacterial disease, spider mites, and the grapeworm. Organic treatments available include pyrethrin for grasshoppers and pheromones for the grapeworm. Research continues on natural remedies for these vineyard pests.

Organic Practices in the Winery

Wines to be labeled "Organic Wine" must be made from at least 95 percent organically farmed grapes and vinified without added sulfites (naturally occurring sulfites may not exceed 10 parts per million) and without genetic modification. Additionally, any yeast that is added must also be certified organic in order for the wine to be labeled organic.

Wines to be labeled "Made with Organic Grapes" are subject to different rules. One hundred percent of the grapes used to make the wine must be certified organic. Additives (like yeast) don't have to be certified organic but cannot be genetically modified. Finally, sulfites can be added—up to 100 parts per million (ppm).

Sulfites and Headaches

One of the largest myths surrounding sulfites is that they give people headaches, especially red wine. While this is true for a very small percentage of the population that has sulfite sensitivity due to asthma, it is largely untrue for the majority of wine drinkers. (Also a sulfite allergy does not typically manifest as a headache—it's more like an asthma attack.) All wines have sulfites—they occur naturally in the winemaking process. Dried fruit, orange juice, and even french fries contain many more parts per million of sulfites—and many wine drinkers claiming that the sulfites in wine give them headaches often have no problem consuming these other sulfite-rich foods. The likely cause of headache while drinking wine might be an allergy to pollen from the vineyard, allergy to oak (used to age the wine), histamines in the skins—especially red wines— or allergy to alcohol in general. Tannins in red wines are another possible explanation. One more theory is that some yeasts create different chemical compounds when dealing with the amount of sugar and alcohol in very ripe grapes, and these compounds cause red-wine headaches. Other explanations include dehydration—since wine is a diuretic, which dehydrates the body further—or unbalanced blood sugar level. Wine has lots of sugar and may cause your blood sugar to drop, especially if you consume it without food, and that can cause headaches.

Sulfites and Organic Wine

Sulfites are sulfur compounds that are naturally produced by yeast during fermentation; some producers add sulfites to their wine at the beginning or end of fermentation. Sulfites act as a preserving agent for the wine, allowing it to have a longer shelf life. Many people assume that organic wine is inherently sulfite free, but this is not the case. Conventional wines are allowed to have 350 ppm of sulfites, while organic wines have less, with a maximum of 100 ppm of sulfites.[22]

The United States has set official rules when it comes to sulfites in organic wine:

- A 100 percent organic wine is made from organically produced grapes only, with no sulfur added. The wine's natural sulfur cannot exceed 10 parts per million (ppm).
- Wines made from 95 percent organically produced grapes and 5 percent conventional grapes, with no added sulfur and not exceeding 10 ppm can also be labeled organic.
- Wine made with 70 percent organic grapes can add sulfur (up to 100 ppm) and be labeled "made with organic grapes," but it will not be labeled USDA-certified Organic.

As a result of the strict regulations, there are few organic wines produced in the United States. Conversely, in Europe, the regulations are more relaxed. Red wine can be labeled organic if it contains 100 ppm, and white or rosé wines can be labeled organic if they contain 150 ppm.

Getting Certified Organic: What Rules Apply?

If a winery is certified organic it means that its practices have been audited and verified by an independent third party. There are many different certifying boards. Each country has different standards and a number of inspecting and certifying organizations authorized by governments.

Also, due to the cost and time associated with organic certification, some wineries simply choose not to apply for organic certification even though they farm in accordance with organic standards and principles.

However, to use the term "organic" in wine labeling or in wholesale grape sales in the United States, certification must be obtained by an "accredited certifying agent," or ACA. These ACAs can be private, public, or nonprofit entities that have received authorization to certify from the USDA. Currently, there are 82 ACAs that are USDA-accredited. Forty-eight are based in the United States and 34 are based in foreign countries. Aside from these entities, there are 20 additional ACAs that are authorized through various agreements between the USDA and foreign governments.

According to Wine Business Monthly, "Organic certification requirements usually include an application, an affidavit, annual submission of an organic system plan (OSP), and inspection of farm fields and processing facilities. Inspectors verify that organic practices, such as long-term soil management, buffering between organic farms and neighboring conventional farms, and record keeping, are followed. This verification is usually only done once and is updated when changes to the requirements occur. Processing inspections include review of a facility's cleaning and pest-control methods, ingredient transportation and storage, and record keeping and audit control. Imported organic wines are certified by entities such as BIOFRANC or ECOCERT, inspection and certification organizations accredited to verify the conformity of organic products against the organic regulations of Europe, Japan and the United States."

While organic practices reduce the amount of chemicals added to the growing process, it would be naïve to assume that organic means "impact-free." In November 2014, *Forbes Magazine* published a criticism of the organic movement. In the article, Henry I. Miller, a physician and molecular biologist, shed light on the dangers of compost and the application of solid organic matter—which can cause significant leaching of nitrites into groundwater supplies and release greenhouse gases.[23]

Those within the organic community express concerns that what was once a movement has become an industry and a resulting commoditization of organic products. They say that large commercial growers and agribusiness firms have entered the market seeking profit opportunities, while not necessarily remaining true to the founding spirit of the organic movement. The ethics of environmental stewardship, for example, was a central aspect of the original locally based organic movement.[24]

Also, in discussing organic certification with several wine producers, I learned that while the NOP sets the national regulations in the United States, the number of auditors and certifiers could often interpret those standards differently. Furthermore, the National Organic Program allows state organic programs (California is the only one) to add more restrictive requirements due to specific environmental conditions or concerns. So, what may qualify as organic in Oregon may not meet the criteria of certifiers in Southern California.

BIODYNAMIC AGRICULTURE

How would Dr. Rudolph Steiner, founder of biodynamic farming, describe biodynamic viticulture today?

Like organic farming, Certified Biodynamic® farming avoids the use of chemical fertilizers, herbicides, pesticides, and synthetic fungicides. Biodynamic (literal translation: life-energizing) farming strives to maintain and even return life to the soil as well as to the farm as a living system. Biodynamic farming originated from Dr. Steiner's advice in 1924 to German farmers who observed a rapid decline in seed fertility, crop vitality, and animal health on their farms.

Rudolph Steiner was an Austrian philosopher, and the beginnings of biodynamic principles are traced to a series of eight lectures he gave to a group of European farmers in June 1924. They were searching for solutions to problems with soil fertility, animal disease, and degenerate seed strains. Steiner died the following year. I am amazed that in such a short period of time one individual could so change the course of sustainable agriculture for nearly 100 years.

In biodynamic farming, agricultural decisions are made with the big picture, long-term view in mind. Outside inputs are minimized. The relationships between all members of the farm (humans, animals, and plants) are regarded as high value and integral to the livelihood of the farm as an ecosystem. On a biodynamic farm, you will find production of many crops at the same time, as monoculture will not benefit the long-term health of the land. Biodynamic viticulture is less a vineyard and more a farm where sustainable wine grapes are produced in addition to other sustainable produce and livestock.

In recent years, biodynamic has become a more respected and coveted way to make wine, purely on the evidence of the quality of the wines it produces.

Several of the biodynamic vineyards I've visited over the years describe themselves as a farm, not a vineyard, because of the high diversity of animal and plant life that exists on their property. At Seresin Estate in Marlborough, New Zealand, there are working horses to pull the plows, sheep to graze the grass between the rows, cows for manure, and even pigs merrily running up and down between the vines.

Horse at Seresin Estate spraying biodynamic preparations across the vineyard using a specially-designed horse-sprayer

Winemaker Clive Dougall commented that the property is designed to be different from the mono-culture that a commercial vineyard can become. Michael Seresin founded the estate based on the mixed farming that he had seen in Italy, where inter-row plantings of vegetables, olive groves, and livestock sit side-by-side with established vineyards. As a result, the 165 hectare Seresin Estate is home to extensive olive tree plantings, vegetable gardens, and orchards, all of which are tended with the same care as the vineyards that surround them. While the vineyards are the part of the estate that brings in the money, these additional plantings and activities are an important part of the unique culture of Seresin Estate. Clive Dougall said, "The idea of providing a working environment free from hazardous chemicals has always been at the heart of the property, but the gardens and livestock also give a sense of balance to the estate, and allow us the opportunity to make good quality organic meat, fruit and vegetables available to the people who work here. In this way, as we choose to look after the land, the land also looks after us."

Two things that distinguish biodynamic farming from other forms of organic farming are:

- the use of a complex system of herbal sprays and composting techniques, known as "preparations," and
- the timing of the operations on the land, which is strictly regulated by the movements of the spheres of the universe (the planet and the moon).

For Steiner, the ideal biodynamic farm was a diverse but self-sustaining ecosystem of plants and animals, surrounded by a belt of forest or wild growth to provide protection from predators. Diseases and pests are less likely to settle on this type of property.

While the above mentality sounds rational and realistic to implement, biodynamic agriculture is still a mystery to many. Why is that? Well, some of the components and rituals of biodynamic farming are pretty strange and may sound a little like witchcraft to some. Many biodynamic farmers admit that some of the practices are unusual, but they harken back to the days of pre-industrial farming, when a farmer would utilize materials found on the farm to create their own on-farm fertilizers and pest and weed control. These include stuffing a stag's bladder with flowers and burying it to make better compost, or relying on the phases of the moon to plan vine planting, pruning, and harvesting, not unlike the use of *The Farmers Almanac* by earlier generations of farmers.

Steiner was a deeply spiritual person who drew from ancient religions such as Zoroastrianism in building his belief system. And so his lectures on traditional farming practices are part practical guide, part sermon; they give "astral-etheric forces" as much weight as cover crops and composting.

I don't pretend to understand the deep and true meaning of biodynamic agriculture. Nicolas Joly, a practitioner of biodynamic farming methods for over 20 years and an acclaimed French winemaker, once said in a speech that explaining biodynamic in three-quarters of an hour is like writing four lines to describe the contents of the Metropolitan Museum of Art in New York.

Steiner lectured that because plants germinate, grow, and bear fruit through their interaction with the sun, earth, air, and water, the universe is a part of this plant's development and growth. Even those who are put off by the spiritual aspect of biodynamics can appreciate the sustainable goals and especially the focus on enlivening the soil, so critical to vine health. Obviously, this is the case, judging by the number of viticulturists who have adopted biodynamic farming in whole or in part in their vineyards. Many renowned European producers have practiced this type of farming for many decades.

The theory is that a farm, or a vineyard, is seen as a living system whose functioning is explained in terms of "formative" forces. If something is wrong on a biodynamic farm, it is because the formative forces of sun, earth, air, and water are out of balance. Biodynamic farmers believe that even the most distant movements of the stars are connected to (and have an effect on) the land. France's most famous soil microbiologist, Claude Bourguignon, maintains that the soil on biodynamic farms contains much more life than organic or conventionally farmed soil, even though he cannot directly prove how or why.

Where organic farming focuses on refraining from adding certain things to the vine and the soil, one of the core principles of biodynamic farming is adding certain preparation elements to the soil and, thus, the plant. This distinction separates biodynamic farming from organic or other sustainable farming initiatives.

There are nine specific preparations, or "preps," numbered 500–508, that are included in composts, sprayed on plants, or added to the soil. These preps are made from herbs, mineral substances, and animal manures and are used in field sprays and compost applications that revitalize the soil with life and aid in photosynthesis. The compost preparations are made from common herbs such as yarrow, chamomile, stinging nettle oak bark, dandelion, and valerian flowers and referred to by number: 500, 501, and 508 are field sprays, while 502 through 507 are compost additives.[25]

Much ado is made about use of the most iconic biodynamic preps 500 and 501, which are prepared using cow's horns, especially preparation 500. Utilizing a cow horn as a receptacle for cow dung, the horns are buried over the winter and then excavated in the spring. The material that results smells of rich earth and looks like beautiful soil. Back in the day, it wasn't unusual for farmers to utilize animal parts as storage vessels, and by putting the horns underground in the winter, the constant temperature allows the dung to ferment, creating a welcoming environment for colonies of microbes to flourish. Once taken out of the horn, this fermented soil is placed in water that is vigorously stirred and applied in homeopathic quantities to the soil. Similar to the effect that healthy fermented foods can have on the human digestive system, prep 500 increases the microbial life of the soil.

Prep 501 is prepared by first burying a cow horn filled with powdered quartz for a few months. Next, you dig it up and put a tiny amount of its contents into a barrel of water. Then, you stir the water in alternating opposite directions for an hour to create a "dynamized" treatment to spray on the plants. Whew! If that seems like too much work, these days it is possible to buy the preparations "ready-made," so vineyard managers need not maintain cows and an herbal garden to implement biodynamic practices.

CERTIFIED
BIODYNAMIC®

Certification

Like organic certification, there is a three-year conversion period before a winery is granted Certified Biodynamic status. The only international certifying body for Biodynamic farming is Demeter International. Demeter Association, Inc. is the United States' representative of Demeter International. Its mission is to support farmers to implement biodynamic practices and principles. The first Demeter chapter was formed in Germany in 1928, and the Demeter symbol and first Standard was introduced to ensure that the farming methods were uniformly followed and monitored.

In 1985, Demeter was formed in the United States. Demeter International is the first, and remains the only, ecological association consisting of a network of individual certification organizations in 50 countries around the world.

Unlike organic certification, which is regulated principally by governments according to varying national criteria, there are international standards for what constitutes biodynamic wine production, so biodynamic wine from France is produced in adherence to the same rules as biodynamic wine from California.

In order for a farm to be Certified Biodynamic, the Demeter Association (the only biodynamic certifying agency in the United States) requires that diverse ecosystems be present. This means that there must be native plant life, various livestock, and a natural supply of water. Additionally, at least 10 percent of the farm's acreage must be devoted to indigenous flora and fauna. This 10 percent of native growth will help attract wildlife that can then protect the farm from harmful pests (like caterpillars or rats).

The use of all the preparations is a requirement for certification from the *Demeter Biodynamic® Farm Standard*. Most of the biodynamic viticulturists I have spoken with say that the biodynamic style of farming, because it is so natural, simply forces them to spend more time in the vineyard. They believe that this increased care translates to purer fruit and, perhaps, a purer expression of the vineyard in their wines.

Biodynamic Practices in the Winery

A Demeter-certified winery must adhere to very specific standards and restrictions. Biodynamic wines are made from 100 percent Demeter certified fruit that must be hand harvested, vinified with natural yeasts, without additives and with limited added sulfites (less than 150 ppm). Biodynamic winemaking has increased since the guidelines for biodynamic wine processing were updated by Demeter (in collaboration with winemakers) in 2009. There are requirements for the highest environmental standards in energy use and handling waste.[26]

The United States now has more biodynamic certified wineries and vineyards than any other country in the world except France and Italy. Winery membership has grown to over 75.

The "mystical" spiritual process described by some practitioners of biodynamic farming discourages many vineyard managers from going all the way to Demeter certification, though they do introduce several elements of eco-farming into the vineyard that are akin to biodynamic preps and composting. Cost is also a deterrent to biodynamic certification as it is with organic. As a result, some wines are produced biodynamically that do not carry a certification or indications as such. A few wineries have complained that Demeter costs are too high. Wineries pay a modest flat rate for audit and certification. Inspection visits, audits, and possible residue testing will be conducted at the product owner's expense.

The certification marks Demeter® and Biodynamic® must always be used in compliance with the Demeter labeling standard. To be sold with the Demeter certification mark, a product profile sheet must be filled out for each wine and submitted to

Demeter, along with the draft label to be used, for pre-approval by the Demeter office before sending in to the United States Alcohol and Tobacco Tax and Trade Bureau (TTB).

However, to carry the Demeter seal on the bottle of wine, a winery must pay ½ cent per dollar on the sale of the wine per bottle for the use of the name and to license the seal, which can be considered too costly by some wineries. As a result, some wineries choose not to certify their wines. It's unfortunate that more biodynamic wineries don't carry the certification seal and promote the quality of their biodynamic wines, both to encourage other producers to adopt these practices and to educate consumers on the quality that can result from these farming practices.

SUSTAINABLE WINEGROWING

What does it mean to be sustainable in the vineyard? When a process is sustainable, it can be carried out over and over without negative environmental effects or impossibly high costs to anyone involved. Sustainable farming is focused on creating healthy relationships among all members of the supply chain—farmers and seasonal labor, producers, consumers, and the local and global community. Some sustainable farmers are reducing their impact on the environment by using local resources and labor, considering alternative sources of energy, and reducing their reliance on harmful chemicals.

Distinct from organic and biodynamic farming (that focus solely on environmental protection), sustainable farming also considers the social responsibility of the farm, as well as the profitability of the end product.

There is no single agency that certifies vineyards or wineries as sustainable. Rather, there are national, industry-led initiatives like Sustainable Wine New Zealand,

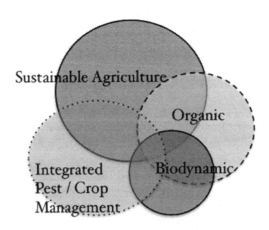

Sustainable Agriculture vs. Organic, Biodynamic

Sustainable winegrowing is a much broader concept, which includes many dimensions.

state-specific affiliations like California Certified Sustainable Wine, as well as organizations such as Fish Friendly Farming, that set standards and certify wineries.

To add one more layer of ambiguity to the mix, there are no national or international standards for what sustainable means, or how one should decipher the various levels of sustainability.

In general, sustainable viticulturists and winemakers work to minimize soil erosion, depletion of soil nutrients, and water pollution. While some of their practices and requirements are like the other responsible farming approaches, it is a much broader concept than either organic or biodynamic. For example, sustainable viticulture emphasizes the use of cover crops and careful canopy management (trellising and pruning) and employs composting. Chemical spraying is permitted, but chemical use is minimized, and spraying events are documented and recorded. Integrated pest management is also an important aspect of sustainable viticulture. Sustainable producers believe their approach is more realistic as the market demands both quality and volume; a vineyard is a business undertaking, which has to be commercially viable.

Sustainability, according to *Wine Spectator Magazine*[27]

"This catch-all category means that grapes are grown with as few chemicals as possible, and minimal additives are used in winemaking. Alternatively, sustainability focuses on not harming the environment. Winemakers who identify as sustainable sometimes choose not to certify as either biodynamic or organic due to the cost associated with certification, while others adhere to their own rules governing organic winemaking. In fact, many old school European winemakers have always been some combination of organic, biodynamic and natural, but don't see the value in labeling as such. These third-party organizations are just some sustainable seals to look out for: Sustainability in Practice (SIP), Low Input Viticulture and Enology (LIVE), Qualité France, California Certified Organic Farmers (CCOF)."

Sustainable wineries focus on the following areas of sustainability:

Waste Management

While aiming to prevent generation of unnecessary waste to begin with, many sustainable wineries reuse or recycle any waste that is generated. This includes repairing damaged items (versus throwing them out), donating unneeded items, and training employees on specific waste management guidelines.

Material Handling

The handling of potentially hazardous waste materials is taken seriously to limit the impact on the environment, local community, and employees. This is one of the primary motivators for adopting sustainable practice—to safeguard the health of workers and family members who apply fertilizers and other chemicals in the vineyard.

A Best Practice In Water Conservation[28]

Water consumption is a huge concern in any agricultural organization, and particularly in drought-stricken California, and so water conservation is also top of mind for the management of Jackson Family Wines (JFW). The industry as a whole uses and average 6 to 9 gallons of water to produce 1 gallon of wine. JFW has reduced its winery water use by 49 percent since 2008 and has halved the industry average for amount of water needed to produce a gallon of wine. In addition, by using native cover crops and letting two-thirds of the land be left unused, JFW takes advantage of natural ecosystem services (like pest control) to cut down on harmful, heavy-duty agricultural practices. JFW is currently at 4.5 gallons for each gallon of wine, with a goal to get that number down to 3 gallons. To make water savings a priority, JFW has put a price on water of 3 cents per gallon so that it can measure savings, even though the company largely uses well water, which is currently "free." They use a variety of technical solutions to reduce water use like drip irrigation instead of sprinklers or flooding. In 2015, JFW began a trial using buried drip tape that can water the roots directly eliminating evaporation.

Delivering the perfect amount of water is a goal. By using new technologies like drones to take close-up pictures of the vineyards, JFW can adjust the water volume in near real time.

Other water-saving efforts include triple-reuse in the bottle washing line, wind inversion props to send warm air to the grapes during a cold snap to keep them from freezing (instead of coating all the grapes in water to create an igloo effect), and sending dirty water from the bottling process out to reservoirs where it can find a second life watering the grapes. Through these efforts JFW has an average water savings of 11 million gallons per year.

Water Management

Nearly every step of the winemaking process involves water, and sustainable wineries must be diligent in conserving their use of water. By sustainably obtaining, using, reusing, and discharging water, wineries can increase their commitment to the environment. Farmers that practice sustainable farming may enhance the moisture levels of their vineyard soil (and thus, reduce the need for irrigation) by mulching, applying composts, or planting cover crops. Mulch and compost help retain water, and slowly leach it into the soil. Cover crops are planted in the vineyard to reduce the impact of natural rainfall on the vineyard soil. Instead of rain falling directly on dirt, the cover crops help buffer the falling rain, allowing it to drip down the plant into the soil.

Energy Efficiency

By using energy-efficient appliances and procedures (and continuing to audit energy use) wineries can significantly reduce their carbon footprint. For example, several wineries in California (like Trefethen, Domaine Carneros, and Chateau Montelena) have installed solar panels and other energy saving devices, which have been subsidized by the state or county government as part of their energy cost reduction efforts. In New Zealand, there is a major groundswell among vineyards to reduce fossil fuel and electricity use. Even though New Zealand draws most of its electricity from renewable sources (water and wind), the rising cost of electricity together with the high energy demands of wine production means the industry focuses on energy as a major sustainability factor, throughout New Zealand's 10 winemaking regions.

An impressive example is New Zealand's Mission Estate, which since 2007 has crushed 1,000 tons of grapes, and bottled over 80,000 cases of wine annually. However, the winery's power usage is similar to that of only four domestic homes. For every liter of wine produced, the power usage is an incredibly low 0.13 KWh. All of Missions' tanks are housed internally, providing considerable energy savings. Unlike most wineries that run on high-powered refrigeration glycol systems all year round, Mission Estate has installed two separate systems—a large, high-powered system to be used during the busy six weeks of harvest, and a smaller, more efficient system to be used during normal operations. (Climate impacts and greenhouse gas (GHG) emissions will be covered fully in Chapter 7.)

Packaging

From a sustainability perspective, there is a close connection between distribution and packaging. Responsible wineries measure CO2 emissions generated by glass production as well as the weight of glass in transport of wine to its market. Many producers are opting for lighter-weight bottles, which saves cost as well as being more environmentally friendly. In 2008, Fetzer Vineyards (one of the largest U.S. wineries) transitioned all of their wine bottles to lightweight bottles. This change is estimated to have reduced glass usage by 16 percent, and carbon emissions by 14 percent.[29] The Province of Ontario, Canada, has taken it one step further by setting a maximum weight for glass wine bottles. As of January 1, 2013, producers are limited to producing wine that is packaged in lightweight, environmentally friendly bottles.[30]

Other producers have opted to bottle some of their wine brands in PET (plastic) bottles to further reduce carbon emissions associated with shipping glass. Backsberg Estate Cellars, the first carbon-neutral winery in South Africa, packages their Tread Lightly Merlot and Sauvignon Blanc varietals in PET bottles. Another great example comes from Yealands Family Wines in New Zealand. Their Peter Yealands line of wines is packaged in sustainable, shatterproof PET bottles.

Many restaurants and bars are starting to serve wines from kegs, as they have found them to be a sustainable alternative to offering wines by the glass. Kegs release much less CO_2 both in manufacture and in transport than wine in bottles. However, the other important aspect is waste: kegs result in little to no waste generation because most are repurposed or recycled, whereas bottle delivery systems result in approximately 1,545 lbs. of waste material per 1,000 liters of wine delivered, despite recycling efforts. A keg holds the equivalent of 26 bottles of wine, and each keg that goes into distribution will save 2,340 lbs. of trash from the landfill over its lifetime.

Another interesting packaging innovation is the paper bottle, actually a flexible pouch of pulp/pouch construction, which can be custom made into bottle shapes with embossing and texture available. Compared to PET or glass container, this paper bottle amounts to 85 percent material weight reduction and up to 50 percent more filled bottles per truck in transport.

Community Outreach

In addition to tangible resource management, sustainable wineries also dedicate time to educating their community of consumers, producers, and vendors about their sustainable practices. These wine producers are also committed to social responsibility and giving back to their communities, both local and around the world, as will be presented in greater detail in Chapter 6.

BEST PRACTICES IN WINE SUSTAINABILITY

Much of the work on sustainability in the wine industry is being done at the industry level to address increasing concerns of consumers, government, retailers, and other stakeholders. In response to trends over the last decade, systems have been developed and promoted by the wine industry at the regional and national level.

Wine industry associations have developed and promoted various environmental management systems for sustainability programs. Most sustainable wine programs began as voluntary environmental management systems (EMS) among a few wineries in the industry. In California, the grape growers in Lodi led the way with a sustainable approach. Similarly, in New Zealand, growers began a common sustainable approach and then worked to bring their customers—the wineries—into the movement.

An EMS is a set of processes and practices that enable an organization to reduce its environmental impacts and increase its operating efficiency. The EMS itself does not dictate a level of environmental performance that must be achieved; each company's EMS is tailored to the company's business and goals. An EMS encourages a company to continuously improve its environmental performance. An EMS monitors environmental performance similar to the way a financial management system monitors expenditure and income and enables regular checks of a company's financial performance. An EMS integrates environmental management into a company's daily operations, long-term planning, and other quality management systems.

The industry association managing the sustainability program is clearly the greatest influence in the wine industry in every region researched, more so than government, except for Europe, where the European Commission wields considerable influence over the wine industry. More specifically, the association represents peer-to-peer influence, as the industry leaders tend to sit on the board and technical committees managing the sustainability program and its certification requirements.

Thus, standards for certifying a winery as sustainable can vary from country to country and region to region. Sustainability decisions and programs for vineyard and winery operations can encompass significantly different elements. Some certification programs only certify the vineyard. Some certify both the vineyard and the winery but use separate (though coordinated) standards for the vineyard and winery. Whether a wine can carry a sustainability certification mark or imprint on its label can be impacted by whether both the winegrowing and winemaking practices have been certified.

The next chapter will examine these established regional certification systems in much greater detail, identifying where each is effective, their comparative strengths and weaknesses—as well as gaps—and how they are being adopted by wine companies in their geography.

KEY TAKEAWAYS

- Certification, water use and quality, soil, air and climatic impacts, energy, chemicals, wildlife, materials, waste, and globalization are all important topics within the discussion of sustainable wine. No single factor is more important, and they are most impactful when considered together.
- Sustainability issues extend beyond the natural environment in the vineyard. Producers and winemakers must also address environmental stewardship throughout the production and distribution of the wine (with regard to packaging and fossil fuel use, among other concerns), as well as maintain social responsibility in their community to be considered truly "sustainable."
- It's costly to transition a vineyard from conventional to organic (or biodynamic), and it takes a few years to rid the soil of all pesticide and chemical residue. And,

as there are so few natural or nonchemical products available as alternatives to traditional treatments, the farmer must focus on growing a healthy vine that is able to feed itself naturally and withstand pests.

- These days, farmers and viticulturists can be organic, but not sustainable, and vice versa. Imagine a mono-cropped farm that substitutes organic fertilizers and pesticides for chemical inputs, its products certified, and then trucks its produce across the United States to its market, with no concern for GHG emissions. This example hardly meets the criteria for a sustainable product. Furthermore, organic certification requires no social or ethical commitments or criteria.

Chapter 2 References

1. Willer, H. et al. *The World of Organic Agriculture. Statistics and Emerging Trends 2013*. FiBL, Frick and IFOAM. Available online: https://www.fibl.org/fileadmin/documents/shop/1606 -organic-world-2013.pdf (Accessed on 24 August 2015.)

2. Greene, C. *Growth Patterns in the U.S. Organic Industry*. United States Department of Agriculture Economic Research Service. 24 October 2013. Available online: http://www.ers .usda.gov/amber-waves/2013-october/growth-patterns-in-the-us-organic-industry.aspx# .Vdsw2rxVikp (Accessed on 24 August 2015.)

3. Rosenthal Duminy, H. *Modern Ecological Wine Grape Production in South Africa*. Cape Wine Masters Diploma. January 2004. Available online: http://www.capewineacademy .co.za/dissertations/CWM_H_Rosenthal.pdf (Accessed on 24 August 2015.)

4. Atkin, T. et al. "Environmental Strategy: Does It Lead to Competitive Advantage in the US Wine Industry?" *International Journal of Wine* Volume 24. Issue 2 (2002): pages 115–133. Available online:http://www.sonoma.edu/sbe/wine-business-institute/research/atkin _gilinsky_newton.pdf (Accessed on 24 August 2015.)

5. Pullman, M. et al., "Sustainability Practices in Food Supply Chains: How Is Wine Different?" *Journal of Wine Research* Volume 21. Issue 1 (2010): pages 35–56. Available online: http:// www.tandfonline.com/doi/abs/10.1080/09571264.2010.495853#.Vds9SLxViko (Accessed 24 August 2015.)

6. Goode, J. "Sustainability, Organics, Biodynamics—New Scientific Perspectives on Viticulture." *Wine Anorak*. Available online: http://www.wineanorak.com/sustainability presentation.pdf (Accessed 24 August 2015.)

7. Callahan, M. "Vintner Unveils Plan for Large Winery Outside Santa Rosa." *The Press Democrat*. 2 February 2015. Available online: http://www.pressdemocrat.com/news/3472664-181 /vintner-unveils-plan-for-large (Accessed 24 August 2015.)

8. Hannah, L. et al. "Climate Change, Wine, and Conservation." *Proceedings of the National Academy of Sciences of the United States of America* Volume 110. Issue 17 (2012): pages 6907– 6912. Available online: http://www.pnas.org/content/110/17/6907.short (Accessed 24 August 2015.)

9. Euromonitor International, *Global Wine: Challenges and Opportunities Facing the Wine Industry*. May 2010. Available for purchase online: https://pdf.marketpublishers.com/euro monitor/global_wine_challenges_n_opportunities_facing_wine_industry.pdf (Accessed 24 August 2015.)

10. Ibid.

11. Savage, G. "France Moves to Tackle Pesticide Risk." *The Drinks Business.* 1 August 2014. Available online: http://www.thedrinksbusiness.com/2014/08/france-moves-to-tackle-pesticide-risk/ (Accessed 24 August 2015.)

12. Penketh, A. "French Organic Winegrower Fined for Refusing to Spray Grapes with Pesticide." *The Guardian.* 7 April 2014. Available online: http://www.theguardian.com/world/2014/apr/07/french-organic-winegrower-fined-refusing-spray-grapes-pesticide (Accessed 24 August 2015.)

13. Matthews, P. *Real Wine: The Discovery of Natural Winemaking.* London: Mitchell Beazley, 2000.

14. Robinson, J. "Spain Leapfrogs France and Italy." *Jancis Robinson.* 29 Mar 2014. Available online: http://www.jancisrobinson.com/articles/spain-leapfrogs-france-and-italy (Accessed 24 August 2015.)

15. Wines, M. "West's Drought and Growth Intensify Conflict Over Water Rights." *New York Times.* 16 March 2014. Available online: http://www.nytimes.com/2014/03/17/us/wests-drought-and-growth-intensify-conflict-over-water-rights.html (Accessed 24 August 2015.)

16. National Agricultural Statistics Service. *Grape Crush Report Overview.* United States Department of Agriculture. Available online: http://www.nass.usda.gov/Statistics_by_State/California/Publications/Grape_Crush/Final/2013/201303gcbnarr.pdf (Accessed 24 August 2015.)

17. Null, C. "How to Make Mass Produced Wine Taste Great." *Wired.* 22 April 2014. Available online: http://www.wired.com/2014/04/how-to-make-wine-taste-good/ (Accessed 24 August 2015.)

18. Klonsky, K., and Healy, B. *Statistical Review of California's Organic Agriculture.* University of California Davis. Available online: http://aic.ucdavis.edu/publications/StatRevCA OrgAg_2009-2012.pdf (Accessed 24 August 2015.)

19. Robin, R. "Defining Organic Practices for Wine and Grapes." *Wine Business Monthly.* April 2006. Available online: http://www.winebusiness.com/wbm/index.cfm?go=getArticle &dataId=42774 (Accessed 24 August 2015.)

20. Agricultural Marketing Service. *Organic Regulations.* United States Department of Agriculture. Available online: http://www.ams.usda.gov/rules-regulations/organic (Accessed 29 August 2014.)

21. Karlsson, B. *Biodynamic, Organic and Natural Winemaking—Sustainable Viticulture and Viniculture.* Edinburgh: Floris Books, 2014. Print.

22. Teague, L. "Wine Headache? Chances Are It's Not the Sulfites." *Wall Street Journal.* 13 March 2015. Available online: http://www.wsj.com/articles/wine-headache-chances-are-its-not-the-sulfites-1426250886 (Accessed 24 August 2015.)

23. Miller, H. "Why Organic Isn't Sustainable." *Forbes.* 19 November 2014. Available online: http://www.forbes.com/sites/henrymiller/2014/11/19/why-organic-isnt-sustainable/2/ (Accessed 24 August 2015.)

24. Conner, D. "Beyond Organic: Information Provision for Sustainable Agriculture in a Changing Market." *Journal of Food Distribution Research* Volume 35. Issue 1 (2004): pages 34–39. Available online: http://ageconsearch.umn.edu/bitstream/27137/1/35010034.pdf (Accessed 24 August 2015.)

25. Demeter Association, Inc. *Biodynamic Preparations.* Available online: http://www.demeter-usa.org/for-farmers/biodynamic-preparations.asp (Accessed 24 August 2015.)

26. Demeter Association, Inc. *The Demeter Biodynamic Farm and Processing Standards.* Available online: http://www.demeter-usa.org/for-farmers/farm-processing-standards.asp (Accessed 24 August 2015.)

27. Hernandez, J. "Do You Really Want to Know What Biodynamic Means?" *Wine Enthusiast Magazine.* May 2014. Available online: http://www.winemag.com/May-2014/Do-You-Really-Know-What-Biodynamic-Means/index.php/slide/Sustainable/cparticle/4 (Accessed 24 August 2015.)

28. Jackson Family Wines, *The Sustainability Story at Jackson Family Wines.* Available online: http://www.jacksonfamilywines.com/sites/default/files/jfw_sustainabilitycasestudy.pdf (Accessed 18 August 2015.)

29. Brown-Forman, *Fetzer Vineyards Converts to Lightweight Glass.* 14 October 2008. Available online: https://www.brown-forman.com/FetzerVineyardsConvertsToLightweightGlass/ (Accessed 24 August 2015.)

30. Copeland, B., and Devendra, A. *Lightweighting Wine Bottles: An Eco-Friendly Trend Becomes Mandatory in Ontario.* Nixon Peabody. Available online: http://www.nixonpeabody.com/files/148136_Beverage_Alcohol_Brief_06_05_2012.pdf (Accessed 24 August 2015.)

CHAPTER 3

SUSTAINABILITY AROUND THE WORLD OF WINE:

*Review of Sustainable Certification Programs
by Region and Industry Association*

I N WRITING THIS CHAPTER, I set out to determine the best and most effective regional and national sustainability programs in the wine sector. My research sought to compare and contrast, assess and judge the various sustainability programs to determine which are the most effective, which require compliance with the highest standards of sustainability, which were models for all others to follow, and which were lacking. The goal was to decide who in the wine industry is setting the pace and raising the bar on sustainability internationally.

In some instances, there were those in the industry who were disparaging of regional sustainability programs, in particular how they compare with biodynamic and organic certification requirements. Often winemakers would tout organic as being somehow better than sustainable programs that simply required record keeping, but still allowed pesticide use. Some biodynamic producers would brand sustainable systems as mere green washing. Organic producers criticize certified sustainable programs as lacking rigor.

Mark Chien, program coordinator of the Oregon State University Wine Research Institute indicated, "There are a group of winegrowers here in Oregon that believe that Oregon LIVE isn't aggressive enough. I believe that each organization has to set their own goals and what they want to achieve at what level. If responsible growers want to have 40% of the vineyard acreage in Oregon certified as anything, then you can't set the bar too high—you can't set it at organic certification. And that's just the reality. Where it gets sticky is when people start touting one thing as better than the other. We have these different systems of viticulture that people can choose to use, and as long as they perform within the guidelines of the systems they choose (and certainly within the legal parameters of whatever farming practices they're using) they're fine; they're all helping to conserve and protect the environment. Don't bother them! They're legal. Don't say one is better than the other."

The fact is that all the wine sustainability programs are quite similar and follow pretty much the same formula(s). All the vineyards, wineries, and regions face the same challenges; it's usually just a matter of degree. And they are all making significant progress in terms of advancing sustainability in viticulture and winemaking, based on climatic and other conditions in their geography and region.

Lodi Rules is the pioneer of sustainability initiatives among all programs—the first structured initiative for sustainable practices in the winegrowing sector established by the Lodi Winegrape Commission in California and set up in 1992. Not only was it the first, but also its author, Cliff Ohmart, set the standard for everybody else. Each of these sustainability programs uses a scoring system, though they pick and choose among the various categories that each group uses to rate their sustainability based on their circumstances. Also among the top programs is LIVE, established in Oregon, which conducts the oldest certification scheme, and is now practiced in the Pacific Northwest region of the United States. These two programs—Lodi and LIVE—set the highest standards. Next comes South Africa, the most comprehensive in terms of environmental protection, conservation, and labor rights and the strictest in terms of its compliance enforcement. Chile, the newest program, has the most comprehensive social responsibility chapter, and New Zealand has accomplished the largest uptake, with nearly 95 percent of all vineyards and wineries certified.

In all of these regions, significant resources are currently being invested in the development and expansion of these programs to improve the sustainability of wine growing and producing processes and to document the progress achieved. In Chile, sustainability has been placed at the heart of a new national strategic plan for wine, which has given rise to a national sustainability program involving certification.

Of the various ongoing programs, some aim exclusively to document and communicate environmental performance, especially regarding carbon emissions, while others focus on the overall sustainability of processes, thus also taking economic and social aspects into consideration.

The programs from Chile, South Africa, and New Zealand have a national scope while the others are regional. For example, McLaren Vale Sustainable Winegrowing in Australia and the program in the Champagne region each have a scope limited to their particular wine region. California has four different programs. VineBalance in New York State is the only program that does not run a certification system, but other initiatives in the state that do lead to certification, such as the newly started Long Island Sustainable Program, were derived from it.

For a visual comparison of the main elements of several wine sustainability programs, there are charts at the end of this chapter excerpted from "Transnational Comparison of Sustainability Assessment Programs for Viticulture and a

Case-Study on Programs' Engagement Processes," an article by researchers at the University of Adelaide.

In the EU, a few important sustainability programs for wine have been developed. Among these it is worth mentioning the Vignerons en Développement Durable and Bilan Carbon initiatives in France; Viticulture Durable en Champagne (VDC) system and label in the Champagne region of France; the FAIR'N GREEN project in Germany; and the recently created Forum for Wine Sustainability in Italy.

For More Information . . .

- Vignerons en Développement Durable (http://www.v-dd.com/en/)
- Bilan Carbone Initiatives (http://www.winenvironment.eu/docs/Bilan-CarboneFrom_the_Vine.pdf)
- Viticulture Durable en Champagne (http://palatepress.com/2015/04/wine/sustainable-growing-in-champagne-finally-more-than-lip-service/)
- FAIR'N GREEN (http://www.fairandgreen.de/en/)
- Forum for Wine Sustainability (http://www.vinosostenibile.org/?lang=en)

Due to the greater breadth and lack of homogeneity in European winemaking systems, programs of national importance like those of the newer wine producing countries have not yet been established. There are of course thousands of wineries certified organic and biodynamic throughout the EU.

There is no international code for sustainable wine growing, and many doubt if that is even feasible given the different climatic conditions, indigenous pests, distinct grape varietals, and different regulatory regimes that exist in different parts of the world, as well as the maturity of wine industries and the homogeneity and relationships that exist in regions. However, the International Organization of Vine and Wine (OIV) has announced resolutions and policies that promote environmental protection and reduction of greenhouse gas (GHG) emissions in the international wine sector, specifically its GHG calculator.

The International Federation of Wines and Spirits (FIVS) worked with its members—national wine and spirits associations—to develop the Global Wine Sector Environmental Sustainability Principles (GWSESP), an international strategy that recognizes that solid environmental credentials are essential to the industry's survival and success. The GWSESP initiative acknowledges that the wine industry is entirely dependent on natural resources: solar energy, suitable climate, clean water, healthy soils, and the successful integration of these elements with ecological processes. Therefore, protection and enhancement of these natural assets through sustainable practices are an imperative. Since 2007, FIVS has been working with the OIV on the development of guidelines for sustainable winegrowing that incorporate FIVS' Principles.[1]

The most significant and relevant sustainability programs for viticulture and viniculture worldwide are fully documented in this chapter. There are others—some recently created, others not as comprehensive, and they will be mentioned summarily.

Compared to sustainability programs in other agricultural sectors, these wine certification programs are quite complex. Most of them are patterned after ISO 14001 guidelines for environmental management systems (EMS) and are characterized by roughly four stages: (1) definition of assessment method, (2) definition of indicators, (3) attributed scores and weights or compliance, and (4) certification (conformance).[2]

Assessment methods can vary: (1) process-based (i.e., is there a plan in place to manage an environmental challenge?), (2) best practice-based, (3) indicator-based, or (4) criterion-based (i.e., compliance to a set of rules). No matter which method is chosen, it is critical to establish benchmarks and performance measures to assist wine growers to improve their sustainability by comparing their performance to their peers and against program goals.

ISO 14000 is a family of standards related to environmental management that exists to help organizations (a) minimize how their operations (processes, etc.) negatively affect the environment, (b) comply with applicable laws, regulations, and other environmentally oriented requirements, and (c) continually improve. They also incorporate a triple bottom line approach, with standards and criteria covering economic, environmental and social factors. The ISO 14001 standard, the most well known of the 14000 standards, is applicable when an organization wishes to:

- implement, maintain, and improve an EMS,
- assure itself of its conformance with its own stated environmental policy (those policy commitments of course must be made),
- demonstrate conformance,
- ensure compliance with environmental laws and regulations,
- seek certification of its environmental management system by an external third-party organization, and
- make a self-determination of conformance.

It is important to point out that the purpose of certification is typically for marketing. The certification aspect is really for the benefit of retailers and consumers, in order to provide a seal of assurance for the public that the requirements of the system have been met at a sufficient level.

Process-based assessments are usually based on ISO standards. The greatest shortcoming of a process-based assessment is that it does not ensure performance outcomes. The practical outcome of process-based methods is the production of written documentation (e.g., management plans)—as you will see in several of these wine sustainability systems—a commitment to do better next year.

The *best-practice-based* assessment method's strongest point is the practical and immediate pathway to objectively deliver net sustainability gains. Education is a core component of this method. Among the described methods, it seems to be the easiest to engage farmers because of its focus on the sustainability output.[3]

Indicator-based assessments rely on reporting of numerical values related to past input use. The weakness of the system is that indicators are just collected data, without being linked to reference levels. Carbon/greenhouse gas accounting and water footprint methods are examples of indicator-based assessments. The strength of this method is the small time required for data recording and ability to readily compare data.[4]

Criterion-based assessments methods are focused on compliance with legislation or rules established by the specific sustainability program. The strength of the method seems to also be its weakness: the method clearly excludes participants who are noncompliant. Unfortunately, exclusion undermines the goal of increasing sustainability progress since participating growers who are in most need of help to improve their sustainability are not certified and thus omitted.[5]

Understanding these methods will help when evaluating the regional programs described in the following pages.

AUSTRALIA

Entwine Australia is the Australian wine industry's national sustainability program—set up to support growers and winemakers in demonstrating and improving the sustainability of their businesses. Entwine Australia was developed by the Winemakers' Federation of Australia (WFA) in consultation with industry and with support from the Australian Government. It is a voluntary environmental assurance scheme that allows winemakers and wine grape growers to receive formal certification of sustainable environmental practices according to recognized standards. It is now managed by the Australian Wine Research Institute (AWRI).

Entwine is as an "umbrella" sustainability program. Under the Entwine umbrella there are two components for members—the reporting of sustainability metrics and participation in an approved certification program. Entwine provides credentials that cover the fundamental components of sustainability (environmental, social, and economic) and can be applied to both the vineyard and winery. The program provides benchmarking tools and resources to enable planning, evaluation, control, and communication. Companies must be independently audited and report annually against a set of defined resource use indicators. Wineries also must report their greenhouse gas emissions.

Entwine is a program designed with flexibility to suit the changing goals and needs of all Australian grape and wine producers and provides information for wine industry research, development, and extension activities and can be used by members for benchmarking.

Members can choose which certification program best suits their business from:

- ISO 14001
- Freshcare Environmental Viticulture/Winery
- Freshcare Environmental Viticulture Code of Practice
- Freshcare Environmental Winery Code of Practice
- Sustainable Australia Winegrowing

Freshcare is the fresh produce industry's own on-farm assurance program, fulfilling both domestic and international market requirements. It is a practical approach to help growers and packers assure customers that their produce is safe to eat and sustainably grown, and thousands of fresh produce businesses have adopted the Freshcare program since its launch in July 2000.

Wine producers also have the choice to be certified instead under Sustainable Winegrowing Australia (SAW), which started as a regional program, the McLaren Vale Sustainable Winegrowing Australia (MVSWGA) and is now accessible to any grower across Australia. It has its origins in the early 2000s. What followed was the development of a series of viticulture initiatives with the objective to improve growing practices, fruit quality, and financial viability in the region. These initiatives included seminars and workshops; a growers' bulletin called CropWatch that provided information from nine weather monitoring stations and pest and disease alerts for the region; and research trials.[6] The association also released a Financial Benchmark for McLaren Vale growers in 2005, and a Pest and Disease Code of Conduct in 2006, which was voluntarily endorsed by the growers in 2007. In this same year the Soil Management, Water Management and Preservation of Biodiversity Codes were also released.

In 2008, the sponsors of the initiative decided they needed to measure results. And in 2009 the assessment workbook was provided to all growers in the region. Next step, 50 growers decided to self-assess.

The MVSWGA method of assessment has three main principles: (1) assessment over time; (2) grower sustainability levels identified on a continuum and not on a pass/fail basis; (3) the assessment and reporting system must be useful for the grower to understand their sustainability status and be able to improve it. In contrast to the other certifications which have a single category of compliance, the MVSWGA places growers into four certification categories: category 1—red, needs attention; category 2—yellow, good; category 3—green, very good; and category 4—blue, excellent. It is expected that very few growers can actually reach the blue level in the program. The program promotes continuing improvement.

Ten percent of program members are randomly selected annually and audited by a third party. Audits are in place to ensure credibility of the growers' sustainability levels based on their responses. There are specific rules and penalties that, in extreme cases, can lead to a member's exclusion in case of discrepancies between inspections and the self-assessment answers and data reporting. Audits are also available to members who wish to become certified. Certification audits are carried out every three years, whereas self-assessment, random inspection process, and data reporting through the online system are annual.

SAW was created to maximize growers' and regional overall sustainability, and aims to minimize environmental impacts. The data capture and reporting provides growers with the best management tool to demonstrate their performance against their regional peers and recognized best practice.

SAW is now available to any grower across Australia and is accredited by the AWRI for full Entwine Membership.

CHILE

One of the pillars of the Chilean wine industry's 2020 Strategic Plan is sustainability: to turn Chile into the largest producer of premium, diverse, and sustainable wines in the New World. The Consorcio I+D Vinos de Chile (R&D Consortium Wines of Chile), the technical arm of the wine industry, designed a comprehensive Sustainability Program—a set of initiatives for wineries to implement, realizing that sustainability represents the convergence of activity that is environmentally friendly, socially equitable, and economically viable. The Sustainability Code is the centerpiece of this project. It is voluntary in nature with requirements in three complementary areas: green (vineyard), red (process), and orange (social). The Code sets standards for the entire value chain of wine making:

- Green Area—vineyard: Includes land owned by the company and land owned by long-term suppliers (contracts of two years or more).
- Red Area—wine making process: Includes the winery, bottling plant, and other facilities related to wine production.
- Orange Area—social: Applies to the company including its land, offices, and facilities.

Recognizing that the production of wine involves many steps beyond simply how the grapes are grown in the vineyards, the Chilean Code investigates business operations at all phases and in all locations of the company—vineyards, wineries, bottling plants and other facilities, and corporate offices. Many codes do not mention social responsibility or they make it a much smaller priority, while focusing primarily on environmental impacts of wine producing. The Chilean code goes much further in the area of social responsibility. For example, the Orange Area of the Chilean code includes a commitment of responsibility to the consumer, ethical practices with suppliers, and a section addressing quality of work life and human rights. This tool could be the most comprehensive and complete of any of the codes evaluated here, based on the breadth of coverage and extent of value chain actors to be included.

In terms of influencing how wineries conduct their business, the code requires:

1. planning, implementing, operating, and maintaining a management system focused on a sustainable wine production,
2. minimizing potential environmental impacts caused in the wine production chain,
3. guiding working relationships inside the company within an ethical framework, and
4. improving communication with their clients, suppliers, and interested parties in the wine production chain and with the communities surrounding their production units.

In my interview with Patricio Parra, general manager of the R&D Consortium of Wines of Chile, he stressed the fact that the Sustainability Code certifies the performance of the winery, not the wine itself. It changes the culture of the management—more so than a line of product itself. "Of course, we don't try to replace other certifications such as those for CO2, water use etc. We're not interested only in the products. It's important for us that the suppliers (of all sizes) can internalize the management of sustainability," he said. "It's not simply a requirement to avoid some pesticide; you need to change your management. The social requirement deals with the change of culture, and our way of thinking.

"The social area of the code is unique among other regional codes of conduct," said Parra. "Many requirements are in our national legislation. What we require from companies is to show us the procedures and tools to ensure that social responsibility will be fulfilled forever. Show us who is in charge, show us the documents. We expect the companies to fulfill the national and international legislation. This part of the code is not just about putting in a requirement—it's 'show me' what you are doing to fulfill these requirements and legislation and how is it being implemented."

The implementation of the code began in January 2011, starting with only the Green Area. In January 2012, 11 wineries were certified to the green area. Certification of all three areas as a whole was under way by January 2013. By the end of 2015, 57 wineries were certified; 57 wineries that represent 70 percent of Chile's bottled wine exports. "We have a biannual cycle of certification—normally after 4 or 5 years participating in the process, the wine itself is going to be certified by default," according to Parra.

There are various bodies with set roles that act independently of one another. The governance, updating, and administration of the Code are the responsibility of Vinos de Chile through the Vinos de Chile R+D Consortium. The audits and certification decisions are the responsibility of certification bodies authorized by Vinos de Chile. As such, the technical decision to certify is completely externalized and independent, but the general review of the process and granting of the certificate remains with Vinos de of Chile.

Certification Requirements

The Code has identified the associated practices of each of the three areas; standards and corresponding checklists have been developed for each sector, which include checkpoints with point totals and forms of verification for each requirement. Some of these checkpoints are considered critical and compliance is mandatory.

"Yes, we have a score we give to applicants, and we are increasing our requirements every 2 years," said Parra. "The minimum requirement at the beginning is 60 percent of the total score, but always you must comply with 100 percent of the critical requirements—from the beginning. As you progress in the rounds of certification, your minimum requirement score must move from 60 percent up to almost 100 percent. Normally, most companies are already starting at 75 percent or 80 percent of the score. And, you must comply within each area independently—it's not a total score. So, one score for vineyard and one score for facilities, and one score for the Orange chapter etc. You cannot get a 40 percent in the vineyard, and then a 90 percent in facilities, and then try to calculate the average. It's all or nothing."

In order for each audited unit in the Red and Green Areas to meet the standard, they must pass 100 percent of the critical control points and obtain a score that is equal to or higher than the score established for its certification cycle, calculated on the basis of the total score obtained. In the Orange Area, the entity must meet 100 percent of the critical requirements and the total score of the consolidated evaluation of the company established based on its certification cycle. The certification lasts for two years.

After obtaining the certification the wine company can apply voluntarily the seal "Certified Sustainable Wine of Chile" on bottles, in all advertising, on its websites, and posters of its vineyards and production facilities.

By fulfilling the Code's requirements, the companies that enter the certification system can show their management capacity to reduce potential environmental and social risks caused by the activities involved in wine production. What is finally "certified" is the company's management and not the end product.

Chile wants its code to assure customers that it is sustainable, but Vinos de Chile also wants to continue innovating in this area. Sustainability is a key aspect of how Chilean wines will be marketed. "This initiative has a lot of innovation, but in two years most other wine producing countries are going to create their own systems, codes, whatever. So, we need to continue to innovate," said Parra.

The Sustainability Code's three areas cover and score practices in all of the following topics:

Green (Vineyard)

Erosion

Soil Management

Nutrition

Diseases, Pests, and Weeds Management

Training

Management and Application of Agrochemicals

Vigor Management

Water Protection Sources

Pre-planting

Established Vineyard

Implementation and Monitoring

Red (Winery)

Waste Reduction and Recycling

Energy Saving and Emissions Reduction

Water Management

Job Safety

Environmental Pollution Prevention

Implementation and Monitoring

Orange (Social Responsibility)

Sustainability Policy

Ethics

Supplier Relations

Human Rights

Environment

Quality of Professional Life

Community

Marketing and Commitment to Clients and Consumers Section

Economic Sustainability

Implementation and Monitoring

FRANCE

There is no single national sustainability system for wine in France, but two programs bear mentioning—a sustainable agriculture system favored by a small group of wineries and a regional sustainability program in the Champagne region.

Haute Valeur Environnementale

The French Ministry of Agriculture developed the Haute Valeur Environnementale (HVE) certification in 2001, a three-tiered system that encourages farms and vineyards to focus on increasing biodiversity, decreasing the negative environmental impact of their phyto-sanitary strategy (i.e., measures for the control of plant diseases, reducing the use of pesticides and fungicides), managing their fertilizer inputs, and improving water management. Once an operation has attained the third and most stringent level of the certification process, it is deemed worthy of the title "High Environmental Value" ("Haute Valeur Environnementale," HVE). The authorities recently established an official label that producers with this status can display on their products and marketing materials.

HVE has strong support from the trade organization Vignerons Indépendants de France (Independent Winegrowers of France) a group of eco-conscious small-scale producers, about 25 percent of which are organic producers. They see a slowing in the number of new entrants to organic certification among wineries in France. HVE is less strict than organic requirements in terms of the elimination of chemical inputs in the vineyard, but it emphasizes other points, such as the promotion of biodiversity, which makes it much more aligned with sustainable agriculture systems that have concerns about vineyards being monocultures.

This is a voluntary approach that involves three levels:

- Level 1 is a prerequisite for access to the process, obtained by carrying out a self-assessment by the farmer, validated by an accredited auditor. Action plans are created.
- Level 2 has 16 "best practices" around four themes: biodiversity, use of pesticides, fertilizers, water management. At this level, a vineyard could receive the environmental certification label; it is validated by an external audit.
- Level 3 is the highest level and provides the certification HVE for the entire farm operation. It includes performance requirements measured either by composite indicators or by global indicators corresponding to the four themes. This level is also validated by an external audit after three years of operating at Level 2.

As of August 2015, 168 farms were certified to Level 3, HVE and 7,000 farms have Level 2 certification. The logo may be affixed to finished products (including wine bottles) containing at least 95 percent of raw materials from farms with HVE.[7]

Viticulture Durable en Champagne

In the early 2000s, The Champagne trade association, Comité Interprofessionnel du Vin de Champagne, hereinafter The Champagne Bureau, sponsored an environmental footprint assessment of the viticulture and winemaking in the region. The result was a Champagne Business Environmental Management Plan with four key action areas:

- The reduction of environmental risks to human health, particularly those arising from the use of agricultural inputs.
- The preservation and enhancement of terroir, biodiversity, and landscapes.
- The accountable management of water, wastewater, by-products, and waste.
- Confronting the energy/climate challenge.

These priorities formed the focus of an environmental policy as a whole, based on internationally accepted standards for environmental management systems.

Then in 2014, the Champagne Bureau decided to pursue a sustainability certification system and on May 12, 2014, launched its own "sustainable" winegrowing certification under the Viticulture Durable en Champagne (VDC) label. Champagne thus became the first French wine region to create its own sustainable label and certification requirements.

Champagne had its own unique reasons for pursuing this direction. For over 40 years following World War II, the champagne region, like most agriculture, used chemical pesticides and herbicides, and an increase in yield was the positive result. But this came at a price: significant erosion in Champagne's sloped vineyards and pesticide residues in the wine. Furthermore, today Champagne is quite concerned about the rise in the mean temperature by 1.8°C (3° F) and predictions of continuing increases in the temperature going forward, which could have detrimental effect on the cultivation of cool-climate grapes and production of champagne as we know it.[8]

Essentially the new VDC certification is very similar to the national HVE—in the sense that a company as a whole is certified. Some of the large Champagne Houses including Bollinger, Duval Leroy, Krug, and Veuve Cliquot were already certified under the HVE. However, HVE applies to all farm products, and as an alternative to organic farming, it is not fully understood by consumers. Like sustainable wine certification programs in "new world" wine countries, Champagne's VDC includes sustainable practices in the vineyard as well as water and waste management.

Certification requires compliance both with 60 critical standards and 31 major standards. There remain 34 minor standards, and at least 20 of those must be complied with as well. It takes three years to be certified, and Champagne Houses are subject to audits every 18 months.

Just one year after this initiative was launched, the system gained recognition through environmental certification from the French Agriculture, Food Processing and Forestry Ministry. As of midyear 2015, about 15 producers representing more than 2,000 hectares—amounting to 6 percent of the land area—have Viticulture Durable en Champagne certification. This may seem like a small number, but remember these types of programs are still new in France and only 100 producers in the Champagne region are even certified organic!

GERMANY

FAIR'N GREEN, founded in November 2013, is a sustainability standard with a focus on economic, social, and environmental implications of an agricultural operation. It was developed by Athenga GmbH, a German consulting firm that specializes in sustainability consulting. With their years of experience in multiple industries—consumer goods and logistics, for example—they see sustainability as an "interdisciplinary interconnection."

Businesses that are operating under the EU Organic standards already qualify for a portion of FAIR'N GREEN certification. FAIR'N GREEN does not aim to compete directly with producers that are certified Organic but rather offers resources to expand on organic certification. However, FAIR'N GREEN is open to those that are not currently operating under the EU Organic standards as well. Overall, the FAIR'N GREEN movement, as it is described by some of its members, aims to reduce the input of artificial substances into the environment and reduce the reliance on fossil fuels.

The central parts of the FAIR'N GREEN system are:

- Four key chapters: environment, society, business management, and value chain
- 150 criteria: 50 percent of all points must be met upon entering the association, as well as a minimum of 40 percent in each of the four sustainability chapters.
- Annual improvement: The companies pledge to improve annually by 3 percent with regard to the previous year and document their measures.
- Sustainability Toolkit: There is concrete assistance and sustainability consulting for achieving the improvement.
- External audit: The QC&I—Quality Certification & Inspection service provides external monitoring and verification for the assessment.

Contents and Measures of FAIR'N GREEN:

- Preparation and analysis of a life cycle assessment.
- Proposals for sustainable energy management.
- Calculation of a carbon footprint for the company.
- Measures for reducing carbon footprint.
- Focusing on social commitment and strengthening CSR.
- Analysis of the supply chain with regard to sustainability issues.
- Hands-on assistance for establishing sustainable procurement.
- Promotion of employees' commitment to sustainability.

Requirements for the certification:
To be admitted into the program it is crucial to consider the principle of near-nature and fair management and comply with the principles of an environmentally friendly viticulture. This includes:

- Environmental protection and natural winemaking.
- Protection of natural resources.
- Focus on measures of cultural techniques for plant protection: good leaf work and soil care are ideal measures to prevent pests.
- Increase the natural resistance of the grapes.
- Preservation of the natural habitat of beneficial animals by greening and an ample variety of flowers from accompanying plants.
- The addition of non-natural substances is only permitted if damage to the vines cannot be prevented otherwise. In this case, selective use is advisable in order to keep the addition of non-natural substances to a minimum.
- Deliberate conservation of biodiversity and preservation of the cultural landscape.
- Systematic and proven reduction of artificial inputs and emissions into the environment and the atmosphere.
- Social commitment.
- Fair wages and social interaction in the company.

Wine growers who already comply with the EU organic farming regulation may find it easier to become FAIR'N GREEN certified; however, this is not a prerequisite.[9]

I know Theresa Breuer, manager of Breuer Estate located in Rüdesheim am Rhein, through our mutual membership in the Magnum Club, where she shared the progress being made in German viticulture. The wine estate Georg Breuer was established in 1880 and has been owned by the Breuer family since the beginning of the 20th century. Georg Breuer, Theresa's grandfather, expanded the vineyard and exports.

Today Theresa Breuer runs the operations at Georg Breuer. Of their membership in FAIR'N GREEN, Theresa says, "For us, sustainable work on the vineyard as well as in the social environment with our team has been a topic for a long time, and we already took first steps. With the membership in FAIR'N GREEN we see a chance to put our ideas in this field into quantifiable numbers and to understand where we are standing in the process. The monitored further development is often forgotten in the hectic of daily routines and for that the topic is just too important for us. We hope to get to know ourselves better and to improve."

Corneilus Dönnhoff of wine estate Dönnhoff was recently elected to the board of the FAIR'N GREEN association, which by the end of 2015 had 30 vineyards as members. He explains his motivation for FAIR'N GREEN as follows: "This holistic sustainability concept is very convincing. We are aware of our historic roots and we carry the responsibility for the landscape and its wine culture. Therefore, it is our duty to pass on healthy vineyards to the next generation, in union with and out of respect for nature. This concept helps us to not only develop our sustainable business but also to measure progress objectively. The goal to protect resources includes social and societal. Respecting people and paying them fair wages is a matter of course for us. We're all working together to fill this philosophy with life."

Forum per la Sostenibilita' del Vino

ITALY

Explicit interest in the subject of sustainable development has emerged later in Italy than in other countries. The question of sustainability seemed important to the wine industry, but specific initiatives were not deemed necessary, as Italian wine growing and production appeared to already have a high level of sustainability. More recently, however, a remarkable level of activism has developed, which has seen the direct involvement of wine growing and producing companies, suppliers of technical equipment and services, producers' associations, research institutes, and public administration, all of which led to the birth of the Forum for the Sustainability of Wine. Established in February

2013, the Forum had the aim of promoting the environmental sustainability of wine as a fundamental element of the qualitative excellence and the competitiveness of Italian wines on the market.

There have been 15 programs with different approaches to sustainable development in the wine sector. (These are listed in the chart below.) Although there are differences in how they process indicators, they have worked to achieve the same objective, highlighting the importance and success of monitoring, controlling, and assessing environmental parameters and agricultural policies.

	Name of Program	Coordinator/Sponsor
1	Biodiversity Friend	World Biodiversity Association
2	CasaClima Wine	Energy Agency of Alto Adige—CasaClima
3	ECO Prowine	CIRCE—Centro de Investigacion de recursos y Consumos Energeticos Universidad de Zaragoza
4	Eko Cantia/Eko Wine	Officinae Verdi/WWF/FederBio/University of Tuscia
5	Gea Vite/Ita. Ca.	SATA Studio Agronomico
6	Magis	Bayer Cropscience s.r.l.
7	Montefalco 2015: New Green Revolution	Ass. Grandi Cru Montefalco
8	Salcheto Carbon Free	Soc. Agr. Salcheto srl/CSQA Certificazioni s.r.l.
9	SosTain*	Ass. Alleanza per la Sostenibilità in Vitocultura/ OPERA
10	Environmental Sustainability of Agrifood SupplyChain by LCA Assessment	CCPB s.r.l./APOCONERPO s.c.a.
11	Tergeo	Unione Italiana Vini Soc. Coop.
12	Vino Libero	Ass. Vino Libero
13	Vite.Net	Horta srl—spin off UNICATT Piacenza
14	V.I.V.A. Sustainable Wine	Italian Ministry of Environment/UNICATT/Agroinnova
15	Vini 3S	DIBAF University of Tuscia/Az. Agr. TREBOTTI

All 15 programs were designed with a holistic vision of sustainability—the triple bottom line—but their emphasis has been almost exclusively on environmental aspects and goals:

- GHG emissions—both direct (including from the use of energy) and indirect—related to the process and/or product
- Water Consumption; direct and indirect water pollution
- Biodiversity maintenance and protection of biodiversity in the ecosystem

These ranged from CasaClima Wine, an architectural-based system focused on constructing "green" winery buildings; to V.I.V.A. Sustainable Wine, an initiative of the Italian Government Environment Ministry focused on sustainable wine; even a city with a major commitment to become a totally green geographic area, Montefalco 2015: New Green Revolution; and of course Unione Italiana Vini (UIV),[10] the trade union for wine producers, which has sponsored Tergeo, a project for gathering, qualifying, and diffusing innovative solutions for improving the sustainability of vine and wine enterprises. Tergeo has been (and remains) a "model" for the dissemination of knowledge and technological know-how among all the actors of the vine and wine production value chain, including vineyards and wine enterprises, scientific and university research bodies, dealers of vine and wine products and services, category associations, and government organizations at the national and regional levels.[11]

Equalitas is a new entity, a stakeholder movement, launched in 2016 with the aim of uniting the Italian wine business into a homogenous and shared vision of sustainability and is the result of a five-year commitment by UIV to Tergeo. While most of the 15 separate initiatives in the Forum make up the new entity, the controlling decision-making power rests with UIV and Federdoc (the national confederation that protects and promotes the Italian Appellations and Dominations of Origin— AOC, DOC, and DOCG). Together UIV and Federdoc hold the 50.5 percent voting majority of Equalitas and have agreed not to vote separately on any issue. This is to ensure that the control of Equalitas is firmly in the hands of the production side of the wine industry.

Equalitas will promote good practices in the following areas:

- agricultural practices such as soil handling, irrigation, biodiversity, no weeding between rows, etc.
- manufacturing practices related to cellar and bottling, and packaging
- social practices, including workers' rights, training, employee satisfaction surveys, and community surveys of neighbors every three years
- economic practices, such as economic incentives for achieving environmental and social improvements, and

- communication practices, including establishing rules to ensure true and transparent communications; social responsibility and environmental reporting to all stakeholders and self-designation as a Sustainable Company.

Equalitas will certify companies (and groups of companies), wines, and territories (i.e., regions). The certification is valid for three years. There are major (M) requisites, which must be complied with 100 percent at the start of the certification validity; minor (m) requisites that demand 30 percent compliance with within the three years of the certification validity, and recommended (R) requisites that must be fulfilled at 10 percent compliance, also within the three years of the certification validity. There are also additional indicators for biodiversity, carbon footprint, and water footprint that should be adopted within three years of certification validity.

SIMEI: UIV is also a major convener of SIMEI, the leading international exhibition for enological and bottling equipment, technology, and packaging of all drinks, which takes place every two years in Milan and Munich. Simultaneous to the exhibition, UIV organizes an international congress to discuss important topics and trends relevant to the wine industry, and in 2013 and 2015 the congresses have been about sustainability. In 2013, the congress entitled Sustainable Viticulture and Wine Production: Steps Ahead Toward a Global and Local Cross-Fertilization convened wine industry leaders, experts, technicians, and stakeholders from around the world and produced a policy paper, "Vision on the sustainable future of our wine and vineyards," which represented a major step by the industry toward harmonization of the various regional wine sustainability systems.

The 2015 Congress expanded the concept of sustainability to a new dimension related to sensory factors in assessing wine. Looking beyond the traditional definition of the triple bottom line (i.e., balancing the social, economic, and environmental needs of today against those of tomorrow), the 2015 SIMEI Congress discussed adding a fourth dimension—taste. Taste and its expression through the techniques of sensory analysis is one very important indicator of sustainability, which has been left out of previous efforts to judge sustainability in wine production. The aim of the 2015 policy deliberation and resulting white paper is to show the relevance of flavor and taste to the creation of sustainable wine, while assessing how these criteria can be scientifically measured. The goal was to introduce this aspect in the overall sustainability debate and to lay the foundation for sensory analysis and a scientific discipline that could become a key factor in communicating sustainability.[12]

NEW ZEALAND

In the early 1990s, the wine industry was undergoing rapid vineyard expansion, and this growth was projected to continue for some time. Along with this expansion there was new pressure on land and water resources, accompanied with issues related to changing use of land. Leaders in the wine industry recognized that the natural resources of the country and the industry were of significant value and needed to be protected and, where possible, enhanced. It was felt that developing guidelines for sustainable viticulture would help establish and retain good practice and would also provide a valuable education tool by which results from industry research could be transferred to producers.

Sustainable Winegrowing New Zealand (SWNZ) was established in 1995 as an industry initiative emanating from New Zealand Winegrowers. It was commercially introduced in 1997 and adopted by growers from the entire grape growing regions. The growers pursued support from their customers—the wineries and introduction of winery standards followed in 2002, a significant development, which further substantiated the industry commitment to sustainable production.

The growth of the industry—as well as its adoption of a more sustainable approach—was primarily driven by significant increases in exports particularly to the UK, which was showing a developing interest in purchase of goods with well-established environmental credentials. Industry leaders felt that taking a proactive approach toward sustainable production would meet this growing demand and assist individual companies to enhance their marketing opportunities.

SWNZ defines sustainability as "delivering excellent wine to consumers in a way that enables the natural environment, the businesses and the communities involved, to thrive." The policy states that wine must be made from 100 percent certified grapes in fully certified winemaking facilities and certification must be through an independently audited third-party program (SWNZ or one of the recognized organic or biodynamic certifications). The program aims to provide quality assurance, and also serves as a "best practice" model.

To become certified, prospects must first self-assess their operations and provide supporting documentation for their responses. Additionally, there is a requirement to supply data for water and input use (electricity, fuel, pesticide/fungicide spray).

The program is based on three pillars: monitor, measure, and manage. Currently, the measures that SWNZ focuses on are water, energy, and agrochemical use. In fact, several prominent wineries have made energy and reduction of GHG emissions a

Arapawa Sheep
Credit: SWNZ

major priority, understandable given the distance they are from their most significant markets in the UK and the United States.

The self-assessment consists of three sets of questions: major, minor, and best practices: Majors are mandatory, minors are generally relevant practices, and best practices are the next step up. Compliance with all major questions and 80 percent of minor questions are required to achieve certification. If 100 percent of major questions are not achieved, corrective actions are required to pass. A second on-site inspection may or may not be requested, depending on each situation.

Third-party auditors work closely with the program managers from the initial inspection in order to be certified and then again every three years to maintain certification. The independent auditors often serve as mentors to growers to help them meet the program's requirements. Certification is issued by SWNZ based on inspection results. Certification is still voluntary; however, since 2010, the New Zealand Winegrowers, the body responsible for promoting the brand New Zealand Wines, made vineyard and wine accreditation to the SWNZ (or one of the recognized organic or biodynamic certifications) a prerequisite to participation in promotional events. As a result, 90 percent of the wines produced in New Zealand became part of the SWNZ.

SWNZ is an integral part of the future of New Zealand wine production. As such, the program aims to deliver the following benefits to its members:

- A framework for viticulture and winemaking practices that protect the environment while efficiently and economically producing premium wine grapes and wine.
- A program of continual improvement to ensure companies operate with a goal of improving their operational practices.

- A platform for technology transfers so that companies are kept up to date regarding any new technology and its application.
- An external audit structure that has integrity and rigor to comply with market expectations, leading to certification as fully sustainable.
- Opportunity to be a part of New Zealand Wine (NZW) industry goal of 100 percent of grape growers and winemakers operating under approved independently audited sustainability programs.

To meet the NZW policies on Sustainability and Vineyard Registration[13] and to enter NZW events, promotions, and awards, wines from 2010 vintage onward had to be recognized as produced by wineries and vineyards operating in accordance with a recognized independently audited sustainability program (or a combination of), the criteria for which are:

- 100 percent of grapes (vineyards) that go into the wine are certified.
- 100 percent of wine processing plant(s) where the wine is produced and bottled are certified.
- If the brand owner does not own *all* the vineyards or the plant in which the wine is processed and bottled (e.g., virtual wineries), it requires a separate membership in the form of a brand certification.

New Zealand succeeded in accomplishing 95 percent certification by 2014 through SWNZ, organic or biodynamic certifications, a distinction among its peers from around the world.

SOUTH AFRICA

Longtime leader in environmental, biodiversity, and wildlife protection and energy efficiency, the wine industry in South Africa has improved its sustainability performance with new labor and health requirements for the entire wine supply chain. Bottle seals now certify three programs.

Two distinct programs—Integrated Production of Wine (IPW) and the Wine and Agriculture Ethical Trade Association (WIETA)—oversee sustainability in the South African wine industry with their focus on environmental practices and labor practices, respectively. A third program, the World Wildlife Fund has long partnered with many wine producers in a conservation partnership—the Biodiversity Wine Initiative (BWI) to protect biodiversity in the Cape Floral Kingdom (CFK), the richest and also the smallest plant kingdom on the planet, where 95 percent of South Africa's wine is grown. Participating winegrowing takes place. The participating wineries are designated "BWI champions" for their work adopting and showcasing biodiversity best practice.

South African wines are also certified as to origin by the Wine and Spirit Board, which also administers IPW.

The Integrated Production of Wine

Integrated Production of Wine (IPW) was established by legislation under the Liquor Products ACT in 1998. Membership is voluntary, but members are legally obliged to comply with the environmental sustainability system's requirements. The 2000 vintage was the first to be certified under this program.

IPW consists of a set of guidelines specifying good agricultural practices related to grape production (farm component), as well as guidelines specifying good manufacturing practices related to wine production (winery component) and packaging activities (bottling). Because wastewater is regarded as the most significant environmental risk at wineries and because water is a limited natural resource in South Africa, IPW also maintains separate additional guidelines for the management of wastewater and solid waste at wineries.

There are 15 guidelines for the farm, 13 guidelines for the winery, and 11 guidelines for dedicated fixed-site bottling facilities.

Compliance with the IPW guidelines is assessed on an annual basis through the completion of a self-evaluation questionnaire and is independently audited on a spot-check basis. IPW Guidelines for farms (vineyards) and cellars (wineries) are very clear in identifying practices that should be followed and directions against those practices that are not acceptable. Recordkeeping is absolutely essential and relevant records must substantiate all points in the self-assessment.

In order for the winery to be certified, the qualifying score of 60 percent or more must be attained. The following criteria must be complied with:

- Grapes must be produced according to IPW.
- No nonpermitted residues may be present in the wine.
- Prescribed record keeping must be up to date.
- Cellar must have all required written permission/permits/licenses for solid waste and wastewater management.

If any of the above criteria are not complied with, an acceptable action plan describing the steps to be taken to ensure compliance during the following season must be submitted with the evaluation forms.

Additionally, 150 grape samples are taken at randomly selected wineries during each harvest season and analyzed by an accredited laboratory for 146 different pesticides residue by means of multiresidue analysis. A wine can only be certified when all the requirements of the Wine of Origin Scheme have been met. The Wine and Spirit Board will certify a wine if all the requirements of the Scheme with regard to origin (i.e., Paarl), cultivar (i.e., Riesling), and vintage (i.e., 2012) have been met and the wine has also been evaluated by one of the tasting panels of the Board and it did not show any unacceptable quality characteristics. Samples of all wines submitted for certification are also scientifically analyzed to determine whether all the legal requirements have been met.[14]

Social Practices and Labor

While IPW establishes standards and audits of environmental practices, WIETA covers fair labor practices on vineyards and in wineries and monitors compliance. Established a decade ago, WIETA is a South African nonprofit association that promotes ethical trade in the wine industry value chain through training, technical assessment, and audits to assess compliance with its code of good practice.

Despite this ethical program, Human Rights Watch exposed some deplorable practices in the South African grape and fruit farming sector, concerning the human rights situation of farmworkers and farm dwellers in the Western Cape province of South Africa, and issued the report of its investigation: Ripe with Abuse—Human Rights Conditions in South Africa's Fruit and Wine Industries, August 23, 2011.[15]

On May 3, 2012, the South African wine industry, in cooperation with worker unions, announced a new fair labor initiative—the creation of an ethical seal under WIETA that will testify to reasonable working conditions, based on rigorous and closely monitored qualification criteria. South African leaders indicated that by introducing the seal, they want to acknowledge and accredit wineries and vineyards that follow ethical practices and to protect them from any potential negative publicity resulting from those who flout the law, referring to the practices exposed by Human Rights Watch. The initiative was intended to increase the confidence in South African wines both domestically and internationally and to capitalize on the industry's global leadership in eco-sustainable production.

The wine industry in South Africa has built a reputation for leadership in advancing environmentally sustainable wine production. This new seal will, industry leaders hope, match that reputation with an infrastructure to promote social sustainability. The WIETA code of good practice is premised on international Labor Conventions and the base code of the Ethical Trading Initiative and also incorporates South African labor legislation.

The WIETA code contains the following important principles:

- Precludes the use of child labor.
- Prohibits forced labor.
- Asserts that employment should be freely chosen.
- Employees should have a healthy and safe working environment.
- Workers should have the right to freedom of association.
- A living wage.
- Protection from unfair discrimination.
- Working hours shall not be excessive.
- Regular employment shall be provided.
- Worker housing and tenure security rights should also be respected.

The fully traceable WIETA seal is modeled on South Africa's environmental sustainability seal developed to promote awareness of the production integrity and required at every stage of the supply chain from vineyard to bottle. Implementation of the ethical program involves three phases: training of workers, owners, and management in labor law and the WIETA code of fair trading principles at regional awareness raising workshops; completion of self-assessment forms to determine their level of compliance and correction of gaps; onsite inspection and audit. Producers have to meet a minimum pass rate of 60 percent. To ensure total traceability, brand owners have to identify all their suppliers, and the whole supply chain (i.e. not just the wineries but all the producers and suppliers) will be audited. This focus on social and labor practices is believed to be a world-first among wine-producing countries.

Each of the above requirements has a separate seal attesting to compliance. Assuming a wine was certified by IPW, by World Wildlife Fund as a BWI, by WIETA and by Wines of Origin (WO), plus any quality awards the wine had received, which typically are also gold labels or seals on the bottle, a bottle could be covered in seals. Imagine how confusing that would be for the consumer (not to mention the clutter).

In recognition of this, beginning with the 2010 vintage, wines could be certified, upon application by the winery, for compliance with the requirements of both WO and IPW. Compliance with the requirements of both schemes is indicated using a new seal on the bottle, attesting to combined verification known as Sustainable Wine South Africa.

Similarly, the World Wide Fund's (WWF) Biodiversity and Wine Initiative (BWI) decided to give its full support to the IPW's program and announced the consolidation of the BWI program into the IPW that will assure wine lovers of a producer's environmental and biodiversity conservation credentials and reinforce the South African wine industry's well-established foundation as a global leader in environmental sustainability.

South Africa's IPW program has had the reputation of being the most comprehensive and strictly managed of all the wine environmental codes in terms of audits and certification. The long-term vision for wine certification in South Africa is for the industry to have one seal, issued by the Wine and Spirit Board, that certifies the Wine of Origin information (vintage, date, variety), the environmental sustainability (IPW), biodiversity protection, and the ethical treatment of workers (WIETA).

United States

Lodi Rules

The Lodi Rules for Sustainable Winegrowing is California's first third party-certified sustainable winegrowing standards. It began with the creation of the Lodi Winegrape Commission in 1991, whose primary goal is to promote the Lodi wine region and market its wines. At the time, integrated pest management (IPM) was thought to be the most important issue for wine grape growers and so the Grassroots IPM program was launched in 1992. IPM is an economically and environmentally sound method for controlling pests. By using information about the life cycle of the pest, farmers can manage pest damage by the most economical means, and with the least possible hazard to people, property, and the environment.

Over the next few years, other issues like ecosystem management and human resources were deemed priorities, and the first edition of the self-assessment workbook was launched in 2000. The third-party certification system was added in 2005, and by 2008 10,000 vineyard acres were certified, 10 percent of the region's wine grapes. The Lodi Rules has two key components. First, the Lodi Rules promotes wine grape grower adoption of 101 sustainability practices, which are termed "standards." The Lodi Rules standards are the backbone of the program, and they meet three criteria: first, they are measurable; second, they address at least one of the three aspects of sustainability: environmental health, social equity, and economic viability; and third, they are economically feasible to implement. The Lodi Rules standards are the most thoroughly and rigorously vetted set of sustainability practices in California's viticulture industry. All standards have been peer-reviewed by scientists, members of the academic community, and environmental organizations.

The second key component of the Lodi Rules is the Pesticide Environmental Assessment System (PEAS). PEAS is a model used to quantify the total environmental and human impact of pesticides applied to Lodi Rules vineyards annually. The PEAS model generates an Environmental Impact Unit (EIU) for each pesticide, which is based on the pesticide's impact on acute risk to farm workers, dietary risks from acute and chronic exposure to people who consume the product, acute risks to small aquatic invertebrates, acute risk to birds, and acute risk to bees and pest natural enemies.[16]

The Lodi Rules takes a comprehensive approach to farming that goes beyond just pest management to promote practices that enhance biodiversity, water and air quality, soil health, and employee and community well-being.

Growers are audited annually by a third party to verify their farming practices and may not exceed a maximum number of "pesticide" points calculated using PEAS. Certification is awarded to an individual vineyard annually.

The Lodi Rules program has grown vigorously since its establishment in 2005. As of 2013, over 26,500 wine-grape acres were "Certified Green." Within the Lodi region about 20,000 acres are certified and over 6,500 acres are certified in other regions throughout California. Approximately 20 wineries produce wines baring the Lodi Rules seal. To warrant use of the Lodi Rules logo, at least 85 percent of the fruit must be from a certified sustainable source.

Protected Harvest, an independent environmental nonprofit organization, specializes in quantifiable sustainability certification and administers the certification process that endorses farmers' use of stringent environmental farming standards. This ensures that the standards have been reviewed and endorsed by an organization that is not connected to the Lodi Winegrape Commission.

Certification Requirements

Under the Lodi Rules program, a vineyard qualifies for certification if it meets these criteria:

1. The farming practices being used must achieve a score of 50 percent or better for each chapter from the Lodi Rules farming standards. Chapters include Ecosystem Management; Education Training and Team Building; Soil Management; Water Management; Vineyard Establishment; and Pest Management. Scoring below 50 percent on any chapter, even if the scores are very high on all the others, disqualifies the vineyard from certification.
2. The environmental impact units for the pesticides being used in that vineyard for the year, as calculated by the PEAS model, cannot exceed 50 units.
3. Each vineyard must qualify for certification every year and must be audited annually through a rigorous process of on-site inspection prior to harvest and pesticide and nutrient usage post-harvest to verify that pesticides used in the vineyard for the year have not exceeded the environmental impact unit threshold.
4. A grower joining the Lodi Rules program must pay a sign-up fee of $2,150, which covers the first year of certification. To continue in the program, there is an annual application fee of $1,300 and an annual dollar fee for each acre the grower seeks to certify. For those growers out of the Lodi appellation, the fee is $3 per acre. These fees pay for administration and auditing of the certification program by Protected Harvest.

Lodi Rules—Certified Sustainable Practices[14?]

INTEGRATED PEST MANAGEMENT

We limit crop protection to only essential measures in our vineyards. We create and maintain habitat for natural enemies of pests.

AIR QUALITY CONTROL

We plant cover crops of native grasses in and around our vineyards to minimize dust. We limit tractor usage to a minimum to reduce air pollution and conserve energy.

LAND STEWARDSHIP

We integrate the management of our vineyards with the ecosystem by providing riparian zones, introducing and preserving native grasses and trees, maintaining vernal pools, protecting wildlife habitat, and installing nesting boxes for owls, birds, and bats.

WATER MANAGEMENT

We constantly monitor soil moisture and measure the vines water needs. We regulate water usage through careful irrigation scheduling, and constantly maintain and service our irrigation systems for maximum efficiency.

SOIL HEALTH

Healthy living soils grow great wines. We add organic matter by planting cover crops and utilizing compost. We control fertilizer and irrigation to maximize nutrition in our soils, which results in higher, more concentrated fruit quality.

HUMAN RESOURCES

People are the foundation of great sustainably grown wines. Our workers receive comprehensive training and development that enables them to perform their jobs safely and maximize their ability for year-round employment.

SUSTAINABLE VISION

We create a sustainable vision for the farm that provides the foundation for sustainable winegrowing, helping ensure the long-term health, biodiversity, and productivity of the farm and surrounding ecosystem. All our farming practices can be evaluated as to whether it moves us toward or away from this vision.

Hand Harvesting
Credit: Wine Institute

The program requires growers to use a wide range of sustainable practices that result in continual improvement of all aspects of their farming operations. "It is not just a do-no-harm program, which consists of practices that should not be used, but rather one that will lead to measurable improvement in the environmental health of the surrounding ecosystem and society-at-large, and wine quality," according to Dr. Cliff Ohmart, formerly Sustainable Winegrowing Director at the Lodi Winegrape Commission and architect of the *Lodi Rules*.[17]

SIP Program

The Sustainability in Practice (SIP) Certification Program is administered by the Central Coast Vineyard Team (CCVT), a nonprofit dedicated to sustainable winegrowing since 1994. Like others it began as a self-assessment tool for wine-grape growers in the central coast region of California to evaluate their sustainable farming practices. After more than a decade, the CCVT decided to move toward third-party certification. CCVT does not grant certification. Instead, an independent advisory council—consisting of academic, regulatory, government, and industry professionals—makes the determination based on the findings of the auditors.

Designed for and within the Central Coast region, the program is available throughout California. SIP Certification is a measurable and recordable set of farming practices, which encompass 10 chapters, and considers the whole farm, verifying the commitment to environmental stewardship, equitable treatment of employees, and business sustainability. SIP Certified substantiates practices in place through third-party inspection, providing certification, not self-assessment, of sustainability. SIP prohibits the use of high-risk pesticides—differentiating it from some other sustainability certifications. SIP Certified allows the seal on the bottle of wine.

The Certification Standards include both Requirements and Management Enhancements. Requirements are practices that must be completed on a foundational level before acquiring Management Enhancement points. Management Enhancements are scores assigned to practices that allow growers to earn points based on additional, nonrequired, but suggested management strategies. Also included within the document is a farm plan, which is required for certification. The farm plan includes documentation, reporting, and written examples of practices throughout the certification standards.

A grower's farming practices and documentation are verified through an independent audit and reviewed by an advisory committee. The purpose of certification is for growers to evaluate and substantiate their farming practices on a whole-farm level. This allows for marketplace authenticity and differentiation.

The shift from self-evaluation to third-party certification began in 2003 when a group of dedicated growers and advisers began developing a set of standards with measurable and verifiable requirements. The program was peer reviewed by over 30 environmental, regulatory, and academic representatives and piloted in 2008.

The SIP Standards evolved from over 15 years of work in sustainable farming and has undergone two extensive external peer reviews. Now in its seventh year, the Standards continue to evolve and incorporate comments by dozens of state, federal, social, environmental, agricultural, and university experts. SIP has a high threshold for eligibility. Rigorous guidelines cover a variety of farming issues, and the minimum eligibility requirements are quite high, addressing everything from air quality, biodiversity, energy efficiency, and water quality and employee benefits.

All of the questions are practice- and performance-based and auditable. To be certified, growers must meet all of the requirements and achieve enough of the management enhancements to receive 75 percent of the total available points. Using materials that fall into specific high-risk pesticide categories is prohibited (e.g., toxic air contaminates, cholinesterase inhibitors, groundwater contaminants). In order to achieve certification, a grower must not use any of the active ingredients on this list. In addition, each point must be proven through documentation and verified by both a records audit and on-site inspection. The advisory committee, comprised of industry, regulatory, and academic experts, grants final certification based on the auditor report. Certification must be renewed annually in a three-year cycle: on-site inspection in the first year and evaluation of demanded records, a combination of paper audits, interviews, and on-site inspections in years 2 and 3.

To use the SIP logo on a bottle, a minimum of 85 percent of the grapes must come from sustainably certified fruit, as verified by a chain of custody audit.

SIP™ Vineyard Certification Standards Point Summary	
Conservation and Enhancement of Biological Diversity	40
Vineyard Acquisition/Establishment and Management	80
Soil Conservation and Water Quality	40
Water Conservation	50
Energy Conservation and Efficiency	36
Air Quality	44
Social Equity	80
Pest Management	70
Continuing Education	20
Product Assurance and Business Sustainability	40
Year End Water and Nitrogen Use Reports	NA
Total Management Enhancement Points	**500**

In 2015, SIP was awarded the Department of Pesticide Regulation Integrated Pest Management Innovator Award. The Innovator Award honors those California organizations that emphasize pest prevention, favor least-hazardous pest management, and share their successful strategies with others.

Certified California Sustainable Winegrowing (CCSW-Certified)

As the state's population exploded and urban areas encroached on traditionally rural farmland, the California wine community decided to take a proactive, precautionary approach to address increasing pressure resulting from public and legislative perceptions, environmental decisions from regulatory and governmental bodies, and other growth-related issues.

The winegrowing members of Wine Institute and the California Association of Wine Grape Growers (CAWG) decided to promote vineyard and winery practices sensitive to the environment, responsive to the needs and interests of society-at-large, and economically feasible to implement and maintain. Wine Institute is the largest advocacy and public policy association for California wine, and the only group representing the industry at the state, federal, and international levels, representing more than 1,000 wineries and affiliated businesses throughout the state of California, responsible for 85 percent of the nation's wine production. CAWG is a public policy advocacy group of wine grape growers, representing more than 60 percent of the total annual grape crush. Together in 2002 they developed the Code of Sustainable Winegrowing Practices workbook as the basis for the Sustainable Winegrowing Program (SWP), providing an educational tool for vintners and growers to assess their practices and learn how to improve their overall sustainability.

In 2003, the California Sustainable Winegrowing Alliance (CSWA) was created to assist in program implementation. Based in San Francisco the CSWA is a nonprofit organization whose purpose is to promote the benefits of sustainable winegrowing practices, enlist industry commitment, and assist in implementation of the SWP.

In January 2010, CSWA announced the next step in its sustainability evolution: third-party verification and certification. The program, known as Certified California Sustainable Winegrowing (CCSW-Certified), uses third-party auditors to verify winery and vineyard adoption and implementation of sustainable winegrowing practices.

The process-based certification includes, from ground to glass, a total of 227 criteria, 58 of which are prerequisites.[18] The prerequisites were established to help achieve an appropriate balance between ensuring the integrity and rigor of the certification program, while enabling broad participation of the California wine industry. The rationale for the prerequisites includes legal requirements, significant stakeholder concern, environmental and social impact, economic feasibility, and potential risk to the company. They cover:

- sustainability business strategy
- soil management
- viticulture
- vineyard water management
- pest management
- wine quality
- ecosystem management
- energy efficiency
- winery water conservation and quality
- material handling
- solid waste reduction

- environmentally preferred purchasing
- human resources
- neighbors and community
- air quality

CCSW-Certified requires that a vineyard or winery:

- conducts an annual self-assessment using the Code workbook (138 vineyard practices and 103 winery practices),
- meets prerequisite criteria (50 vineyard prerequisites and 32 winery prerequisites,
- identifies priority areas and creates action plans that are implemented and updated annually, and
- demonstrates continuous improvement.

The process for certification is to complete the self-assessment, indicating whether a vineyard or winery's practices fall within category 1 (the lowest level of sustainability), category 2, category 3, or category 4 (the highest level of sustainability). If category 1 is indicated then an action plan must be developed. If it is a certification prerequisite, then they must move up to a 2 or higher. Not all criteria require action plans. If an action plan is required by a prerequisite, in most cases they must move up to a category 2 or higher in their second year of certification or they cannot continue to be certified. For some prerequisites, the applicant must register a category 2 or higher in order to be certified. In other cases, a category 2 is required the first year and category 3 or higher in subsequent years. Timely completion of action plans is necessary to meet the certification program expectation of continuous improvement and to satisfy the auditor so that certification will be recommended to the CSWA Certification Review Panel.

Regarding whether a certification label will be authorized for wineries to use, CSWA has not yet made a final determination if and how a logo or claims can be used on the bottle. Certified wineries and vineyards are given documentation of certification to use on their website and in marketing materials. CSWA set 2016 as the year it would develop additional certification requirements to allow the use of the logo on the bottle.

"It's a very complicated issue because we must take into consideration eco-label protocols, chain of custody issues and the interface with other existing and future certification programs that may be relevant for wine," said Allison Jordan, Executive Director at CSWA. "At this point, the primary audiences for the SWP and for CCSW-Certified are policymakers, regulators, and market gatekeepers including retailers, restaurants and the media that influence them."

Some stakeholders I spoke with, including journalists and even some California vineyard owners, complain that the CSWA standards are quite relaxed and set a low bar at the urging of the very large industrial wine companies that are influential on the board of the CSWA and the largest members of the Wine Institute.

Other stakeholders and journalists I spoke with, like Cyril Penn at Wine Business Monthly, offered a different perspective, cautioned against being overly critical of the program, and stressed that all progress is good. "There is much progress among California wineries in terms of water conservation and energy conservation that is being recognized with awards and in the media. All the California wineries are trying to do the right thing in terms of the environment and sustainability," Penn said. Of course, in the past there has been some cynicism among smaller California wine producers about the influence of large companies, and also cynicism on the part of organic and biodynamic producers regarding those who pursued sustainable certifications. But now it seems they are all pulling together. For example, the large wineries have been very supportive of direct-to-consumer advocacy, which primarily benefits the smaller producers who don't have the longstanding relationships with and access to the major national wine distributors, like the larger wine companies.

Of the 82 prerequisites for certification, only 11 require an assessment at category 2 or higher. All the others can be met at the lowest level of sustainability—category 1. Most of the remaining prerequisites require action plans and that the vineyard or winery must move up to a category 2 or higher in their second year of certification or they lose their certification. The lowest category is sufficient to gain certification on the large majority of points.

Yet certification isn't the only goal of the California program. It has developed tools for wineries to use in assessing its environmental footprint and has offered performance measurements to help track water use, energy use, applied nitrogen use, and GHG emissions. These projects funded by CSWA, and educational in nature, provide growers and vintners with tools to measure, manage, and track their use of natural resources to optimize operations, decrease costs, and increase sustainability.

An important aspect of the California program is the communications of ongoing improvement, for the statewide industry as a whole. The Sustainable Winegrowing Program is unique in measuring and publicly reporting performance for the entire state industry. The California Wine Community Sustainability Report 2004 was the first time an entire industry has used a common assessment tool to publicly report on the adoption of sustainable practices. A second report was released in 2009, and its most recent report, the program's 2015 report, shows broad participation in the SWP and wide adoption and implementation of sustainable practices in vineyards and wineries around the state. The report also shows growing participation in Certified California Sustainable Winegrowing, providing third-party verification of sustainability practices.

Participation in both the SWP and CCSW-Certified continues to grow. By 2015, over 10,000 vintners and growers had attended over 250 targeted education workshops. According to the 2015 report, since CSWA was founded in 2002, 2,091

California vineyard and winery organizations had participated in the SWP Self-Assessment Program. These organizations represent over 421,000 acres, 69 percent of California's wine grape acreage, and more than 212 million cases, 79 percent of cases produced in the state. In 2015, 483 vineyards and 91 wineries achieved CCSW-Certification. The 483 vineyards represent 102,327 CCSW-Certified wine grape acres, accounting for 17 percent of California's total acres. The 91 CCSW-Certified wineries produce 171 million cases, 64 percent of total cases from California.

Napa Green and Fish Friendly Farming

The Napa Valley Vintners (NVV) also developed a third-party certification program under its Napa Green label, a voluntary program for Napa Valley landowners, in partnership with the Fish Friendly Farming program, which focuses on restoring fish and wildlife habitat and improving water quality in the Upper Napa River Habitat to protect the endangered Coho salmon and steelhead trout. The objectives of the program are to ensure compliance with all local, state, and federal environmental regulations including the Clean Water Act, Endangered Species Act, California Department of Fish and Game Code, and County Conservation Regulations.

New York: Long Island Sustainable Winegrowing

Long Island wineries are confronted by environmental challenges from many different directions. Their vines sit atop the island's sole drinking-water aquifer. Soil erosion and chemical runoff can spread via creeks into the estuaries that support fish nurseries, migrating birds, and oyster and clam beds. Where they don't face a river, bay, or ocean, the island's North Fork and the Hamptons appellations bump up against the suburban sprawl of New York City.

In an attempt to protect that fragile ecosystem, and under pressure from the Environmental Protection Agency (EPA), a group of producers came together in 2012 to create a sustainability code specific to their circumstances and set an example. Inspired by sustainable wine certifications in West Coast states such as California and Oregon, the group wanted to create a local program—the first in an East Coast wine region—that reflected the best practices in use. Started by four wineries—Bedell Cellars, Channing Daughters, Martha Clara Vineyards and Shinn Estate—Long Island Sustainable Winegrowing (LISW) provides education and certification for Long Island vineyards.[19]

Many Long Island winegrowers have been following the New York state-recognized program of best practices called VineBalance, developed in 2004 with Cornell

Cooperative Extension, the New York Wine & Grape Foundation and New York Farm Viability. The foundation of the program is its grower self-assessment workbook—134 questions in eight sections covering the multitude of management decisions made by New York State grape growers. Designed to both document sustainable grape growing practices already in place and promote sustainable practices throughout the industry, the workbook is primarily an educational tool to bring awareness to the economic, environmental, and social implications of specific viticulture practices. The self-assessment provides a baseline for potential modifications detailed in an action plan after completing the workbook. When it was created, Vine Balance did not involve audits or certification.

The Long Island Group used VineBalance as a basis and took it further, adapting guidelines to deal with their unique conditions on Long Island. LISW uses international standards of sustainable practices in quality wine grape production that have been refined for the northeast and utilize the VineBalance Workbook and other materials developed by Cornell Cooperative Extension of Suffolk County. These practices are based on an independent third-party-verified checklist system consisting of recommended and prohibited practices and materials.

Among LISW's big concerns are preventing pesticides and excess nitrate-nitrogen in fertilizers from leaching into the groundwater, then harming the health of the island's estuaries and bays. For example, the program stresses that at least two-thirds of the vineyard must have permanent cover crops rather than bare soil—grasses, legumes, and flowers help minimize erosion, improve soil health without chemicals, and support beneficial insects that fight pests, among other things. The organization also stresses preserving local biodiversity.

Out of a total of 56 wineries in the region, 19 wineries were certified by 2015. To qualify for certification, participants must complete the VineBalance Workbook self-assessment and earn a qualifying score, with special emphasis on 18 core requirements, such as having a plan to mitigate runoff, use and storage of pesticides, and a plan to create ecological areas on the farm for insects, native wildlife, and plants that are not crops. Accompanying that are detailed score sheets for weed management, disease management, and insect control. Some herbicides, fungicides, and insecticides are prohibited altogether because of their tendency to leach into and persist in the water. Others are limited to use once or twice per season.

Reduced-risk, bio-pesticides or organic materials are allowed, and in the case of fungicides, must make up more than half of applications each season. For fertilizer, the program requires that at least some of it be organic, such as compost or mulch.

Participants must then undergo an independent, third-party inspection involving an on-site visit and a review of all records, earning passing scores on all criteria, and create an action plan for future improvements. The following year they must show progress on that plan. A winery has to be certified the first two consecutive years, and then the inspections take place every third year, in keeping with organic and Demeter biodynamic standards.

Long Island vineyards encompass about 3,000 planted acres and a wide range of grape varieties, dominated by Merlot, Cabernet Franc, Cabernet Sauvignon, and Chardonnay.

Oregon LIVE

One of the pioneers in developing a third-party sustainable certification program is the Oregon group LIVE or Low Input Viticulture and Enology, Inc. This refers to the production of wine grapes through integrated science-based, environmentally sensitive production practices. The outcome is a conservative use of raw materials (inputs such as pesticides, fertilizer, water, chemicals, fuel, etc.) applied in vineyard and winery production to only that which is needed to maintain the highest quality fruit.

A voluntary organization, LIVE was established in 1997 by a group of Oregon wine grape growers. The pilot project started with about 20 vineyards, and the group was voluntarily inspected through a partnership developed with Oregon State University. The objective was to understand their level of compliance with the guidelines. In 1999, LIVE was incorporated and certified by the International Organization for the Biological and Integrated Control of Noxious Animals and Plants (IOBC) to certify individual farmers. That same year inspections were conducted by independent third-party contractors with integrated pest management expertise. In 2006, the program was expanded to include growers from Washington State.

Membership is a key feature of the LIVE system. Growers need to join the program to have access to a username and password to access all functionalities of the online system and to have their data saved and considered for inspection by the program management. All educational resources and administrative documents are available as well. LIVE stresses the triple bottom line, promoting environmental preservation and conservation of the vineyard and surrounding areas, a farm's economic viability and support to its social, cultural, and recreational aspects.

LIVE goes beyond most other sustainability certifications in that it takes a whole-farm and whole-winery approach to sustainability. The entire property, including non-grape crops, landscaping, building operations, labor practices, even packaging must be managed to LIVE standards.

The program assessment is comprised of mandatory record keeping (pesticide, fertilizer, and irrigation), 5 percent of farm area is to be set aside as a biodiversity and ecological compensation zone, and a checklist of 13 chapters, each one with a series of topics, called "control points." The checklist follows a color scheme rationale where Red control points on the checklist are considered the most critical and 100 percent required, which means that full compliance is mandatory to become part of the program. LIVE requires 90 percent of the Yellow control points (very important but somewhat less critical than Red control points) and 50 percent of the Green control points. The system was developed to avoid members concentrating too heavily on any one given area of assessment.

LIVE is Northwest-based and recognizes that the Pacific Northwest is a unique biome with ecological conditions different from other wine regions, such as California, Virginia, and upstate New York. Therefore, wherever appropriate, LIVE's standards are specific to the Northwest. There is a list of approved pesticides, specific to two vineyard locations based on climate: Region I refers to cool-weather maritime climate—Willamette Valley, the western part of the Columbia Gorge, and northern Umpqua Valley—and region II refers to warm-weather continental viticulture climate—Walla Walla Valley, Eastern Oregon, Columbia Valley, Southern Umpqua and the Rogue Valley, Idaho, and British Columbia.

LIVE members must complete a series of reporting requirements each year that document their compliance with LIVE standards. Each of the following areas require documentation and third-party assessment:

VINEYARD

Farm records, training and traceability

Biodiversity

Site selection

Varieties and rootstock

Plant nutrition and fertilizer use

Irrigation

Integrated plant protection

Animal density and welfare

Worker health and safety

Watershed and riparian health

WINERY

Winery records and training

Grape sourcing and enology

Energy use and greenhouse gas emissions

Materials management

Water management

Worker health, safety, and benefits

Community impact and education

Certification is only achieved after completion of two years of farming under LIVE standards. Farmers have to be inspected in the first two years of the program.

Regarding inspections, authorized inspectors of the LIVE organization will review the program with each member by means of the Checklist Evaluation system. All required soil and tissue tests must be available for evaluation. Any unsatisfactory rating by the inspection service will be discussed on-site with the participating member.

After passing the second-year inspection, they can be certified by an independent third party, if program requirements are met. Certification must be renewed every three years, but any member is subjected to random inspections at any time. Additionally, members certified or not, must submit their records every year.

LIVE's goal is to encourage farming practices that create a high biological diversity in the whole vineyard. The vineyard program looks at biodiversity and all inputs into the vineyard. The winery program looks at energy use, worker health and safety, and inputs in the winery, such as chemicals used in the winemaking process, including cleaning products.

Through its partnership with the Northwest's Salmon-Safe, LIVE is supporting the mission to transform land management practices so Pacific salmon can thrive in West Coast watersheds. This partnership was the first joint certification effort concluded by Salmon-Safe, which results in vineyards adopting Salmon-Safe standards as part of their LIVE certification.

LIVE certifies the entire property the vineyard resides upon and takes a holistic approach. So if a farmer is growing hazelnuts or boysenberries next to wine grapes, LIVE requires these crops to be certified by Salmon-Safe as well. LIVE members who pass their first inspection year also become certified Salmon-Safe.

At the start of 2015, there were nearly 300 vineyard and 40 winery members of LIVE. Membership covered 10,913 vineyard acres 26,053 farm acres. Wineries can source fruit from wherever they wish. However, only bottles of wine produced from 97 percent LIVE–certified fruit can carry the LIVE certified label.

EMERGING SUSTAINABILITY PROGRAM

Argentina

Bodegas de Argentina, an association of Argentine wineries, launched its Wine and Viticulture Sustainability Protocol in November 2012, developed in partnership with the Catena Institute of Wine. Bodegas de Argentina is an association of 254 wineries, representing 90 percent of Argentine wine production. Laura Catena, founder of the Catena Institute of Wine, brought this idea to Bodegas de Argentina along with the idea of using the California CCSW as a model. Catena Zapata is a family-owned winery that has been producing wines for 110 years, and Laura Catena, the fourth generation, is now leading the company with her father Nicolas Catena, patriarch of Catena Zapata.

Catena had been working for years with sustainable practices, but they saw the need for all Argentine producers to have a protocol that gives directions about how to work in a more sustainable way. The process of developing the protocol was very inclusive from the start. Bodegas de Argentina had already established a special commission for sustainability issues (carbon footprint, water footprint, recycling, etc.). The protocol was evaluated by this commission for three years.

Both Nicolas and Laura Catena have a love of California and its wines. Nicolas lived there and taught at the University of California Berkeley; Laura Catena is an emergency doctor who studied in the United States. She lives part time in San Francisco with her family and part time in Mendoza, where she is the managing director of the winery. For the Catena family, California was an obvious inspiration for the sustainability protocol, but also Bodegas de Argentina was convinced that the natural environment of California is closest to theirs, so many practices can be compared.

In 2015, the Sustainability Commission of Bodegas de Argentina added provisions and requirements to the sustainability protocol for certification. And in June 2015, Bodegas Esmeralda (Catena Zapata) received certification to become the first sustainable certified Argentine winery, after passing an audit by SGS Argentina.* Annual audits will be required to maintain the certification.

KEY TAKEAWAYS

- While it is ultimately the decision of the viticulturist and vintner as to which system is best for their climate, region, land and circumstances, successful change is only achieved with record keeping, reporting, independent audits, and verification. However, certification is critical so that the retailer and consumer have assurance and confidence in the system applied.
- In terms of regional and national sustainability programs, Europe is catching on to the New World approach and recognizing the limitations of organic certification that remain in consumer perception of organic wine.
- A lot of progress is being made the world over in terms of sustainability in the wine sector. To those adherents of organic certification and biodynamic philosophy and practice who describe sustainable as "greenwashing," the rebuttal is that biodynamic and organic do not cover or include air quality, water quality, energy use, carbon footprint reduction, and community engagement and social advancement. These aspects are all covered—and being improved—in the sustainable certification programs.

The tables below are excerpted from *Sustainability Journal* (MDPI) article "Transnational Comparison of Sustainability Assessment Programs for Viticulture and a Case-Study on Programs' Engagement Processes," by Irina Santiago-Brown et al.[5]

---

* SGS is the world's leading inspection, verification, testing, and certification company whose certification services demonstrate that products, processes, systems, or services are compliant with national and international regulations and standards.

TABLE 3.   Wine growing sustainability programs comparison.

	Lodi Winegrowers' Workbook/ Lodi Rules	Sustainable Winegrowing New Zealand (SWNZ)	Vineyard Team/ Sustainability in Practice	Low Input Viticulture and Enology (LIVE)
Country	United States	New Zealand	United States	United States
Scope	Regional, mainly Lodi but also California	National	Regional (California)	Regional (Oregon and Washington States)
Year of establishment	1992 (as the Grassroots IPM program)	1995 pilot (commercially in 1997)	1996 (Positive Points System) 2008 (SIP)	1997 (pilot) 1999
Year of establishment of certification	2005	2000	2008	1999
Wineries certification	Yes**	Yes	No	Yes
Number of members/ vineyards	Not available	94% of the total vineyards in New Zealand	300 (VT)	289
Vineyard area acres/hectares	Not available	33,600 hectares	80,000 acres in Vineyard Team membership	10,639 acres
Certified Vineyard area	25,709 (Lodi Rules)	33,600 hectares	31,600 acres	9342 acres
Number of certified members/ vineyards	72 members	1784	174	251
Educational objectives	Yes	Yes	Yes	Yes
Program content peer-reviewed	Yes	No	Yes	Yes

Integrated Pridcution of Wine (IPW)	Sustainable Winegrowing Program (SWP)*	VineBalance	McLaren Vale Sustainable Winegrowing Australia (MVSWGA)	Sustainable Wine Chile
South Africa	United States	United States	Australia	Chile
National	Regional (California)	Regional (New York State)	Regional (McLaran Vale)	National
1998	2003 (CSWA)/ 2002 (SWP)	2005	2009	2009
2010	2010	NA	2012	2011
Yes	Yes	No	No	Yes
3000 farms— 95% of the wines produced in South Africa	954 (SWP)—55% of statewide acres	75 (2008)	119 members 191 vineyards	79 (level 1 & 2) vineyards or wineries
93,155.96 hectares (92.6% of total in South Africa in 2011)	293,404 acres— 69% of statewide areas	6,560 acres	2929 hectares—39% of total area under vine in McLaren Vale	Not available
93,155.96 hectares (92.6% of total in South Africa in 2011)	62,455 (11.6% of statewide acres)	NA	Not available	Not available
3000	187	NA	22	46 vineyards or wineries
Yes	Yes	Yes	Yes	Yes
Yes	Yes	No	Yes	Yes

TABLE 3. Wine growing sustainability programs comparison. *(Cont.)*

	Lodi Winegrowers' Workbook/ Lodi Rules	Sustainable Winegrowing New Zealand (SWNZ)	Vineyard Team/ Sustainability in Practice	Low Input Viticulture and Enology (LIVE)
Country	**United States**	**New Zealand**	**United States**	**United States**
Different sustainability levels for certification	No	Yes	No	No
Prohibited chemicals list	PEAS requirements (Lodi Rules)	Yes, from New Zealand legislation	Yes (highh risk pesticided are not allowed)	Yes. Two distinct lists based on climate of vineyard location
Certification	Pass or fail (must exceed 70% of the overall points available plus at least 50% in every chapter	Pass or fail (must reach 100% of major questions and 80% of minor questions)	Pass or fail (Participants must meet 75% of total points including all requirements)	Pass or fail. 100% (Red control points) + 90% (Yellow conrol points) + 50% (Green control points) + 5% farm area set aside for biodiversity
Assessment type	Best practice based + indicator based	Best practice based + indicator based	Best practice based + indicator based	Best practice based + indicator based + criteria based
Promotion of viticultural training	Yes	Yes	Yes	Yes
Third party certification	Yes (Lodi Rules)	Yes	Yes (SIP)	Yes

Notes: * California Sustainable Winegrowing Alliance; ** Lodi wineries' certification only on the change of custody (proof of segregating certified from non-certified grapes); *** list from AWRI [75]

Integrated Pridcution of Wine (IPW)	Sustainable Winegrowing Program (SWP)*	VineBalance	McLaren Vale Sustainable Winegrowing Australia (MVSWGA)	Sustainable Wine Chile
South Africa	United States	United States	Australia	Chile
No	No	N/A	4 levels. Higher level demands 75% of available points	Yes
Yes	No	NA	Yes, adopted from AWRI***	Yes, for herbicides
Pass or fail (must reach at least 60%)	Pass of fail. Certification requires scoring a 2 or higher for specific criteria, or have an action plan in place to improve performance*	NA	Sustainability level validation: Red (from 0 to 25%), Yellow (from 25.1 to 50%), Green (from 50.1 to 75%), and Blue (more than 75.1%)	Pass or fail (must reach 100% of critical points and at least 60% of the score)
Best practice based + criteria based + indicator based	Process based	Best practice based	Best practice based + process based + indicator based	Best practice based
Yes	Yes	Yes	Yes	Yes
Yes	Yes (Certified SWP)	No	Yes	Yes

CHAPTER 3 REFERENCES

1. FIVS, Environmental Sustainability. Available online: https://fivs.org/wm/strategic Initiatives/fivsForesee.htm (Accessed 31 August 2015.)

2. Santiago-Brown, I. et al. "Transnational Comparison of Sustainability Assessment Programs for Viticulture and a Case-Study on Programs' Engagement Processes." *Sustainability Journal* Issue 6 (2014): pages 2031–2066.

3. Ibid.

4. Ibid.

5. Ibid.

6. Government of South Australia, *Crop Watch*. Available online: http://www.pir.sa.gov.au /research/services/reports_and_newsletters/crop_watch (Accessed 31 August 2015.)

7. Ministry of Agriculture, France, *Farms: Environmental Certification*. Available online: http: //agriculture.gouv.fr/exploitations-agricoles-certification-environnementale (Accessed 31 August 2015.)

8. Henry, C. "Sustainable Growing in Champagne: Finally More Than Lip Service?" *Palate Press*, 27 April 2015. Available online: http://palatepress.com/2015/04/wine/sustainable -growing-in-champagne-finally-more-than-lip-service/ (Accessed 31 August 2015.)

9. FAIR'N GREEN, *Requirements*. Available online: http://www.fairandgreen.de/en/about-fair-green/requirements/ (Accessed 31 August 2015.)

10. Union Italian Vini, http://www.uiv.it/ (Accessed June 6, 2016.)

11. Tergeo, http://www.tergeo.it/en/ (Accessed June 6, 2016.)

12. White Paper, *Wine Sustainability: Past, Present, Future Sensory Characterization of Wines as an Integral Dimension of Sustainability* (26th Edition of the SIMEI exhibition, Milan, 3–4 November 2015. http://www.simei.it/en/congress/sustainability (Accessed June 6, 2016.)

13. New Zealand Wine, *Sustainable Winegrowing New Zealand*. Available online: http://www .nzwine.com/sustainability/sustainable-winegrowing-new-zealand/ (Accessed 31 August 2015.)

14. Wines of South Africa, *Certification of Wine as Guarantee to the Public*. Available online: http://www.wosa.co.za/The-Industry/Wines-Of-Origin/Certification-Of-Wine-as-Public -Guarantee/ (Accessed 31 August 2015.)

15. Human Rights Watch, *Ripe with Abuse: Human Rights Conditions in South Africa's Fruit and Wine Industries*. Available online: https://www.hrw.org/report/2011/08/23/ripe-abuse /human-rights-conditions-south-africas-fruit-and-wine-industries (Accessed 31 August 2015.)

16. Lodi Winegrape Commission. *The Lodi Rules for Sustainable Winegrowing Certification Standards, Second Edition*. Lodi Winegrape Commission, 2013. Available online: http:// www.lodigrowers.com/wp-content/uploads/2014/01/LR-binder-COMPLETE-V14.pdf (Accessed 31 August 2015.)

17. LoCA: The Wines of Lodi, *California Press Kit 2014*. Available online: http://www.charles comm.com/assets/client_files/Lodi_PressKit_2014.pdf (Accessed 31 August 2015.)

18. Intardonato, J. "Sustainable Certification Programs." *Wine Business Monthly*, July 2009. Available for members online: http://www.winebusiness.com (Accessed 31 August 2015.)

19. Certified California Sustainable Winegrowing, *Certification Pre-Requisites*. Available online: http://www.sustainablewinegrowing.org/amass/library/1/docs/CCSW-Certified %20Pre-Requisites%20-%203rd%20Edition.pdf (Accessed 31 August 2015.)

20. Long Island Sustainable Wine, *What Is Sustainability?* Available online: http://www .lisustainablewine.org/sustainability (Accessed 31 August 2015.)

21. Forum per la Sostenibilita del Vino (Italy), *First Report on Sustainable Winegrowing.* Available online: http://www.vinosostenibile.org/wp-content/uploads/2014/11/First-Report -Wine-Sustainability-Ocotber-2014.pdf (Accessed 31 August 2015.)

CHAPTER 4

SUSTAINABILITY AND THE CUSTOMER:

Educating and Marketing Sustainability to the Consumer

SUSTAINABILITY is increasingly becoming more popular in the wine industry. From farmers to producers, marketers to researchers, participants throughout the supply chain are making changes. The decision to invest in sustainable winemaking often originates with growers and winery owners who are motivated by family legacy, their health, and the health of vineyard workers. Their big challenge, they have told me, is how to recoup this investment in their value chain and ultimately in the marketplace.

Wine marketers are keen to sell organic wines to consumers who desire green lifestyles, and they know that many consumers are willing to "pay for the privilege of buying green" and for the confidence that their food and health are protected from harmful chemicals. But it's not clear yet whether wine consumers are ready for a more sustainable future. Today, American wine drinkers have a wide choice of wines produced within the United States or around the world.

Why do consumers choose to purchase certain bottles of wine? There is no simple answer, as the selection process is subjective and unique to each consumer's specific circumstances on any given day. Not only must consumers decide whether they want red or white wine and which grape or region they prefer, they're also faced with other questions, such as how much must they spend to ensure they are getting a "good" bottle of wine; what is the difference in alcohol levels between various wines that are appealing; which wine pairs with the food they want to eat, and which wine will favorably impress their dinner host?

Several consumer research studies have investigated the factors that could lead to purchasing decisions, including involvement and interest in the wine industry; generational differences; gender differences; lifestyle differences, and packaging and wine label preferences.[1] Wine consumers are also presented with myriad "good wine" choices: organic, biodynamic, natural, biologique (bio), and sustainable.

The industry, of course, uses these different categories to educate the consumer, differentiate their products, and create the perception of added value by describing their earth-friendly, ecologically responsible practices. However various studies have shown that though consumers like the idea of sustainable or organic wines, they are often confused by the different terms used to describe eco-friendly viticulture and winemaking, though they like the idea of sustainable or organic winemaking. In fact, they actually don't know much in general about how wine is made and tend to assume that wine is inherently "natural."[2]

The rules, regulations, and processes surrounding organic, sustainable, and natural wines can be confusing even to industry representatives. Alternative materials such as lighter bottles, bag-in-box (BIB), Tetra Pak, and cans, which bring wine to market in unfamiliar shapes, and dispensing methods such as wine on tap in restaurants and wine bars, may be very unfamiliar developments to consumers who cling to old purchasing habits. And since consumers rely on the sales and marketing people within the industry for that education, it's clear that further education in the retail, winery, and hospitality sectors is needed.

To the degree that the wine industry can make these new sustainable products intelligible and attractive to consumers, they will succeed in bringing the sustainable model to market. Consumer demand for wine and for knowledge about how specific wines are produced are an important opportunity for wineries to provide information and justification of their practices, and bring the "eco" factors alive in the story of their wines.[3]

Practical Implications

In the coming years, the wine industry must work to give the public clear definitions of what sustainable, codified certification and transparent eco-labeling mean. While sustainable wines are still a niche market, it's possible that with a change in the overall marketing strategy, these wineries could achieve a competitive advantage. Marketers need to examine if and how certification and labeling systems might drive consumers' purchasing decisions in the wine sector.

But consumers do not necessarily need to know all the jargon and how it is used. Rather, they need to learn that wines from sustainable wineries have direct and global benefits for them as purchasers. Research published by the American Association of Wine Economists indicates that if consumers understand that the purchase of "green" products will benefit them in one way or another, they are more likely to purchase said products. Consumers tend to purchase green products more for the private benefits (quality of product or health benefits) than the public benefits (the environment).[4]

Studies in 2013 sponsored by the Wine Institute revealed that the eco-friendly attributes of sustainably produced wine do impact the purchasing decisions of both environmentally conscious wine consumers and the wine trade (e.g., distributors and retailers).[5]

For the consumer research, the Wine Institute partnered with the Natural Marketing Institute in conducting its 11th annual LOHAS Consumer Trends Database™, which quantifies the size of the consumer market for environmentally and socially responsible products. For this research, they specifically segmented adult wine consumers.

Among the key findings were that 34 percent of wine consumers across all segments of the survey consider environmental/sustainable attributes when making wine purchases. Sixty-six percent of these wine consumers said they identify the eco-friendly, sustainable attributes of wine at the point of purchase via labels and information on the shelf or in-store. Of the LOHAS consumers—the greenest segment of consumers who describe themselves as active stewards of the environment and buyers of eco-friendly, socially responsible products—43 percent reported purchasing wine in the past three months, higher than the general adult population; 52 percent of these consumers consider the environmental attributes of their wine selections compared to 34 percent of all wine consumers.

Among consumers, market response to organic or natural wines has not been as definitively positive. Often, consumer attitudes toward these types of wines contradict one another.

Studies in Europe show the existence of consumers who refuse to value "bio" (i.e., organic) credentials. Furthermore, it has been shown that while bio production methods have a positive impact on the price of the bottle (presumably due to higher quality grapes), this effect lasts only as long as the "green" attributes remain undisclosed; the moment the bottle starts to carry a bio label the price is dragged down. If the wine isn't of high quality, consumers have a hard time accepting bio certification as worth the higher price. "Green" labels do little to improve a wine's image if it is not perceived as quality regardless of the environmental certification.[6]

How to Reconcile These Conflicting Views

Between these extremes, we find the average consumer, for whom taste is paramount: "If you're not giving someone a pleasurable experience they won't come back for another bottle," says Tony Norskog, owner of Orleans Hill Winery in Nevada City, California. "It's the repeat sales that I live on. That's where the wine has to be good whether it has sulfites or not."[7]

The same conclusion was reached by Cornell University in 2013: taste alone is a strong predictor of wine preference, across all types of wine. Even if an organic label influences the first purchase of a wine, the overarching implication for wine manufacturers is that they must focus on taste and other intrinsic attributes if they want to stimulate repeat purchases of organic wine.[8] The typical wine consumer also cares about price and value for money.

These conflicting consumer views must be weighed by the winery to decide whether implementation of an environmental management system (EMS) will result in any marketplace benefits. While consumers do indicate a level of concern for the environment, this may not be matched by their actual purchasing behavior.

The research is mixed. Many believe that wineries should regard the implementation of a formal EMS as being an offensive strategy because consumers perceive a positive relationship between product quality and wines that are marketed as being environmentally friendly. Cecil Camilleri, director of sustainability for Australian wine brand Yalumba, considers their environmentally focused activities as an intrinsic aspect of wine quality. Analysis of consumer views regarding sustainable wines in the New Zealand market indicates that just over half of respondents thought the use of environmentally sustainable wine production practices would result in no change in product quality, while almost 40 percent believed that quality would actually increase.[9]

Trust in a winery and its brand equity significantly increases when a winery implements a pro-environmental business strategy. Furthermore, there is some evidence that implementation of environmentally friendly practices by a winery may lead to product differentiation, competitive advantage, and increased sales.[10] Similarly, a 2002 case study conducted by Mary Pugh and Richard Fletcher of the Australian wine brand Banrock Station noted that its support of environmental conservation projects was a unique positioning strategy, which differentiated its products, created a competitive advantage, and increased its market share.

Although price and taste are still perhaps the most important factors in purchase decisions, wineries have unique opportunities to promote sustainability as a key marketing message. Sustainability could become the "icing on the cake" or perhaps the deciding factor between two wines, one sustainably produced, one not—all else being equal. Producers should focus on well-branded, quality wines, with sustainability as simply part of their story.

THE WINE INDUSTRY MUST TAKE THE LEAD: FROM VINEYARDS TO RETAILERS

The greater wine industry should take the initiative to shape consumer demand: providing better information and labeling; promoting incentives to change consumer behavior; and ensuring that sustainability takes center stage when it comes to product innovation. Much of the work to educate professionals and consumers is being undertaken by the trade associations and research organizations that support the industry.

The California Sustainable Winegrowing Alliance (CSWA) has an online course for sommeliers and others in the wine trade to help them understand sustainability and learn the vocabulary to talk about sustainably certified wines. The Wine Institute has material on their website designed to educate the consumer, "Discover California Wines" being just one. There is also a training course and online exam for Sustainable Winegrowing Ambassadors. The Institute published a beautiful coffee table book in 2014, *Down to Earth*, which is a compilation of winery profiles and personal stories about winemakers throughout California to introduce consumers to the world of sustainable wines and bring to life the connection between sustainability and high-quality wines.

Even though California does not have a bottle seal attesting to certification under the Certified California Sustainable Wine (CCSW) certification system, there are over 5,000 wines in the state that use the term "sustainable" on the bottle label. The Wine Institute also now gives an annual award for Leadership and another award for Community Engagement—putting a spotlight on wineries that exemplify the best sustainable practices.

Marketing to and Educating Consumers

Consumers want to feel they can make a difference in addressing the world's social and environmental challenges through the products they buy. Organizations that want to thrive in the future must find a way to communicate their values to engage and inspire these savvy consumers.

Yet many U.S. companies hesitate to promote sustainability as part of their marketing and advertising strategies. Marketers cite lack of consumer interest, presumed high risk factor, and perception that sustainability is boring, expensive, or too complicated[12] as reasons for not promoting a green business model or featuring sustainability in their marketing.

Marketers seek to understand the needs of the audience they want to reach and respond to those needs in ways that drive demand for their product or service. Consumers' needs for environmental sustainability and social responsibility should be no exception and should be promoted along with other important attributes of the wines they seek.

Is marketing sustainability good for business? A study published in June 2013 found that so-called meaningful brands outperformed the stock market by 120 percent. The study's researchers defined the most meaningful brands as those that systematically improve personal and collective well-being of consumers, including environmental performance and community giving, and are rewarded by stronger brand equity and attachment.[13] These findings resonate with the wine industry, where the product's essential role is to contribute to the quality of leisure time and social interactions.

For example, some consumers prefer organic over nonorganic wines and are willing to pay a premium price for such products. Consumers who exhibit high environmental attitudes strongly prefer organic wines and are willing to pay more to purchase them than consumers with low environmental attitudes are willing to pay. Consumers who value a healthy lifestyle express a significantly stronger preference for organic wines and are also willing to pay a premium.[14] The industry must respond to those preferences with adequate marketing and communication.

The wine industry in the United States has become much more sophisticated. How did that happen? Brand managers understood the customer's need for a simpler approach to wine culture. It is possible for marketers to also make the sustainable message clear and simple and in a way that enhances the consumer's enjoyment of what is in their glass. Just as Starbucks made its socially responsible and ethical messages part of a new coffee culture and lifestyle, so too can wine marketers include a sustainable aspect as part of the behavior and sociology of wine drinking. Marketers have the tools to make the environmental message simple and integral to their brand strategies.

A word of caution: Key to this strategy of effective marketing and communications is actually adopting sustainability before attempting to communicate a green message. You have to do the work first and not engage in premature communication or over-claim. Otherwise you'll be accused of "green washing" and never regain the consumer's trust.

BUILDING BRAND EQUITY THROUGH SUSTAINABILITY AND SOCIAL RESPONSIBILITY

In today's world, brands are an increasingly powerful component of a company's value, and developing a relationship with consumers grounded in values and purpose is essential. Although there are many topics that can and should be addressed to make a brand stand out, authentic sustainable practice is an increasingly important one to consumers. So it is not so much about what is produced as it is about the perceived wants and needs of the target audience.

Sustainability branding is the process of creating and maintaining an identity of a specific product, service, or business that reflects special added value in terms of environmental and social benefits. Sustainability helps maximize that value. And while these branding efforts are primarily directed to consumers, stakeholders within the company must be given a solid concept of what the brand stands for through internal branding campaigns.

The automotive sector is one for which sustainability is a big issue, and Honda has been a leader in incorporating sustainability into its brand equity.

CASE IN POINT

Honda recognized early on that mineral fuels are limited and prices of petroleum would continue to rise. This motivated it to adapt its product range to fuel-efficient cars. Honda was one of the first movers in this direction, and this is paying dividends today. More than 40 years ago, the Honda engineers who embraced the challenge of developing the revolutionary CVCC engine had a simple vision—they wanted to ensure blue skies for our children. That is their brand positioning—Blue Skies for Our Children—and its work in making sure its plants are reducing emissions is captured under the brand positioning—Keeping Blue Skies Blue. Today that vision continues to inspire the advancement of sustainability and reduction of CO_2 emissions in Honda products and manufacturing plants. It was the first mass-market automaker to offer an entire lineup of cars and light trucks that meet or exceed low-emissions vehicle standards and the world's first commercial application of a fuel cell electric vehicle. Its Accord becomes the world's first V-6 hybrid vehicle. And in 2014, Honda America installed two power-producing wind turbines at its Ohio Transmission Manufacturing plant, becoming the first automaker in the United States to derive a substantial amount of its power from turbines located on its own property.

While reducing dependence of gas-guzzling cars and increasing the number of fuel-efficient models became a "must do" in the automotive sector, Honda was first to differentiate its offerings and its brand. Its record U.S. sales have been attributed to fuel-efficient Civics, electric and hybrid vehicles. This leading behavior has contributed to annual increases in Honda's brand value since 2004. International consultancy Interbrand has recently published the 2015 edition of its Best Global Brands ranking, placing Honda as the nineteenth most valuable global brand. Honda's brand was valued in excess of $22 billion, an increase of 6 percent compared with 2014.

Building brand equity is not strictly an external marketing effort. Branding strategies have to be embraced by the entire organization, from the salespeople, to the winemakers, to the person employed to pour wine in the tasting room—every person in every functional department needs to understand and believe in the brand in order for it to be successful. In many ways, the culture of the organization is closely aligned with the firm's brand. (And be clear about the differences between a company's brand—its externally perceived mission, values, and reason for being—as distinct from specific product brands and labels or logo.) Also, marketing is not branding, though marketing is an essential part of brand building.

The modern wine industry is extremely competitive and fragmented, thus building brand equity, while necessary, is particularly difficult. According to the Wine Institute, there are over 4,285 bonded wineries in California alone, and 10,417 in the United States. It has been said there are over 50,000 registered wine brands produced in the United States, the vast majority in California. Although many of these brands are dormant, probably about 10,000 wine brands are being produced at any one time in the United States (again, the vast majority, about 80 percent, are from California). Consider also the vast number of imported brands.

Furthermore, except for regional origin or grape variety, most products are similar from a consumer point of view and lack a main differentiating point. Authentic sustainability marketing and social advertising connected with the CSR strategy are important ways to differentiate brands.

Avoid Greenwashing

Show, don't tell. Actions speak louder than words, so demonstrate solid sustainability practices. A well-designed, credible sustainability program supports a positive reputation. Focus on how the winery's sustainability efforts align with the values of consumers, such as ethics, environmental performance, and commitment to communities. A sustainability program that is consistent with a brand's positioning will create value for the business.

Keep messages simple and relevant. Avoid vague, unsubstantiated messaging such as "all-natural," "made using organic methods," or "sustainable." Third-party verification and certification are key to consumer trust. Look for synergies between the company's brand and associated social causes—not just charitable donations—and also ethical products and services that will change consumers' behavior and help them live a more "sustainable" life.

A leading brand translates to customers what is relevant in today's world, influencing buying behavior. It also develops a strong relationship with customers because of its distinct offerings, leading to repeated purchasing. In other words, a brand creates value in two ways: 1) generating demand, and 2) securing future earnings for the business.

Sustainability is not a fad. It's a new way of doing business. Companies need to assess the relevance of sustainable issues to their business, current perceptions about their brands on this matter, the potential upsides of investing in sustainability projects, and the reputation risk of not doing so. Brand value is a way to summarize all of this.

The challenge is to embed true sustainable behavior in everything a company does, not only to attract new customers but also to help define future behavior and shape the market. The transformational challenge is to make "green" a part of the DNA of the enterprise, just the way businesses had to make globalization and digital technology a part of nearly every business consideration.

The relationship between brands and people is a connection that takes place on an emotional level. That deep emotional connection with customers translates into unwavering consumer loyalty. This goes above and beyond the quality of the product or taste of the wine. Customers define themselves through brands they use—the clothes they wear, the cars they drive, the drinks they consume, the university they attended, their favorite restaurants. Creating an emotional bond with customers requires more than good marketing—a company engaged in emotional branding puts the needs of its consumers ahead of the product it's selling. Consumers want to feel they are reducing their personal impact on the environment. They have a desire to be more aware, more ethical, and to live a sustainable life. Sustainable branding can help fulfill those needs.

SUSTAINABILITY CHAMPIONS: FOUR MARKETING CASE STUDIES

Kunde Family Winery

The first grape vines on what is now Kunde Estate in Sonoma County, California, were planted in 1879. The property, then known as Wildwood Ranch, comprised 640 acres and was purchased by Louis Kunde in 1904. During Prohibition, they were one of the few wineries to obtain a license to sell sacramental wine and non-fermented grape juice, both allowed by law. Several generations have managed the Kunde property, which over the years has gone from producing wine to only growing grapes to sell to other wineries.

In the late 1980s, they built a new winery and aging caves, and in 1990 they had their first crush at the Kunde Family Estate Winery. In the early 2000s, Jeff Kunde, the current head of the company, took over Kunde Family Estate with his sister Marcia as VP of marketing.

Today, they have 750 acres planted to grapes that produce about 1,600 tons per harvest. The ranch's 1,850 acres constitute the largest contiguous vineyard estate in Sonoma County. With less than 40 percent of the estate planted to vineyards, the remaining native habitat is integral to the health and vitality of the entire property. They produce approximately 100,000 cases of estate-made wines each year. After several years of supplying almost its entire grape output to the winery, the vineyard operations are again supplying other wineries.

In 2001, Jeff conducted a sustainability self-assessment of the estate and decided there was much that could be done to connect positively with the community and with employees by communicating these commitments internally and to customers. From a marketing perspective, Kunde promotes three company attributes to its customers: 1) It is family owned, 2) the wines are estate grown, and 3) the land is sustainably farmed.

Family owned: Kunde focuses heavily on the concept of "family owned" and seeks to leverage the history of the long family ownership of the company to encourage support of a small family company in an era of large and multinational corporations, and to engage the consumer, especially those visiting the tasting room, in the romanticized concept of old-fashioned, family-run winemaking. Having their fourth generation running the business with the fifth following in their footsteps certainly validates this claim.

Sustainably farmed: Kunde initiated a tradition of guided eco-hikes for the community and visiting consumers, where they learn about many of the sustainable practices on the estate. These eco-hikes can be as long as four hours and cover four miles—several straight uphill—for adventurous and fit consumers! Eco-hikes and mountaintop tastings get both consumers and community members beyond the tasting room and into the real workings of the vineyards and winery. They see sustainability practices at work first-hand, including cover crops; erosion prevention; the large areas of undeveloped land; wildlife; owl boxes for vertebrate control; use of grape waste in composting; cattle to graze land prior to planting (instead of fuel-powered mowers); use of weather stations to indicate when disease and pest pressure is high and avoid unnecessary pesticide spraying; creek bed restoration with native flowers; solar thermal panels (which have a lower carbon footprint than pure solar panels) for the hot water system for the offices and tasting rooms; and insulated and energy efficient wine tanks.

Consumers sense that these practices show a genuine commitment to responsible stewardship of the land, rather than purely a marketing technique to increase sales.

Jeff Kunde argues with some justification that the long-term benefits of an environmentally sustainable enterprise reap its benefits not in annual financial performance but in the long-term success and very survival of the company by ensuring the land and environment on which the company depends remain viable and productive into the future and for successive generations.

Yalumba Family Vignerons

Yalumba is Australia's oldest family-owned winery. It was founded in 1849 by Samuel Smith, a British migrant and English brewer. After purchasing a 30-acre parcel of land, Smith and his son began planting the first vines by moonlight. Samuel named his patch "Yalumba"—aboriginal for "all the land around." Today its wines span the gamut from shiraz to cabernet sauvignon to Rhone styles to Mediterranean whites and many blends in between. Yalumba leads the industry in environmental performance, reducing carbon emissions, increasing biodiversity, exploring organic viticulture, and operating its vineyards as ecosystems where everything is connected to everything else.

Its sustainability program has developed over 30 years into a Life Cycle Analysis program and runs through the entire business from soil to grapes, winery to production, corporate citizen to the consumer.

Yalumba's commitment to sustainable business practices is comprehensive and a life cycle approach model for the wine industry. At Yalumba, environmentally friendly practices are considered integral, an intrinsic aspect of wine quality.

In order to substantiate this aspect of quality, Yalumba is implementing a brand stewardship program that reflects authenticity, due diligence, product safety, and credible environmental management.

Dr. Cecil Camilleri, senior environmental manager, has been the main architect of Yalumba's environment programs, promoting a comprehensive approach that fully covers all aspects of sustainability and life cycle of the product.

Through its product stewardship program, where over 98 percent of its packaging materials are recyclable, Yalumba seeks to encourage its customers and consumers to dispose of product packaging in an environmentally and socially responsible manner. In 2011, it developed a five-year plan to fulfill its product stewardship goals, including the requirements of the Australian Packaging Covenant—an agreement between government, industry, and community groups to find and fund solutions to address packaging sustainability issues—fully accepting the challenge of including significant stakeholder involvement, specifically suppliers and consumers.

Yalumba believes that external communication is as important as accomplishing its environmental goals. Consumers must be made aware of the commitment, the progress, and the challenges. The winery's communication program includes strategic tracking of stakeholder awareness, attitudes, and behavior. It assists with consumer environmental education through such avenues as point of sale materials, in-store signage and labeling, and the development of appropriate consumer information, made available through Yalumba's website and product label.

Yalumba's criteria[15] for assessing its eco-friendly packaging includes asking a number of questions directly related to consumer needs for information:

- Will the package carry an environmental claim about its components?
- Does the marketing strategy for the product include environmental claims, logos, and consumer education?
- If recycling logos or information is provided on the packaging, has the company verified that appropriate recycling systems are in place to enable the recycling of the packaging components?
- If recycling logos or information are provided on the packaging, are they clearly visible?
- Is anti-litter information included on the packaging, particularly if the packaging is likely to occur in the public litter stream and/or if a component of the packaging is problematic for the litter stream?

Villa Maria Estate

Villa Maria, located in Auckland, New Zealand, was founded by George Fistonich in 1961. During Villa Maria's early years, George and his wife Gail did everything themselves, without staff, and bought grapes from farmers in the region. In the 1970s, sales increased, employees were hired, and grape growers were rewarded for growing better quality grapes. These efforts resulted in an impressive number of medals and wine competition awards.

In 1988, the winery started to sell to overseas markets, especially the UK. Seven years later, Villa Maria became an early pioneer of the sustainable wine movement. Significantly, in 2001, still in the early days of awareness regarding the quality advantages of screw-cap closures, Villa Maria became the first major winery in the world to switch totally to screw caps. Unlike its competitors, the winery took the trouble to explain this decision on the capsules of its bottles so that consumers would understand and support the environmental aspects and importance of making this move.

What sustainability means to Villa Maria is finding ways to minimize the impact of their business on the environment and communicating that externally. There is no endpoint: it's a continuous journey of improvement and they're committed to trying harder. Villa Maria produces wine that is Certified Sustainable New Zealand, but they also produce certified organic wine. They believe that great wine starts from an intimate relationship with the land. In fact, Villa Maria was the first major New Zealand winery to achieve Bio-Gro organic certification from the vineyard to the

Villa Maria Estate, Hawkes Bay, Twyford Gravels Vineyard

winery, to the bottling facility and warehouse. Bio-Gro is a not-for-profit organic producer and consumer society actively working to grow increased demand for organic products in New Zealand.

It's important for consumers to understand Villa Maria's commitment to both sustainability and organic grape growing and winemaking. The wine company currently has four vineyards under organic management and plans to progressively implement organic practices throughout all of its vineyards. It is New Zealand's most awarded winery, and they recognize that the awards provide excellent assurance to consumers that what they're delivering also meets the highest standards of quality and sustainability.

Sustainability plays a huge part in the ethos of Villa Maria Estate and the design of both the Auckland and Marlborough wineries, encompassing the drive toward reducing carbon emissions. Their wineries are open to the public and include on-site cafes or restaurants. Customers who visit immediately understand the winery's commitment to sustainability.

HEAT RECOVERY

Both Villa Maria wineries have installed heat recovery systems, which take waste heat from the refrigeration plant and store it for use in the winemaking process. The recovered heat is used to warm grape juice prior to and during fermentation, and to warm the wine before it is bottled. The heat recovery plant complements gas and electric energy and enables the winery to significantly reduce its total energy consumption.

NATURAL LIGHTING

Villa Maria's wineries are designed to use natural light as a source of daytime illumination. This provides a healthier environment for staff and significant energy savings.

RECYCLING

Villa Maria encourages recycling in its wineries. Grape pressings are either recycled as cattle feed or composted as nutrient for the vineyards. The company has an ongoing commitment to separating all plastic, glass, and metal waste, and approximately 70 percent of the packaging used for a bottle of Villa Maria Private Bin wine is made from recycled material.

HYBRID VEHICLES

Since 2007 Villa Maria has been progressively changing its sales team fleet to low-emission hybrid vehicles.

These sustainable practices and accomplishments may not be well known to the many American consumers of Villa Maria wines, but they are part of the winery's communications strategies at New Zealand wine fairs and for visitors to their tasting rooms, cafes, and restaurants.

Sonoma County Grapegrowers

Sonoma County Winegrowers

In January 2014, the predominantly family-owned wine grape farms of Sonoma County announced their commitment to be a 100 percent sustainable wine region within five years. The group, known formally as the Sonoma County Winegrape Commission (also known as Sonoma County Winegrowers), is actively promoting this commitment and their progress through articles in *Wine Spectator*, *Wine Enthusiast*, and *Food and Wine* magazines and the *San Francisco Chronicle*, as well as through a "Sonoma County Certified" public awareness campaign. The grape growers issued their first CSR report in 2015, discussing their progress toward the 100 percent goal in year one.

They decided to go even further and launch an ad campaign to inform and educate wine consumers on the eco-friendly benefits of buying a Sonoma County wine. This is the first national advertising campaign specifically focused on sustainable winegrowing practices. Rather than take a typical wine ad profiling local farmers and their families or picturesque vineyards, Sonoma County's wine industry, including grape growers, vintners, master sommeliers, and others came together to develop an advertising campaign that would communicate directly to wine consumers with a tutorial on sustainability.

"Research continues to show that sustainability and eco-consciousness matters to consumers when choosing a bottle of wine, but they can't always define what sustainability is," said Karissa Kruse, president of the Sonoma County Winegrowers. She added, "We want consumers to be knowledgeable about the 138 vineyard practices that wine grape growers in Sonoma County are utilizing so that they can buy any bottle of wine from Sonoma County with confidence knowing that it has been produced in a manner that protects the land, improves the quality of life for those working in the industry and enhances the community where we live and work."

The first ad in the campaign series, called 138, appeared in the November 2014 issues of *Food & Wine*, *Wine Spectator*, and *Wine Enthusiast* and focused on vine balance using content taken directly from the California Code of Sustainable Winegrowing.

The next ad in this campaign, *Sonoma Wine: "Sustainable Agriculture in a Glass,"* was launched in Chicago, March 2015. Sonoma County Winegrowers, in conjunction with Sonoma County Vintners, partnered with Binny's Beverage Depot for a month-long promotion in March 2015 throughout their 30 stores across the Chicago metro area. This partnership included staff training on Sonoma County as a wine region, in-store tastings for consumers, and lots of branding and promotional material showcasing Sonoma County's commitment to sustainable agriculture. The

theme "Sustainable Agriculture in a Glass" was shown on posters, case cards, end cap displays, fact cards, and more. At the beginning of the promotion, 16 winemakers and winegrowers from Sonoma County poured their wines at four Binny's locations in Chicago during the Sonoma in the City trade, media, and consumer program. Toward the end of these activities, Binny's hosted another in-store tasting for consumers to showcase Sonoma wines.

MARKETING ORGANIC WINE

Long before California, South Africa, and New Zealand developed wine sustainability certifications, organic wine was introduced to the marketplace and remains the most widely recognized environmental certification for wine and the most clearly understood by the consumer as a result of their experience with organic foods.

Many consumers presume that organic foods provide greater health benefits and generally taste better than their conventionally grown counterparts. But do organically minded consumers also opt for natural or organic wines? It seems likely that choosing organic or biodynamic wines should be a natural extension of their food preferences—to avoid wines made with chemicals and pesticide sprays.

As with organic food, consumers want to believe that sustainable wine is the healthy choice. Many champions of natural wine like authors Alice Feiring and Jamie Goode, founder of RAW Wine fair Isabelle Legeron, natural wine importer Jenny Lefcourt, and organic wine marketer Annie Arnold all agree that wine made with minimal intervention tastes better and is better for you.[16]

In fact, it has been proven that wine itself has many health benefits:

- Consumed in moderation, white wine can improve lung function.
- Drinking a modest amount of red wine increases cardiac output and arterial elasticity.
- Drinking even one glass of red wine a week may reduce the risk of senility or Alzheimer's disease.
- Some studies show wine helps eradicate the bacteria that cause peptic ulcers.

The obvious conclusion is that wines produced with fewer chemicals are even healthier for consumers.[17]

Despite these findings, however, some consumers tend to view wines with organic labels on the bottles in a negative light. This can be attributed to the early days when organic wines entered the marketplace and consumers were disappointed in the taste. Indeed, many consumers will remember organic wines of the late 1980s and early 1990s as almost undrinkable. However, advances in winemaking technology and natural viticulture have allowed the quality of organic wine to increase dramatically.

Alas, while the quality has improved, the stigma associated with the early poor-tasting organic wines has run deep, and marketers are afraid people will prejudge the wines against that older standard.[18] Wine is a short-term luxury, and customers don't want to gamble on a wine that might not meet their pleasure expectations, especially if the wine costs $15 or more. Some vineyards and wineries don't want to label their wines as organic or sustainable, as they are worried such labeling will adversely affect sales.

Organic foods are readily available and have a reputation for quality and health despite the higher price. This could happen with organic wine. Continued exposure and increased education on the benefits of organic and biodynamic wines could improve these consumers' perceptions.[19]

In my interviews with a number of importers, brand representatives, and marketers of organic wine, I discovered unique approaches to marketing these wines in the distribution chain to retailers and ultimately to consumers.

All agreed that there is a new generation of young people who expect their wine choices to include organic or sustainable offerings. These young consumers don't have the experience with the way organic wine tasted years ago, when it really wasn't very good. They have a lot more experience with buying organic meats, vegetables, fruits, and home care products. They will carry organics up a notch and are buying $10 to $15 bottles of organic wine. Yet the wine doesn't have to be an expensive organic wine in order to be high quality and good tasting.

An outspoken advocate for the organic wine industry is Annie Rabin Arnold, founder of the Organic Wine Exchange, an online retail wine sales company.

Annie actually grew up in the wine business. Her grandfather started selling wine in 1938. Early on, she decided to pursue another line of work only to come back to learn more about the family business. That's when she noticed a niche that was not clearly defined or well represented—organic—so she decided to go off on her own and fill that niche. Her dream of representing organic wineries from around the world is now a reality.

Annie was motivated to get into the business of promoting organic wines because she felt organic farmers were not being recognized for their efforts in introducing organically certified grapes into our wine supply. She wants to raise consumer awareness that conventional wines include other additives beyond the pesticides and chemical fertilizers that are applied to the vines and soil. "People think that wine is only fermented grapes, and the big wine companies that own the majority of the wine brands like it that way," she says.

When Annie started her business, she relied on an online presence as her primary marketing channel, posting videos, winemaker interviews, and other info. But the business only took off when people could taste the wines. "You can talk all day long about how good the wine is for you, how well made it was in the vineyards, how it has treated the land and how it is preserved for future generations, no chemicals added etc., but the real proof is in the tasting. Consumers have to feel good about their purchase. When they have the opportunity to participate in a tasting, the wines speak for themselves."

In Annie's business model, "Consultants take the wines into people's homes for a wine tasting party. The wine is priced so it is affordable and the consultant is there to help them understand the wine, food pairing, taste preferences," she explained. "This experience helps the customer really understand not only what's behind the organic wine movement, but also what wines best suit their palate."

In addition to in-home tastings, Annie presents many tastings at farmers markets, primarily to educate people. By doing this she has met a lot of chefs who shop at the farmers markets, and as a result she can get the chefs to add her wines to their wine lists. "Most consumers buy wines on what's familiar to them or what the label looks like. They need to see brands multiple times in order to recognize and feel comfortable with purchasing them again. By getting these wines into restaurants we are familiarizing, educating and marketing organic wines at the same time."

Like many who produce and promote organic and biodynamic wines, Annie believes that sustainable is a bit of greenwashing. "Being certified sustainable has many great attributes, like using solar energy, recycling, reclaiming water, and being overall environmentally conscious. However, it doesn't mean you are not adding pesticides and chemicals to the vines or additives to the wine. Eliminating chemicals in the vineyard is easy for consumers to understand. If the consumer understands the impact of an organic carrot, then they will appreciate the organic grape. Due to insufficient information required on the labels, consumers are kept in the dark about all the legal additives many wineries are using in their final product. It is common practice for some producers to try to expand or extend their vintage by using additives or buying cheaper grapes and enhancing it."

Edward Field is a co-owner and founder of Natural Merchants, Inc., one of North America's leading importers and distributors of the finest organic wines direct from the European and Mediterranean regions. Natural Merchants Selections includes more than 150 carefully selected natural, organic, and biodynamic wines from France, Italy, Greece, Austria, and Spain, all family owned and, according to their marketing materials, "grown in unique organic terroir, each vineyard producing clean, fresh superior wines that are both good for the earth and tantalizing for the palate."

These wineries are top organic producers in each country. Natural Merchants does not work with *négociants*,* traders, or cooperatives. They work directly with the family, and these are producers who have enough hectares and have been doing it for long enough to supply to a market with the size and diversity of the United States. Organic wines from their portfolio can be found in conventional and natural retail stores including Whole Foods nationally, accessed through traditional U.S. wine distributors across the country.

Field finds it is more difficult educating U.S. consumers and retailers compared to Europeans, because of the way USDA has developed their organic standards.

"The USDA, by creating two different labeling standards—'organic' (organically grown grapes without any added sulfites) and 'made with organically grown grapes' (with small amounts of added sulfites)—is just a little bit too much for people to understand. In Europe, all wines made with organic grapes are simply labeled as 'organic wine.' It's an uphill battle to convey the differences to all of our partners in the U.S.," Field said.

---

* Négociant is the French term for a wine merchant who assembles the produce of smaller growers and winemakers and sells the resulting wine under its own name.

Field says another challenge for organic wine is placement in retail stores. "If you look at a typical grocery store—even a Whole Foods—you will see organic products right next to the same conventional product. But most of the times, if a retailer sells organic wine, they'll designate a rack or a certain wine section. In Whole Foods, for example, they will have a rack labeled "Eco-wines" almost to show that they have it and are environmentally responsible.

"My preference is for a retailer to 'cut that wine in,'—to place organic Pinot Grigio for example right in the middle of all the rest of the Pinot Grigio bottles, because you will sell 10 times more of the organic wine if somebody's looking for Pinot Grigio then see the organic label. The customer may decide to treat themselves just like they are treating themselves in any other aisle and feel good about making that organic choice."

When asked about advertising, most of the organic marketers or representatives pointed out the huge cost implications. "Wine Spectator charges a healthy, healthy amount [for advertising]. There are European subsidies for advertising that will help with promoting organic wines there. But in the U.S., size matters. Large wineries and big wine corporations have the ability to do major advertising." "Our answer," says Ed Field, "has been to focus on our social media efforts. We're a small company, so we have to make it fun and allow the public to get to know our wineries.

"We participate in industry-specific events, like Expo-West—the largest organic show in the nation. We'll sometimes participate in their advertising vehicles because we know they have a certain type of retailers that are going to attend. Or, we'll spend our marketing budget on attending wine trade shows where organics are the focus and where we can be hands-on with our distribution partners."

Natural Merchants also values wines that contain no genetically modified organisms (i.e., non-GMO), and the bottles they import carry a hang-tag attesting to their status as non-GMO verified. According to the LOHAS survey, 2014 is the first year that non-GMO overtook organic as a deciding factor on brand selection. The United States is the only major country that does not require labeling products as containing GMOs.

Lisa Bell is the owner of Crescendo Communications in Boulder, Colorado, and handles marketing for Natural Merchants. She says a primary challenge is that organic wines still have a bad reputation with a lot of wine critics. Lisa's primary goal for a number of years has been to get samples of their best offerings to as many wine reviewers and reputable rating organizations as possible. "We've been pretty successful at that—have gotten some highly rated wines, and many of the major wine critics are starting to take notice. But it's a long, long process. The wine reviewers have a hard time getting 'organic wine is bad' out of their heads."

For example, Lettie Teague, who writes the *Wall Street Journal*'s "On Wine" column, said on March 13, 2015, that she couldn't find a single NSA (no sulfite added) wine she liked in her local grocery wine section. The salesman at her ShopRite store in Little Falls, New Jersey, indicated he wasn't very impressed by NSA wines, although he did point out a couple he liked. Teague summarized her tasting experience as, "They were among the worst wines I've ever had. All three looked and tasted like old apple cider and smelled oxidized. Upon tasting the wines, a friend of mine said, 'Bring on the sulfites!' There wasn't a single NSA wine from my selection that I could recommend."[20]

Bell indicated that "some retailers say they have a 'sustainable wine' section, and there are mainstream wines in there that have nothing to do with sustainability. And yet, some distributors and winery reps have gone in and sold them a sustainable story that just isn't accurate. The retailer is misinformed and that adds to the confusion for the consumer.

"Certification means too many different things to too many people. It's the same thing when you go to the grocery store and you buy 'natural' chicken. What does that mean? If it says on the package 'grown without growth hormones or antibiotics,' that may be as far as it goes. They might not be getting fed organic grains, or they might not be raised humanely. Yet the 'natural chicken' commands a price premium that people will pay because they think they're getting a healthier meal from it. And the same thing applies to wine—if you see a sustainable wine in the grocery store you naturally assume that it's made in a healthier fashion."

How to educate the trade? Lisa sees two challenges: One is for people to get over the past bad image of organic wines, but then also it's to get people to understand all these various certifications and to distinguish them and understand that organic certification is rigorous.

"With the trade, especially the wine reviewers, it's critical to keep submitting wine samples and information about the wine, to enter valid competitions and to keep spending the money to do it. When an organic wine gets a 90+ rating from Wine Enthusiast or some other recognized wine rating system, everyone starts paying attention.

"Unfortunately with a large distributor a wine from a smaller organic wine producer can get lost. It's very difficult when they have a portfolio of 500+ wines. So it's completely understandable that the bigger wineries are the ones that come to the top." The marketer of organic wines also spends a lot of effort in the restaurant industry. "It's kind of up to the distributor. If they have a strong on-premise program it works great. Wines from Natural Merchants do extremely well by the glass, especially in restaurants that are a 'farm-to-table' format. These are becoming prevalent in major markets across the country. And now there are a few chain restaurants that are starting to serve organic wines such as LYFE Kitchen and True Food Kitchen— which can be a great boost to sales of organic wines."

MARKET SEGMENTATION AND OPPORTUNITIES

Women and young people are the new targets of the wine industry. These segments present unique opportunities for appropriately marketing sustainability in wine.

Millennials and GenXers are the particular favorite of marketers and the wine industry. Millennials are inclined to drink wine more than beer (though artisanal and craft beers run a very close second).

Millennials (those born between 1980 and 2000) have come of age, and they do drink wine. For millennials, wine is "in"—in movies, on TV, in every bar, restaurant, grocery store, specialty store, at every party, in every convenience store, at family gatherings.

Recently the number of young wine drinkers has been increasing. According to the Wine Market Council (WMC), 70 million people aged between 17 and 34 are growing fonder of wine.[21] Six percent of millennials are drinking wine daily, 26 percent are drinking wine several times a week, and 19 percent drink wine once a week on average. (The Wine Market Council is a nonprofit association of grape growers, wine producers, importers, wholesalers, and retailers with the aim of providing consumer research to help support and strengthen the industry.)

This comprises the core wine-drinking segment of millennials, accounting for 51 percent of them, compared to only 37 percent five years ago. The Council's research shows that Generation X (ages 35 to 46) was late in coming to the table for wine but is making up ground. Now 62 percent are core wine drinkers compared to only 41 percent five years ago.

Millennials are especially attracted to imports from New Zealand, Chile, South Africa, and Argentina. There are 76 million millennials in the United States, compared to 44 million GenXers (born between early 1960s and 1980) and 77 million baby boomers (those born in the years following World War II). So the millennials are the next "boom" generation, judging by their size and birthrate.

According to the Wine Market Council's research, millennials also rely on wine reviews for information and ratings about wine, and more often the opinions of their friends rather than wine critics. So expert reviewers and wine journalists have an opportunity to present information to this segment that fulfills their information needs, including the sustainability credentials of wines reviewed. If magazines like *Wine Spectator, Wine Advocate*, and *Wine Enthusiast*—which seem to be more focused on the older, more established, male wine collector—don't attempt to reach this demographic, we'll likely see new "experts" emerge in publications that millennials consider more "relevant" to their lives.

Already, we see social media as influencing their wine purchases. Almost every day a new site is launched and a new smartphone app is developed and released to serve the international wine consumer online.

SOCIAL MEDIA AND WINE

Thanks to the Internet, wine lovers can experience how wine is made. They can buy wines from online shops such as The Wine Atelier, Club W, and Naked Wines. Millennials use social media to learn—the grape variety, the history of the region, and the fascinating story of the winemaker or the family that owns the winery. They also share this information with their friends and their network, which makes them very attractive to marketers and provides a great opportunity to share the sustainability credentials of a winery.

The Top Six Wine Apps Millennials Love

Vivino

This app enables users to snap a photo of a wine label and instantly get information about the wine—including community ratings, average pricing, and descriptions. Users can store certain wines to their library to help them remember what they've tasted. Users can add their own reviews and tastings notes to the wine. Similar to Trip Advisor, reviews are from a user database, not wine professionals.

http://www.vivino.com/

Delectable

Similar to Vivino in that users can snap a photo of a wine label and instantly get information about the wine—including community ratings, average pricing, and descriptions. In addition to storing wines to their library to help them remember what they've tasted and adding reviews and tasting notes, Delectable also offers the option for users to order a certain wine directly through the app.

https://delectable.com/

Cor.kz

Cor.kz is an app designed to help users choose bottles of wine that they'll like. By typing in the name of the wine (or scanning the barcode), users gain access to reviews and tasting notes on CellarTracker.com. Users can keep track of wines they've purchased in the app as well.

http://cor.kz/

Wine-Searcher

The app for the popular wine search engine, Wine-Searcher, allows users to search for information on over 7 million bottles of wine, beer, and spirits. Additionally, the app will connect users with over 50,000 merchants around the world that carry the wines they want and show who has the best price.

http://www.wine-searcher.com/app.lml

Hello Vino

This user-friendly app acts a personal wine assistant to help users pick out the perfect bottle of wine. Allowing searches by occasion, pairing with a meal, shopping for a gift, or seasonal varietals, the app lets the user guide the selection process. They can store wines they've tried and scan bottles to get more information.

http://www.hellovino.com/

Crushed

Similar to Vivino or Delectable, Crushed is a social wine app that allows users to take photos of wine labels to gain information about the wine, add reviews, and share what they're drinking with their friends via social networks.

http://crushed.com/app/

These more relevant media and apps should be sure to feature information on organic, biodynamic, and sustainably produced wines in their reviews, as those are significant to this demographic.

The importance of this demographic trend was an important feature of Wine Vision 2014 in London, a premier annual event attended by CEOs and senior level decision makers in the wine business from over 20 countries. The 2014 event brought 200 attendees and included a presentation by Tyler Balliet, co-founder and president of Wine Riot, who shared insights into the millennials market and how to educate them about wine.

Wine Riot was started in 2008 by two millennials with a simple concept: create a fun, non-intimidating place where people learn about wine. They wanted to give participants the tools to find cool wine tastings, talk to experts, explore wine regions, and constantly discover new favorites. Wine Riot events are held in cities around the United States for millennials to learn tasting terminology, taste wines at winery booths, attend 20-minute seated crash courses on wine, get tattoos, listen (and dance) to the latest music hits, download a mobile app to navigate the event, rate and remember every wine, and find their favorite wines in stores.

Tyler's advice on how to market to millennials:[22]

- Thirty-eight percent of attendees use the mobile app and 80 percent of attendees return within a month to see what wines they liked at the Wine Riot event.
- Millennials trust friends' opinions of the wine more than any other source. In five years, Wine Riot has collected 266,032 wine reviews from 36,025 people. So expert wine reviews are secondary.
- The average Wine Riot attendee is willing to spend up to two times the price they normally spend if they know they really like the wine.
- When shopping for wine, they are overwhelmed by too many choices on the shelf; when no one is available to help, the information is confusing, so 23 percent say they leave the store without buying at all.
- Do education as marketing.
- Market to women.

Sustainability and the Millennials

The millennials are also a prime target market for sustainably produced wines. They are more focused on the environment than their parents' generation—76 percent to 24 percent, according to a 2014 poll commissioned by the Clinton Global Initiative and Microsoft. The poll found that 66 percent of millennials say there is "solid evidence" the earth is getting warmer, and 75 percent of those respondents say human activity is responsible for it. Also, more than two-thirds of respondents said they are willing to pay more for products from sustainability-focused companies.

The poll found more than half of the respondents optimistic about their chances at improving the state of human rights during their lifetimes. Millennials also appear to be optimistic that they can fix gender income inequality, with 69 percent of respondents saying they think their generation will make progress in closing the pay gap between men and women.[23]

Another survey, conducted by the Pew Research Center, shows that millennials in the United States are most likely to pay a little more for responsibly made products. Additionally, 80 percent want to work for companies that care about the impact they have on the world, and many of them want to ride their bike or a bus to work (instead of driving).[24]

Pew found that millennials have also taken the lead in seizing on the new platforms of the digital era—the Internet, mobile technology, and social media—to construct personalized networks of friends, colleagues, and affinity groups. Eighty-one percent of millennials are on Facebook, where their generation's median friend count is 250, far higher than that of older age groups.[25]

THE IMPORTANCE OF THE FEMALE WINE CONSUMER

Women are another primary new market for wine purchases, and they are also more likely to purchase sustainably produced wines. In fact, women are purchasing wine more than ever before. Research shows that 70 percent of wines sold in the UK are purchased by women in supermarkets as part of their regular grocery shopping routine. In the U.S. market, some have reported that women make over 60 percent of wine purchases. An Australian study reported that females purchase wine more often, spend disproportionately more, and buy more expensive wine than their male counterparts; this helps to illustrate why the female wine purchaser has been of such significant interest to wine producers and marketers in recent years.[26]

The introduction of wine sales through supermarket stores in many nations has been one of the key factors that has dramatically changed wine purchasing gender roles. The observed increase in wine purchasing by females has resulted in wine marketers paying special attention to this consumer segment. According to the Wine Market Council, 53 percent of wine drinkers in the United States are women. In 2009, women matched men as "core drinkers"—those who drink wine at least once a week.

The WMC annual survey of 2015 trends showed that women in particular are driving a surge in U.S. wine consumption, accounting for 57 percent of wine volume in the United States. The survey found that "highly involved" female wine drinkers are mostly older millennials who tend to be "urban educated professionals" and are generally more ethnically diverse than the typical female wine drinker. Looking at women's wine preferences, the survey found that 38 percent of females felt that organic or sustainably certified products were important factors when purchasing wine, compared with 32 percent of males.

But men and women approach wine in very different ways. The collector profile is still predominantly male, while high-end wine buyers—those who regularly spend more than $15 on a bottle of wine—are mostly women. Men tend to focus more on ratings, aging time, type of oak used, and other technical details, often to impress a woman or business colleagues. For women, it's about value, taste, and pairing wines with food. These aspects are intrinsically tied in the world of women and wine.

In the United States, women buy supermarket brands (i.e., private label) but also premium wines. Thus, the wine industry believes that women are the future of wine. American advertisers feature more and more women-only gatherings in their wine ads and websites.

However, these advertisers often treat women as if they are unsophisticated, obsessed with dieting, and attracted by a pair of long legs in high heels on the label. They assume women like "girly" brands and prefer ripe, fruit-forward wines without tannin and oak.

In 2012, I organized a group of women of various ages in Washington, D.C., for a wine club for monthly wine tastings, with in-depth lessons in wine regions, history, wineries, winemaker profiles and food pairing. These were women who enjoy wine, but most were novices and eager to learn about terroir, barrel aging, grape origins, the business of wine, and the winemaking process, including sustainability approaches and organic certification. I learned through them that women are quite serious about wine purchases and not enticed by the so-called girly wines.

Women are more likely than men to support environmental causes through voting, activism, and consumer purchasing choices.[27] According to the World Bank, "Women play an essential role in the management of natural resources, including soil, water, forests and energy, and often have a profound traditional and contemporary knowledge of the natural world around them."[28]

Eco-feminism, a set of movements and philosophies that link feminism with ecology, stresses that women are closer to nature than are men. This closeness, therefore, makes women more nurturing and caring toward their environment. Some indicate the biology of women as the reason behind the closeness, while others credit culture and historical factors.[29]

Eco-feminists believe that these connections are illustrated through traditionally "female" values such as reciprocity, nurturing, and cooperation, which are present both among women and in nature. Women and nature are also united through their shared history of oppression by a patriarchal Western society, eco-feminists believe.[30]

Repeated studies have shown that women have a stake in the environment, and women give greater priority to protecting and improving the capacity of nature, maintaining farming lands, and caring for nature and environment's future.[31]

My favorite example of female prominence in the defense of natural forests dates back to 1906 India. As forest clearing was expanding, conflict between loggers, government, and peasant communities increased. To thwart resistance to the forest clearing, the men were diverted from their villages to a fictional payment compensation site and loggers were sent to the forests. The women, left in the villages, protested by physically hugging themselves to the trees to prevent them being cut down, giving rise to what is now called the Chipko movement, an environmentalist movement initiated by these Indian women (which also is where the term "tree-huggers" originated). This conflict started because men wanted to cut the trees to use them for industrial purposes while women wanted to keep them since it was their food resource, and deforestation was a survival matter for local people.[32]

THE GREEN BELT MOVEMENT IN KENYA

One of the biggest women's environmental movements in recent history is the Green Belt Movement, founded by Nobel Prize winner Wangari Maathai on World Environment Day in 1977. The starting ceremony was very simple: a few women planted seven trees in Maathai's backyard in Kenya. By 2005, 30 million trees had been planted by participants in the Green Belt Movement on public and private lands. The Green Belt Movement aims to bring environmental restoration along with society's economic growth and development. This movement, led by Maathai, focused on restoration of Kenya's rapidly diminishing forests as well as empowering the rural women through environmental preservation, with a special emphasis on planting indigenous trees.

Not to take us too far afield from our topic of opportunities for marketing sustainability in wine, the conclusion here is that, like the millennials, the rising level of female wine consumers in many countries and their keen personal affinity for environmental protection would make them amenable and very receptive to messages regarding sustainability in wine. Women will greatly value the environmental aspect and, if educated in this regard, will seek out sustainably produced wines when they purchase.

KEY TAKEAWAYS

- Among consumers, the market response to organic or natural wines has not been definitively positive. "Green" labels do little to improve a wine's image if the wine isn't of a high enough quality or just doesn't taste as expected, regardless of the environmental certification.

- The values and benefits that come from implementing sustainable practices have been compelling and attractive to growers and winemakers. Making these benefits apparent to consumers will be a crucial activity for sustainable winegrowers.
- To effectively reach consumers and keep a brand and its overall enterprise viable, "green" must become part of the DNA. Doing so will become expected across the board, much like globalization and digital technology.
- Consumers respond to brand equity grounded in values and purpose. It is not so much about what is produced as it is about their wants and needs. But actions speak louder than words, so demonstrate solid sustainability practices.
- Expressing strong brand differentiation can be a powerful element in building brand equity; for the wine industry, authentic sustainability can be that purpose.
- The rising tide of environmental awareness in emerging market segments will help to meet the challenge by educating these consumers about sustainability and its connection to quality wines.
- Building brand equity is not strictly a marketing effort. These strategies must be embraced by all employees throughout the organization, from the vineyard manager and the winemakers, to the salespeople and the person employed to pour wine in the tasting room. Embedding true sustainable behavior in everything you do will not only attract new customers but will help define future behavior and shape the market.
- Marketers need to focus their efforts on women (who buy and consume more wine than men) and millennials, who are more focused on the environment than their parents' generation. These segments present unique opportunities for appropriately marketing sustainability in wine.

CHAPTER 4 REFERENCES

1. Nuebling, M. et al. "Environmental Impacts of Wine Production: A Pilot Study Exploring Consumer Knowledge and Environmental Concern." *Academy of Wine Business Research.* 28 June 2014. Available online: http://academyofwinebusiness.com/wp-content/uploads /2014/07/SUS05_Nuebling_Michaela.pdf (Accessed 24 August 2015.)

2. Sogaria, G. et al. "Sustainable Wine Market and WTP: An Insight of Consumers Attitudes." *American Association of Wine Economists.* 2013. Available online: http://www.wine -economics.org/aawe/wp-content/uploads/2013/07/Sogari_Mora_Menozzi.pdf (Accessed 24 August 2015.)

3. Ibid.

4. Jolly, D., and Norris, K. "Marketing prospects for organic and pesticide-free produce," *American Journal of Alternative Agriculture.* Volume 6. Issue 4 (1991): pages 174–179. Available for purchase online: http://journals.cambridge.org/action/displayAbstract?fromPage =online&aid=6355772&fileId=S0889189300004227 (Accessed 24 August 2015.)

5. Wine Institute. "New Research on Sustainability's Impact on Wine Buying Decisions," 7 May 2013. Available online: http://www.wineinstitute.org/resources/pressroom/05072013 (Accessed 24 August 2015.)

6. Chameeva, T., and Krzywoszynska, A. "Barriers and Driving Forces in Organic Winemaking in Europe: Case Studies in France and Italy." *Academy of Wine Business.* 9 June 2011. Available online: http://academyofwinebusiness.com/wp-content/uploads/2011/09/5 -AWBR2011-Bouzdine-Chameeva-Krzywoszynska.pdf (Accessed 24 August 2015.)

7. May, T. "Adding Organic Wines to the Retail Mix." *Natural Foods Merchandiser.* 24 April 2008. Available online: http://newhope360.com/beverage/adding-organic-wines-retail-mix (Accessed 24 August 2015.)

8. Rahman, I. et al. "A Comparison of the Influence of Purchaser Attitudes and Product Attributes on Organic Wine Preferences." *Cornell Hospitality Quarterly.* 21 August 2013. Available online: http://cqx.sagepub.com/content/early/2013/08/20/1938965513496314?patient inform-links=yes&legid=spcqx;1938965513496314v1 (Accessed on 24 August 2015.)

9. Forbes, S. et al. *Consumer Attitudes Regarding Environmentally Sustainable Wine: An Exploratory Study of the New Zealand Marketplace.* Lincoln University. 2009. Available online: https://researcharchive.lincoln.ac.nz/bitstream/handle/10182/3439/Consumer _attitudes.pdf?sequence=1 (Accessed 24 August 2015.)

10. Nowak, L., and Washburn, J. "Building Brand Equity: Consumer Reactions to Proactive Environmental Policies by the Winery," *International Journal of Wine Marketing.* Volume 14 (2002): pages 5–19. Available online: http://www.emeraldinsight.com/doi/abs/10.1108 /eb008743?mobileUi=0 (Accessed 24 August 2015.)

11. Pugh, M., and Fletcher, R. "Green International Wine Marketing," *Australasian Marketing Journal* Volume 10. Issue 3 (2002): pages 76–85. Available online: http://wwwdocs.fce.unsw .edu.au/marketing/amj_10_03_pugh.pdf (Accessed 24 August 2015.)

12. Walshe, S. Interview with Tensie Whelan: "We Meet Resistance Every Step of the Way." *The Guardian.* 26 October 2011. Available online: http://www.theguardian.com/sustainable-business/behaviour-change-tensie-whelan-rainforest-alliance (Accessed 24 August 2015.)

13. Havas Media Group. Meaningful Brands. 7 November 2011, Havas Media Group. Available online: http://www.havasmedia.com/press/press-releases/2011/meaningful-brands-havas -media-launches-global-results (Accessed 24 August 2015.)

14. Forbes, S. et al. *Consumer Attitudes Regarding Environmentally Sustainable Wine: An Exploratory Study of the New Zealand Marketplace.* Lincoln University. 2009. Available online: https://researcharchive.lincoln.ac.nz/bitstream/handle/10182/3439/Consumer _attitudes.pdf?sequence=1 (Accessed on 24 August 2015.)

15. Camilleri, C. *Yalumba's Sustainable Winemaking Programmes: An Action Plan for the Australian Packaging Covenant 2010–2015.* Sustainable Wine Programmes. 25 January 2011. Available online: http://203.23.76.110/yalumba/library/Yalumba%20Action%20Plan% 2025012011.pdf (Accessed 24 August 2015.)

16. Schneider, L. "Natural Wine Can Learn from Natural Food." *Huffington Post.* 18 January 2013. Available online: http://www.huffingtonpost.com/lee-schneider/organic-wine _b_2498941.html (Accessed 24 August 2015.)

17. Organic Authority. *Organic Vines for Better Wines.* 18 October 2006. Available online: http://www.organicauthority.com/organic-food/organic-food-articles/organic-vines-for -better-wines.html (Accessed 24 August 2015.)

18. Ibid.

19. Delmas, M. *Perception of Eco-Labels: Organic and Biodynamic Wines.* University of California Los Angeles Institute of the Environment, 2010. Available online: http://www.erb.umich

.edu/News-and-Events/news-events-docs/09-10/conferencePapers/4836_Delmas -Wine-04-01-2010.pdf) (Accessed 24 August 2015.)

20. Teague, L. "Wine Headache? Chances Are It's Not the Sulfites." *The Wall Street Journal.* 13 March 2015. Available online: http://www.wsj.com/articles/wine-headache-chances-are-its -not-the-sulfites-1426250886 (Accessed 24 August 2015.)

21. Korman, A. "Wine's 2011 Report Card." *Wine Enthusiast Magazine.* 2012. Available online: http://www.winemag.com/Web-2012/Wines-2011-Report-Card/ (Accessed 24 August 2015.)

22. Sterling CreativeWorks. *3 Things to Know About Millennials and Wine.* Available online: http://www.sterlingcreativeworks.com/3-things-to-know-about-millennials-and-wine / (Accessed 24 August 2015.)

23. Timm, J. *Millennials: We Care More about the Environment.* MSNBC. 22 March 2014. Available online: http://www.msnbc.com/morning-joe/millennials-environment-climate -change (Accessed 24 August 2015.)

24. Pew Research Center. *Millennials in Adulthood: Detached from Institutions, Networked with Friends.* 7 March 2014. Available online: http://www.pewsocialtrends.org/2014/03/07 /millennials-in-adulthood/ (Accessed 24 August 2015.)

25. Pew Research Center. *Millennials in Adulthood: Detached from Institutions, Networked with Friends.* 7 March 2014. Available online: http://www.pewsocialtrends.org/2014/03/07 /millennials-in-adulthood/ (Accessed 24 August 2015.)

26. Forbes, S. et al. *Women and Wine: Analysis of This Important Market Segment.* Academy of Wine Business Research Conference, February 2010. Available online: http://academy ofwinebusiness.com/wp-content/uploads/2010/04/ForbesCohenDean-Women-and-wine. pdf (Accessed 24 August 2015.)

27. Gould, K., and Hosey, L. *Women in Green: Voices of Sustainable Design.* Oregon: Ecotone Publishing, 2007.

28. The Global Development Research Center. *Gender and the Environment.* Available online: http://www.gdrc.org/gender/gender-envi.html (Accessed 24 August 2015.)

29. Agarwal, B. "Conceptualizing Environmental Collective Action: Why Gender Matters." *Cambridge Journal of Economics*, Volume 24. Issue 3 (2000) pages 283–310). Available online: http://www.binaagarwal.com/downloads/apapers/conceptualizing_environmental _collective_action.pdf (Accessed 24 August 2015.)

30. Gard, G., and Gruen, L. "Ecofeminism Revisited: Rejecting Essentialism and Re-Placing Species in a Material Feminist Environmentalism." *Academia.* Available online: http:// www.academia.edu/2606383/Ecofeminism_Revisited (Accessed 24 August 2015.)

31. Jiggins, J. *Changing the Boundaries: Women-Centered Perspectives on population and the Environment.* New York: Island Press, 1994.

32. Breton, M. J. *Women Pioneers for the Environment.* Boston: Northeastern University Press, 1998.

CHAPTER 5

ROLE OF THE TRADE— DISTRIBUTORS, RETAILERS, RESTAURANTS:

Educating the Crowd

SINCE THE EARLY 1980S, the supply chain for wine has experienced the conflu- ence of a changing consumer base and a change in the locus of distribution chan- nels. Previously, the supply chain was characterized by localized trading where wines were sold within 30 miles from where they were made. Wine sales to négociants and merchants were direct from the producer/cooperative, with the négociant or wine broker organizing the on-sale of the wine to the wine merchant.

That has all changed. The transformation of retailing that has happened in the last 30 years has also been felt in the wine industry, as the locus of control has shifted from the vineyard to the supermarket and hypermarket.[1]

CONSOLIDATION IN THE FOOD RETAIL INDUSTRY

Throughout the 1980s, regional and local supermarket chains dominated the food retail landscape. In the 1990s, large grocery store chains merged or bought out other regional retailers, while large warehouse clubs and large discount general merchan- dise stores expanded into grocery products.[2]

Between 1996 and 1999, there were 385 grocery mergers—nearly 100 each year. In the decade that followed, grocery store chains focused on consolidation, mergers, and takeovers in an effort to compete with the giant retail warehouses and nontradi- tional food outlets, such as Walmart and Costco.[3]

Meanwhile, new national supercenters and discounters emerged as grocery pow-erhouses. Walmart, for instance, became the largest food retailer in the United States within a dozen years of opening its first supercenter that sold food products.

The share of groceries sold by the four largest food retailers has more than dou-bled in a decade. By 2009, the top four food retailers—Walmart, Kroger, Costco, and Supervalu—controlled more than half of all grocery sales. Grocery store concentra-tion can be considerably higher on the local level.[4]

These evolving events in the retail sector resulted in concentration that forced a critical mass requirement for a winemaker to be able to effectively access and trade in the retail supply chain. Supermarkets and hypermarkets form the leading distribu-tion channel in the global wine market, accounting for over 40 percent share of the total market's volume.[5]

Likewise, in the United States, consumers are buying more wine at grocery stores. A recent Nielsen's study found that nearly 80,000 grocery stores in the United States sold wine in 2014, a significant increase (9 percent) over the number of grocers who sold wine in 2010. Supermarkets, grocers, and warehouse stores such as Costco and Sam's Club sold $8.6 billion of wine in 2014—42 percent of all off-premise wine sales—this despite the fact that in 15 states, selling wine in grocery stores is still prohibited or restricted.

The top five states for wine sales in grocery stores:

California—$1.5b

Florida—$852m

Texas—$603m

Ohio—$357m

Virginia—$351m

And supermarkets aren't just selling a few scattered varieties of wine. Nielsen research shows that the average grocery store sells about 360 different wines in a week—and that number continues to grow, which is good news for consumer choice. Nielsen's also found that when shoppers buy wine they tend to buy more food, to pair with the wine. And of course, the wine purchase increases their overall sales ticket, all good news for the store manager.[6]

Retailers: Grocery, Wine Shops

The various partners in the greater global wine trade connect wine producers with wine importers and distributors worldwide. They each play important roles in how wine gets to market—to retailers, including wine shops, grocery stores, supermar-kets, restaurants, and wine bars. In turn, all these have the potential to influence consumer adoption and purchase of sustainable wines.

Although the majority of wine shoppers don't take notice of terms such as organic, biodynamic, sustainability, natural, carbon neutral or "wine miles," the businesses that sell to those consumers—retail chains, restaurants, hotels—increasingly demand purpose-made plans that show the wineries' commitments to environmentally friendly approaches. Notable examples are UK retailers Tesco and Marks & Spencer, Whole Foods, Walmart, SAQ of Quebec, LCBO of Ontario, Systembolaget of Sweden, and other Nordic liquor monopolies.

More wine retail shops, grocery chains, hotels, restaurants, and event planners are making sustainable procurement of wine a priority. Some independent wine and spirits shops are focusing the majority of their wine inventory on sustainable, organic, and biodynamic wines.

One very important reason why sustainable wine has become a big focus in major wine regions and is happening so strongly right now is the need to satisfy supermarket buyers, (i.e., procurement managers). According to several wineries, retailers have erected a "sustainability hurdle" that must be traversed, either because of the retailer's overall CSR commitments and corporate brand positioning or because they don't want to have their reputation tarnished or be embarrassed by an unsustainable product that lands on their shelves and becomes the subject of stakeholder concern.

CASE STUDIES

Whole Foods

Importers and distributors of organic wines have high hopes that Whole Foods will become the major outlet for organic wine sales. In all Whole Foods stores, there is an offering of "Eco-Wines." Three stores in northwest Washington, D.C., have shelves designated as Eco-Wines, but in differing amounts. In one store, there are twice as many shelves in this section as the others, and in another store there are also shelves dedicated to box wines—Bota Box, Big House, and Black Box. In the largest of these stores, there are far fewer shelves of Eco-Wines and a much smaller offering. All three stores include a separate display of Our Daily Cab, an organic wine from California also branded "Peace Love & Organic," though in one store the sign above the display described it as biodynamic (it's not; it's organic and vegan), and in the other stores the description was correct. (So even a sophisticated organic retailer like Whole Foods gets confused by all these designations!)

In London, the Whole Foods Market in Kensington has the largest collection of organic wines I have ever seen in any grocery store. Clearly, the Eco-Wine selections vary by region and neighborhood. In the Whole Foods store in Charlottesville, Virginia (just three hours from Washington, D.C., and in Virginia wine country) the organic and sustainable wine selections were far outnumbered by local Virginia wines.

In 2012, Whole Foods Market announced that their shoppers were not only trying new varieties, but they also were turning to organic wines with no sulfites added (NSA). To meet this demand, the company expanded its offerings to become the only national retailer to carry the first USDA Certified Organic NSA wines from Italy and Spain.

"We see more and more interest in these wines from wine enthusiasts who believe NSA wines provide the most pure expression of the grape and from those who have sulfite sensitivities or allergies," said Geof Ryan, national wine buyer for Whole Foods Market, in a press release.

Depending on the store, approximately 10 to 20 of the wines on Whole Foods Market shelves are organic NSA wines, including wines from U.S. producers.

Lettie Teague, acclaimed *Wall Street Journal* wine columnist, wrote about Whole Foods wine departments and her visit to one in particular. The Highland Park Whole Foods in Dallas, Texas, had a small wine selection but very warm reception:

"It was perhaps the friendliest grocery store I've visited—especially in terms of its consumption policy. 'You can open any bottle of wine you want and drink it in the store,' said the store's wine buyer, Holly Vaughan. Did she mean I could drink it at the store's wine bar? Yes, but I could also drink it walking around the store. 'Some carts even have attachments for stemware,' said Ms. Vaughan. I pictured tipsy shoppers toppling artfully piled bunches of produce, open bottle of Kendall-Jackson Chardonnay in hand. She assured me this wasn't the case. 'Thankfully everyone keeps it pretty tame.' There are a few other Whole Foods outlets—in Chicago and Austin, for instance—where drinking and shopping can be done simultaneously."[7]

Walmart and the Sustainability Consortium

Today, Walmart and Sam's Clubs have codified their sustainability expectations. They require all their suppliers to respond to its 15 Sustainability Supplier Assessment Questions as a way to assess suppliers' commitment to sustainability. These questions ask whether the supplier and its supply chain have measured and set publicly available improvement targets in the areas of 1) Energy and Climate: Reduce energy costs and green-house gas emissions; 2) Material Efficiency: Reduce waste and enhance quality; 3) Nature and Resources: High-quality, responsibly sourced raw materials; 4) People and Community: Vibrant, productive workplaces and communities.

Wine distributors and wineries must complete this assessment if they are to sell their products in Walmart stores or Sam's Clubs. I have been told by a couple of wineries, whose price points are above those wines sold by Walmart, that their distributors still ask them to provide this information and complete the assessment, since often Walmart expects the distributor's entire "book" (i.e., list of wines offered) to be compliant.

Lisa Bell, owner of Crescendo Communications, a full-service marketing firm, recalled early commitments by Walmart to stock organic food. "Trends in the organic industry seem to ebb and flow—as far as consumer acceptance, as far as mainstream acceptance. In Chicago in 2006, the Organic Trade Association's trade show called 'All Things Organic' was on fire! The show attracted buyers from Walmart, Target, and the big chain stores that were seriously considering competing with the Whole Foods of the world, and trying their hand at an organic line. Walmart had just made a pledge to convert a significant percentage of their produce to organic—it was a big deal at the time. But within months, they pulled way back, and slowed down their organic product commitment. As quickly as this became a hot thing for them, it dissipated. And I think that's very interesting."

Today, however, Walmart is a founder and leader in The Sustainability Consortium (TSC). TSC is an organization of diverse global participants working to promote science and integrated tools in order to improve informed decision making for product sustainability throughout the entire product life cycle across all relevant consumer goods sectors. Other members include Tesco, Ahold, and Marks & Spencer.

The aim of TSC is to work collaboratively and develop an approach that drives better understanding, standardization, transparency, and informed decision-making regarding the sustainability of products. TSC is developing a standardized framework for the communication of sustainability-related information throughout the product value chain. The framework, called the Sustainability Measurement & Reporting System (SMRS) serves as a common, global platform for companies to measure and report on product sustainability. SMRS enables rigorous product level life cycle assessments to be done at a fraction of today's time and cost, and provides a platform for sustainability-related data sharing across the supply chain.

With the SMRS, companies can improve the quality of decision-making about product sustainability. This enables companies to manage the sustainability of upstream supplies and suppliers and communicate product sustainability downstream to consumers, while also partnering with auditing and certification firms to create assurance standards.

TSC has identified these consumer drivers for more sustainable products and standardization:

- Desire for product transparency and increasing demand for responsible products.
- Confusion on what constitutes a sustainable product.
- Proliferation of single attribute eco-labels and increase in green claims and green washing.
- Call for help in making informed decisions.

TSC provides material for education and training to its members and their suppliers. Their members can use the data created by TSC to teach their buyers the right questions to ask when speaking to suppliers about their sustainability. TSC is creating practical solutions and data, called Key Performance Indicators (KPIs), that support and give background for real conversations that that take place at the "buyer-supplier" table.

In addition, TSC has created Product Sustainability Toolkits and access to TSC Learning Centers. Product Sustainability Toolkits are interactive tools that highlight environmental and social issues relevant to a product category, practices that can be used to drive improvement on those issues, and KPIs to track and measure performance against these issues.

The Toolkits are designed to facilitate decision-making by retailers, manufacturers, and suppliers along the value chain, with an emphasis on impact and improving product sustainability. The Toolkits are science-based and stakeholder-informed, with input from companies, academics, civil society organizations, and government agencies.

The TSC Learning Center is an online educational platform that provides guided practice on using TSC tools and services to maximize effectiveness and impact. The training material currently available provides users an opportunity to practice responding to TSC Key Performance Indicators in order to accurately measure and track product sustainability. Future additional training modules will focus on prioritizing issues, setting goals and policies and identifying their sourcing regions, and training global teams all through the use of TSC tools and services.

For the wine sector, TSC starts with brief Sustainability Insights. These one-page documents include relevant information from TSC research on the known and potential social and environmental impacts across product life cycles. While other issues exist in the supply chain, the Sustainability Insights are the most relevant to the decision-making teams for retail and manufacturing.

TSC has also developed KPIs that retail buyers should ask of wineries and distributors regarding:

- Supply Chain Engagement, Transparency, Communication, Data Sharing
- On-Farm Biodiversity and Ecosystems Management
- Monitoring Soil Fertility, Degradation, and Erosion
- Fertilizer Tracking and Goals
- Standard and Certification Adoption
- Use of Copper-Based Biocides
- Integrated Pest Management
- Fuel Tracking and Goals
- Water Consumption for Irrigation
- Water Use and Scarcity
- Use of Renewable Energy
- Energy Use in Winemaking
- Water Consumption for Winemaking
- Water Emissions in Winemaking
- Packaging

- Glass Production: Recycled Content
- Container Lightweighting
- Distribution Fuel Use
- Container End-of-Life
- Labor rights; Worker Safety

TSC has also organized these KPIs according to the point in the value chain where these activities take place:

1. Crop Supply Mapping
2. Deforestation and Land Conversion—Growing Operations
3. Fertilizer Application—Growing Operations
4. Greenhouse Gas Emissions Intensity—Growing Operations
5. Irrigation Water Use Intensity—Growing Operations
6. Labor Rights—Growing Operations
7. Pesticide Application—Growing Operations
8. Worker Health and Safety—Growing Operations
9. Yield—Growing Operations
10. Greenhouse Gas Emissions Intensity—Processing
11. Wastewater Generation—Processing
12. Water Use Intensity—Processing
13. Packaging Raw Material Sourcing and End-of-Life
14. Sustainable Packaging Design and Production
15. Transportation to Retailers

Costco

Costco is the second largest global retailer and a dominant importer and retailer of wine. In Fiscal Year 2015, Costco's Fine Wine Sales amounted to $965M and its Total Wine Sales $1.69B. Their private label business, Kirkland Signature brand, has grown since its launch in 2003 and now represents less than 15 percent of its wine business. The Kirkland label also gets good reviews and ratings. For example, Kirkland's 2010 Columbia Valley Red blend of Cabernet Sauvignon, Merlot, Syrah, Cabernet Franc, Petit Verdot, and Sangiovese received an 87-point rating from *Wine Spectator*. Additionally, Kirkland Signature 2013 Russian River Chardonnay received 90 points from *Wine Enthusiast*.

On June 5, 2015, Costco's CFO Richard Galanti announced that it has surpassed Whole Foods to become the biggest organic grocer, with warehouse club's sales of organic products exceeding $4 billion annually—up from a previous $3 billion-plus estimate given in 2014. By comparison, the industry leader, Whole Foods, sells about $3.6 billion in organic food every year.

It's still small, relative to Costco's total sales in 2015 expected to reach $114 billion, but growing faster. In terms of the organic food industry, it's a huge number: It means more than 1 out of 10 dollars in organic food sales are made at a Costco. The Organic Trade Association, a U.S. lobbying group for the industry, estimates total organic food sales to be around $36 billion. Costco's organics business has doubled in the past couple of years, according to its CFO.

The numbers underscore how organic food, once the domain of alternative co-ops, farmers markets, and specialty retailers, has become a mainstream phenomenon—especially among so-called millennials, the elusive younger demographic that warehouse clubs like Costco are eager to attract.

Yet this growth in organics is not reflected in Costco's tremendous wine sales, though wine is part of Costco's Food and Sundries Division that registered such impressive organic sales. In my interview with Annette Alvarez-Peters, Costco's wine executive and Assistant GMM (Beverage Alcohol), she readily admitted that wine is lagging in this regard. "Overall as a company, we're now the largest in organics. But, as it pertains to this particular department [wine], we're still behind. There are a couple of reasons for this. It's difficult to know the awareness level of our member base as it relates to organic wine. We don't have sales people, and we don't use a great deal of signage, so communicating the messages of organic, biodynamic or sustainable can be difficult. We're also very limited in the amount of items we can carry. Every item has to be able to stand on its own sales performance. To this point, the number of organic wine items that have been able to justify the space base on sales have been limited."

Alvarez-Peters's team is composed of 12 buyers across the United States, and they carry an average of 150 SKUs. At Costco, each buyer is responsible for wine, beer, and spirits for their region, including the necessary paperwork and supplier/distributor relationships to run their business. Domestic wines comprise approximately 65 percent of total wine business, though imports tend to be a bigger player in the Midwest and on the East Coast than in the West. Each buyer has the autonomy to purchase all categories for their region, and they do support local wineries. For example, Washington State will have a larger selection of Washington wines, and Oregon will have various pinot noir and pinot gris from the area, while California Central Coast stores will include wines from Santa Barbara and Paso Robles.

In the Food and Sundries department, according to Alvarez-Peters, Costco performs a lot of in-store "roadshows" and "treasure hunts," and twice a year, that includes an organic feature. "We haven't figured out exactly which to offer in these promotions. Of course, there are many wines that are organic, biodynamic or sustainable, but that isn't necessarily called out on their labels. When we've asked any of these wineries why they don't take advantage of this growing movement towards sustainability or organics, their overwhelming response is that they don't want to be pigeonholed. For many wineries, quality comes first. If they also happen to be organic, so be it, however, they don't want to be separated from the rest of their fine wine counterparts. The wineries prefer to sell their wines along with their particular varietal or appellation, and not be relegated to an 'organic section.' The last time I was in Bordeaux, France, I met with a well-known Pauillac Classified Growth producer. They know they could make world-class wine with their organic and biodynamic vineyards. The Chateau felt they would elevate the quality of their wines as well as being the right thing to do for the environment. Their bottles of wine sell for approximately $200. Their message is similar to what we'd heard in the past, they do not want to be separated from the other fine wines."

Costco's business model and approach to business is very simple: As big as they are, they still do a lot of their procurement, and special events are conducted on gut feelings: Is this wine great? Does it meet this price point? Does it make this quality level? Do they think their members will buy it? Once these questions are answered, they go to market. They bring the wine in, sell it, and rotate the item in and out of the system within a few weeks (though it may return at some point in the future).

When asked about the possibility of focusing on sustainable or organic for Kirkland Signature, their private label,* as a competitive differentiator perhaps, Alvarez-Peters indicated, "As a general rule, our winemaker and grower partners want to do the right thing for the environment. Most of them operate in a sustainable way by limited spraying for diseases or pests if it isn't absolutely necessary. However, we haven't found a supplier to partner with on a wholly organic wine for Kirkland Signature."

Alvarez-Peters admitted that being at the forefront of sustainable wines is also difficult for Costco, because they lack the in-warehouse staffing to educate their member base. They have a few wine sales persons in limited locations, but the lack of permanent staffing in each building makes the message difficult to get out. "We operate a cash and carry business. Generally speaking, when a member goes into the warehouse, they already know about the product. However, when a trend is on the upswing, and we make a decision to enter that business or category, the learning curve sometimes can be difficult."

When asked about the role that distributors play in this, Alvarez-Peters mentioned that their 12 buyers across the United States do work directly with distributor partners. "For example, our Midwest buyer has 13 states to oversee. Let's say he is working with Constellation on a program for his 13 states. He needs to talk to three 'territory' Constellation people, plus 13 or more distributors in each state for one item placement. Multiply that by 150 items and it can be quite time consuming. The best way for an importer or distributor to sell Costco is to do their homework by getting into the stores and review our selection. They can offer items from their portfolio that will round out our selection. The same would ring true for organics or sustainable items, each item must meet a sales volume criteria to become a rotation item in our program."

---

* Private-label products are usually created by retail chains that buy a product from a major manufacturer at a discount bulk price, rebrand the product under their own name, and capture a greater proportion of the retail sale. This trend in the wine industry is especially evident in Europe and is expanding in the United States.

Marks & Spencer

Plan A is the name Marks & Spencer (M&S) gives to its ethical and environmental goals. It was launched in 2007 as a 100-point, five-year plan. In 2007, M&S published its original 100 Plan A commitments, setting a 2012 deadline and grouping the commitments under five pillars to achieve five broad objectives: 1) become carbon neutral; 2) send no waste to landfill; 3) extend sustainable sourcing; 4) set new standards in ethical trading; and 5) help customers and employees to live healthier lifestyles. These five objectives are also called Plan A Qualities. In 2010, M&S added 80 new commitments, extending some of the original 100 and adding two new pillar headings: "Involving customers" and "How we do business," with a new 2015 deadline. They also declared an aspiration to become the world's most sustainable major retailer by 2015. Their goal: ensure that by 2020, every M&S product has Plan A quality built into it, making sustainability a new norm.

Having achieved their major aim of making their UK business carbon neutral, M&S has now introduced Plan A 2020, which consists of 100 new, revised, and existing commitments, with the ultimate goal of becoming the world's most sustainable major retailer. M&S's aim is to have at least one Plan A attribute in all M&S General Merchandise and Food Products by 2020. As of April 2015, based on the volume of items sold worldwide, 64 percent of M&S products had at least one Plan A quality (compared with 57 percent the year before).

Plan A attributes must have clear sustainable benefits, meet minimum standards, and demonstrate positive or significantly lower environmental and/or social impacts. M&S has committed itself to responsible sourcing and is currently developing a series of Plan A attributes applicable to their wines. M&S analyzed the key hotspot areas throughout the life cycle of its wine products, identifying environmental and social risks at the vineyard, bottling, transport, and packaging stages, and is working to address these issues.

Existing attributes applicable to wine suppliers include fair-trade certification, significant packing reductions, and bulk shipping practices, but regional sustainability schemes, including the Sustainability Code of the Wines of Chile, Sustainable Winegrowing New Zealand, and the California Sustainable Winegrowing Alliance, are among some of the schemes approved as Plan A attributes in 2015 that encourage sustainability in operations from vineyard to glass.

M&S recognizes the regional challenges facing its wine suppliers and is trying to build this into its approach to sourcing wine, recognizing different approaches to sustainability in the wine industry. Suppliers are encouraged to participate in these regional schemes to instill sustainability in their products and are encouraged to take ownership and find more sustainable ways to work.

In my meeting with M&S wine buyers, they indicated that wine is a high priority, though they have had some difficulty implementing Plan A with wine suppliers. Wine had not seemed to be as high of a priority product for them as more "hot spot" items such as sourcing of palm oil, soy, coffee, cocoa, and Brazilian beef. However, with more suppliers realizing the benefits of improving the sustainability of their products, from reduced costs to more engaged staff, M&S can communicate the value of Plan A attributes to wine suppliers more clearly.

One Plan A commitment relates specifically to environmentally efficient food packaging where the aim is to use the most environmentally efficient forms of packaging systems throughout the supply chain to help reduce the overall carbon footprint of packaging and products. M&S are making reductions in its carbon footprint through reductions in weight, moves to lower carbon types of packaging, or use of recycled materials. M&S has recognized the environmental impact of glass bottles and is continually working to find new sustainable approaches to packaging; for example, developing a carbon neutral wine product, Beaujolais Nouveau.

Marks & Spencers's case study for The Sustainability Consortium, of which it is also a member, describes its approach to employing more bulk shipping of wine for bottling closer to point of sale. (In these case studies, TSC Members share how they are implementing TSC Product Sustainability Toolkits in their businesses to identify hotspots and improvement opportunities in their supply chains, communicate the issues to buyers and suppliers of their products and services, and to create internal tools to track and measure the sustainability progress in their business practices.) The M&S Case study indicates that M&S has a bonus structure with measurements based on attributes in sustainability. Bulk shipping is one of the KPIs for wine and aligned with the M&S goal in Plan A to reduce the carbon footprint of its supply chain.

Systembolaget of Sweden

Systembolaget, a government-owned chain of liquor stores in Sweden, is the only retail store allowed to sell alcoholic beverages in the country. Systembolaget takes a very proactive approach, setting standards and guidelines, conducting field trips to wine growing regions, and publishing an annual Corporate Social Responsibility (CSR) Report to share their findings and results with stakeholders. The monopoly's long-term goal is to ensure that all drinks products are manufactured under conditions that are good for both people and the environment while meeting customers' demands in terms of quality, product range, and value for money.

As Sweden's government-owned liquor retail monopoly and perhaps the largest retail buyer of wine and spirits in the world, Systembolaget is in a unique position to drive questions of sustainability. Indeed, the core reason for Systembolaget to exist as a monopoly is one of social responsibility in its home market: limiting the harmful effects of alcohol. From this core aspect of social responsibility, Systembolaget has found it easy to expand the social sustainability concept to include the production side.

Sara Norell heads the buying department at Systembolaget. She illustrates the special position of the monopoly. "All the government-owned companies in Sweden are supposed to act as industry role models. We can work long-term rather than focus on short term profit. A supermarket can earn more from an organic bottle through premiumization but for Systembolaget it is rather a matter of taking responsibility all the way down the supply chain," she says.

Nordic Buyers' Joint Code of Conduct Through BSCI

It's no doubt an advantage to be a big buyer when you want to push for change. Though Systembolaget is most likely one of the world's largest buyer/retailer of alcohol, their sustainability efforts carry additional clout through collaboration with the other Nordic state-run monopolies—Alko in Finland and Vinmonopolet in Norway—to create a common code of conduct. In January 2011, the retail monopolies within Denmark, Finland, Iceland, Norway, and Sweden adopted a shared Code of Conduct to apply to all purchasing agreements (both old and new).

They joined Business Social Compliance Initiatives (BSCI), an international organization based in Brussels that seeks primarily to improve working conditions in factories and farms, and as of 2015, all Nordic monopolies were members of BSCI.

The Business Social Compliance Initiative Code of Conduct

Enacted on January 1, 2014, the BSCI Code of Conduct is a set of principles and values that reflect the belief of BSCI participants and the expectations they have for their business partners. The Code of Conduct is summarized below:

BSCI participants acknowledge their ability to create change in their supply chains through their purchasing activities. They are to always seek ways to abide by principles that provide the highest amount of protection to workers and the environment and act with due diligence if any human rights issue is detected in their supply chain. Additionally, they are to continuously train and educate employees on health and safety policies and procedures.

The Code of Conduct covers the following categories to ensure worker safety, health and protection:

- The Rights of Freedom of Association and Collective Bargaining
- No Discrimination
- Fair Remuneration
- Decent Working Hours
- Occupational Health and Safety
- No Child Labour
- Special Protection for Young Workers

- No Precarious Employment
- No Bonded Labour
- Protection of the Environment
- Ethical Business Behavior

In 2012, Systembolaget implemented this code of conduct into their general purchasing conditions applying to any importer selling their goods to Systembolaget. The importers accept responsibility for compliance in the production chain including their producers and their respective sub-suppliers. "The code is very long and for a small importer it is a huge amount of work even if it is not difficult per se," says Andreas Karlsson who is CEO of the mid-sized Swedish importer Terrific Wines, which focuses on smaller, sustainable family producers. "As an industry we should definitely do this, but the work it requires from the importers is not negligible," he says and notes that importers with larger producers or blended bulk wine products are more challenged to keep track.

Since 2013, Systembolaget has been conducting site inspections of large suppliers in high-risk regions, regions where there might be potential for environmental degradation and human rights violations or lax enforcement of labor laws. The sites are selected through a risk analysis that takes into account location, volumes, and price segment of the products delivered. In their agreement with BSCI, Systembolaget expects inspection of two-thirds of the sales volume in predefined risk countries. BSCI does not conduct the audits themselves, but there are several well-reputed auditing companies accredited to do audits according to BSCI standards.

During the first year's inspections, Systembolaget found both significant and minor deviations from the code. During the 2013 revisions, two producers had significant problems complying with human rights issues, and all 14 inspected producers had minor digressions. During reinspections in 2014, 9 still lacked full compliance. None were banned from delivering wine to the monopoly, and, according to Systembolaget, conditions improved significantly between inspections. The compliance problems ranged from absence of policy (for example, no policy against child labor) to discrimination, excessive work hours, and severe limitations on freedom to unionize. Starting in 2015, Systembolaget began looking not only at producers but also at their sub-suppliers and farmers selling grapes to the producer.

In the past few years, Systembolaget has been criticized for not acting more forcibly when significant deviations are discovered. This is especially true of a few cases in South Africa where union representatives sounded the alarm directly to Systembolaget about violations of human rights and working conditions at named sites supplying wine to the monopoly. Even in the cases when these infringements were not solved from one year's inspection to the follow-up, the deviance did not lead to sales stops or fines.

Terminating a relationship is the very last resort, and although it's clear that some producers struggle to cope with the code, Systembolaget wants to be part of a long-term change and intensify the focus on those producers rather than terminate, which for sure wouldn't lead to driving any improvement by those particular producers.

The focus countries for inspections in 2015 were Italy and Mexico, as well as continued inspection in Chile and South Africa. "We are working hand in hand with the other Nordic monopolies to present a stronger front and also to acknowledge audits made by the other monopolies," says Sara Norell. "We are also starting to look at other comparable codes and certifications in order to avoid double auditing and to really focus our efforts where they will be making the biggest difference. This will probably also result in collaborations with the other big buyers' codes of conduct, such as Tesco's," says Norell, who does recognize that audits can be time consuming for producers.

Norell defends why producers in another sustainability program, or in regions where the law is stricter than the program, can still be subject to BSCI inspection. "If there is an initiative, such as California Sustainable Winegrowing Alliance, we would of course like to accept it. However, it is self-assessed," she notes. "If we are to consider this as good as Fair Trade or Fair for Life or other initiatives, we have to assess it to see that it is just as good. It is generally difficult to compare different programs and initiatives with each other. Even those with very similar codes can have quite different protocols for monitoring." But as Systembolaget does not find that they have the resources to do this themselves, they require a third-party checkpoint. "If not, it could leave space for greenwashing," says Norell. But in addition to collaborating with other international buyers, they review programs already in place, such as regional sustainability programs. "We are looking for programs that are at the same level as BSCI. Laws are not enough. South African labor laws are perfect but we know there is a history of problems around this so we still want to be there to check implementation," she concludes.

Separate Environmental Initiative

As BSCI has a focus on social sustainability and is admittedly weak on environmental issues, Systembolaget wants to strengthen their focus on environmental sustainability. A life cycle analysis of the impact of packaging (not only carbon) in 2011 showed that packaging was clearly the category with the largest carbon footprint—30 percent of the total. For this reason, Systembolaget has implemented a fine for heavy glass bottles, inspired by the one already launched by the The Liquor Control Board of Ontario (LCBO)—a provincial government-owned retailer in Canada, also with CSR standards and sustainability requirements. The weight limit for glass bottles for still wine is set at 420 grams, and the fee is 6-cents/100g for additional weight exceeding 420 grams after this. The new rules apply to still wines starting with the 2016 harvest. Beer, sparkling wine, spirits, and fortified wines are next in line for bottle weight review. According to Sara Norell, Systembolaget has looked to confirm that bottle suppliers providing lightweight bottles are available in the regions where they purchase wine. Systembolaget communicates to the consumer that bottle weight does not reflect quality, but rather that heavy bottles come with an environmental disadvantage.

Systembolaget has communicated a goal to reduce their CO_2 release by 14,000 metric tonnes by 2020, down from 171,090 metric tonnes in 2014. Of these 14,000, 10,000 are expected to come from the switch to lightweight bottles.

Marketing Advantages Require Third-Party Inspection

Organic and socially responsible (Fair Trade/Fair for Life) products are categories that are clearly marked on the shelf talkers at Systembolaget. Also, wine in PET bottles is specially marked—as a more sustainable alternative to glass bottles. In 2015, only approximately 1.3 percent of sold wine volume was in PET bottles, but it is growing by more than 25 percent in both value and volume. However, getting this prominent placement and signage requires that the product is certified by an internationally recognized organization and inspected by a third party. "Sustainably farmed," "natural," or similarly vague categories are not marked for customers.

Issues: Price Pressure and Sustainability

Importers and producers frequently report that Systembolaget regularly issues government tenders (i.e., request for procurement) for wines at the absolutely lowest price point—prices below market price for that type and quality in the region—even below the cost of production at times.

This focus on price has drawbacks for both quality, typicity,* and of course sustainability. The risk of cheating increases and the chance for conscientious smaller producers to compete decreases. "It goes without saying that if you press the prices too hard, someone will pay. It's not the monopoly and often not the importer, so it's the producer or the worker," says Andreas Karlsson. "Consumers will always want cheap wine but it goes against the purpose of Systembolaget for them to repeatedly push the price of the tenders to the absolute minimum for a region. They could take their commitment all the way and make the choice to not buy the very cheapest levels, levels where it is likely that the process is not economically sustainable," says Karlsson.

---

* Typicity is the characteristic of a wine that makes it typical for the region or grape of origin. Typicity describes the degree to which a wine reflects its origins and thus demonstrates the signature characteristics of the area where it was produced, its mode of production, or its parent grape.

Regardless of price point, Norell confirms that they cannot assign all of the responsibility for the supply chain over to their suppliers with the code of conduct. "We have a responsibility to look deep into our supply chain. That's why we do audits and round table discussions where we meet with government representatives, small-holders, large producers, trade unions, Fair Trade and so forth, asking where the biggest risks and opportunities are and where we can support them," she concludes. Through communication and collaboration, the Scandinavian monopolies hope to use their size to be a force for good in the world of wine.

DISTRIBUTORS

Nearly all importers, brand representatives, and restaurant wine directors interviewed indicated that the largest distributors in the United States do not carry very many, if any, organic, biodynamic, or natural wines; and when they do, they rarely promote them because they are typically smaller production and basically the commitment just isn't there. Those establishments—wine shops, restaurants, and wine bars that want to have a large number of sustainable wines in their inventory—rely on small- to medium-sized, typically regional, distributors who have made sustainable wines and buying from smaller family-owned wineries a priority. These include the following:

Winebow

The wine inventory list of Winebow, a distributor with their main office in Montvale, New Jersey, contains a variety of sustainable wines from many different regions of the world and the United States, in all price ranges. They seek to meet the growing interest among retailers and consumers in the mid-Atlantic region in having sustainably produced wines available for purchase. Their sales people are quite knowledgeable about organic, biodynamic, and sustainable wines.

Country Vintner

Likewise, this distributor, based in Ashland, Virginia, proved to have an interesting offering of sustainably produced wines. When Country Vintner chooses to offer a sustainable selection, it always starts, as it does with any other wine, with the wine itself—the outstanding quality. Country Vintner is not seeking out sustainable wines per se, but has a focus on small production, family-owned wineries: fine wines that reflect their place of origin. These wines are characterized by intention, good practices, and care for the land and for the future of the earth. In other words, none of these are industrial grade wines. Very few of these wines are labeled organic, but they are either certified organic or made using organic practices.

The winemakers they work with understand that they can recoup their investment in sustainable practices because certain consumers want these better quality wines.

Vintage 59 is a good example; most of their wines are organic or biodynamic. All the growers they work with take a common-sense sustainable path and none produce using conventional methods. They reject "post-harvest wizardry" and modern enological tricks that may be used in the winery to turn ordinary grape juice into acceptable wine.

Unfortunately, consumers don't know the questions to ask about sustainability because they don't understand the winemaking process. According to a Country Vintner representative, "It's the purists who are producing some of the highest quality wines these days and that bodes well for the future of sustainable wines."

Both distributors were quick to point out that despite what people say about distributors not approaching or promoting sustainable wines, distributors don't act blindly. They take an optimistic view and will deliver what the consumer wants. But actually the winery and their representatives bear a great responsibility to do the education, so that consumers do understand what goes into making a bottle of wine. The wine industry has the responsibility for the marketing, to "make" people want sustainable wine.

Mountain People's Wine & Beer

Michael Michel is president of Mountain People's Wine & Beer Distribution, the leading organic wine and beer distributor in California, an independent, family-run distributor focused on providing California with the largest selection of organic.

Founded as an extension of the natural and organic food distribution business United Natural Foods Inc., a pioneer in the natural foods business, the owners believed it was important to make available high-quality organic wine and beer to its customers in order to further the growth of the organic industry and to provide consumers with organic choices. They already had a distribution network in place for organic foods, and they started by working with small wineries like Frey Vineyards, Nevada County Wine Guild, La Rocca Vineyards, Hallcrest Vineyards, and others to build a portfolio of organic wines.

Mountain People's left the fold of United Natural Foods Inc. over 10 years ago, and now its mission is to change the way people think about organic wine and offer the most complete line of organic wines available. Their motto is "Supporting Organic Family Farms." They believe in working with small family wineries, importers, and farmers who are committed to producing the highest quality organic wine while caring for the planet and the palate.

Michael Michel pointed out some of the factors inhibiting the growth of organic wine sales in the United States. "A majority of the wine sold in the US is sold at the retail level in the $6–$15 range per bottle and retailers and the large wine companies control most of that market. They have matured in the industry and have built name brands that consumers are looking for and they control the shelf space. It is difficult for niche and smaller segments like organic wine to secure the coveted shelf space," he stressed. "Also, organic wine is difficult for the average consumer to understand with confusing designations required on wine labeling by the U.S. Department of Agriculture (USDA): *Organic Wine—No Sulfite Added* and *Made with Organic Wine—with limited sulfites added.* They both indicate 100 percent Certified Organic Vineyards and Wineries, but to get the USDA label you must not add any sulfites, Michel explained.

"Whole Foods is probably selling the most Certified Organic wine in the US and taking a leadership role in promoting Organic Wine. They and other retailers have the opportunity to take a leadership role in promoting and educating consumers about Organic Wine and if they focus on it in the next few years we could see tremendous growth. The Organic Wine industry, except for Bonterra, has not developed into a mature industry and doesn't have the capital to promote their vision and wine brands. Right now we need to rely on the leadership of the retailers. The wine quality is there—we just need education and promotion. "

Another challenge to expanding sales of organic wine is the amount of organic juice available. There's not enough juice to increase volume dramatically domestically.

Also, the three years it takes to get the vineyards converted and certified as organic is yet another factor. Therefore, if demand increased, it might not be met. According to Michel, "The other item to consider is that if we do have large increase in demand, there is limited organic acreage which would possibly drive a premium for organic wines and create demand for more organic acreage."

Top Wine Distributors in the United States

By contrast the larger distributors don't have a focus on distributing sustainably produced wines, although surely some of their wines are organic or sustainably certified. A few of these large companies have "social and environmental responsibility" programs that include such commitments as working against underage drinking and overconsumption, and supporting charitable events and scholarship programs in their communities. Two distributors, Southern and Young's, stress environmental responsibilities.

Top U.S. Wine and Spirits Distributors

1. **Southern Glazer's Wine and Spirits**—a 2016 merger between Southern Wine and Spirits (SWS) and Glazer's Family (previously the tenth largest) became the largest distributor in the country. SWS has made strides to improve their fleet vehicles' carbon emissions (http://www.southernwine.com/)

2. **Charmer Sunbelt**—http://www.charmer-sunbelt.com/
3. **Republic National**—http://www.rndc-usa.com/
4. **Young's Market's**—their corporate headquarters was "built to surpass Silver LEED standards," and their "fleet of clean diesel delivery trucks are maintained to standards far ahead of California Air Resources Board (CARB) compliance." (http://www.youngsmarket.com/)
5. **Wirtz Beverage**—http://www.wirtzbeveragegroup.com/
6. **Martignetti Co.**—http://www.martignetti.com/
7. **Johnson Bros.**—http://www.johnsonbrothers.com/
8. **Allied Beverage**—http://www.alliedbeverage.com/
9. **Fedway Associates**—https://www.fedway.com/

Despite the few examples of sustainable goals by large distributors, they are typically considered a bottleneck for organic and sustainable wines. Wine is big business in the United States, and its distribution is like many other packaged goods destined for retail. Annie Arnold, founder of The Organic Wine Exchange, said, "Many distributors are only concerned about their bottom line. As much as we like to romanticize the beautiful vineyard and the humble winemaker with his family all working the harvest, this really is a big commercial industry. It's no different from any other industry whose products you see on the shelves in the grocery store where margins are fiercely guarded and negotiated. Wine has turned more into a mass-distributed commercial product."

Organic producers and importers worry that they don't have the resources to compete with the big distributors in getting their wine onto store shelves or into restaurants. Every importer and every winery has to assume that they're paying the salaries of the distributors' employees and/or paying for incentives, for sales, and so forth. There just aren't enough big players in the organic industry to play that game. The incentives that large distributors can offer just can't be matched by a small or medium-size distributor, according to several organic importers and wineries interviewed. These incentives—such as buying large numbers of wine glasses for the restaurant; reprinting the menu and wine list; buying expensive gifts for the restaurant manager, owner, and wine director—keep organic and natural wines off the list, at least until the restaurant decides to re-do the list, and then the large distributors aren't happy if some organic wines show up on the new list (the list whose printing they paid for!).

These organic representatives seek out a medium-sized distributor that maybe carries craft beers. They are the ones in the marketplace that are accustomed to telling a story. They want to make a name for themselves. They can position themselves as having a unique (and authentic) portfolio and are proud to say they're in the organic wine business. They want to be consultants in a way and talk to their retail partners in a way that isn't purely sales pitching, but actually a source of information on how to market these organic products more effectively.

Of course, there are distributors devoted to organics, as you find in California.

The Wine Institute partnered with PE International (a sustainability consulting firm) to survey over 50 members of the wine trade in 2013. Retailers, restaurant owners, and distributors (among others) participated to share their insight on sustainable wine as it relates to their roles in the industry.

Across all segments, 37 percent of respondents said that sustainable attributes were frequently or very frequently a factor in wine selection. A larger segment (86 percent) indicated that the attributes were at least occasionally a factor in wine selection. The majority of respondents reported that they rely on winery marketing materials or testimony from a winery representative for information on sustainable practices. Aside from that, the vast majority relies on third-party certifications, bottle seals, or label information.

Putting a seal, logo, or information about sustainable practices on the wine bottle is a sentiment supported by the majority of respondents to the trade survey, who indicated that sustainability certification programs are helpful (71 percent), as are seals on bottles (81 percent). The survey also revealed that Biodynamic (63 percent), USDA Organic (53 percent), and California Certified Sustainable Wine (CCSW-Certified) (49 percent) are the certifications most frequently associated with wines offered by the trade responding to the survey.[9]

Similarly, according to a Wine Institute study, 66 percent of consumer respondents said that they depend on information they get from bottle labels and/or from information provided by the retail store where they purchase the wine. So, clear and informative bottle labeling (and marketing materials) seems to be one way to increase the selection of sustainably produced wine by both retailers and consumers.[10]

THE ROLE OF IMPORTERS AND BRAND REPRESENTATIVES

Négociants International, based in Australia, has become one of the world's preeminent premium wine exporters, with branch offices in the United States, the UK, and New Zealand. They are also the export department of Australia's oldest family-owned winery, Yalumba. Owned by the Hill Smith family for over 150 years, Yalumba has grown into one of the finest independent wine companies in the world. Négociants is also the U.S. representative of Yalumba and several other Southern Hemisphere wines, notably Australian brands owned by the Hill Smith family such as Janzz and Oxford Landing.

All Hill Smith brands are committed to rigorous sustainability standards. For example, Yalumba recently purchased 100 acres of land next to Oxford Landing vineyards and publicly committed not to plant vines on this property for 100 years.

Instead they are planting native bushes to revitalize the soil and contribute to carbon neutrality. So far they have planted 25,000 trees.

Négociants also represents other nonrelated wineries from the Southern Hemisphere, including Henschke of Australia, which is biodynamically and organically farmed, and Two Paddocks of New Zealand, a small, family-owned estate founded by actor Sam Neill in 1993, that specializes in pinot noir, in the Central Otago region, most admired for the pinot noir varietal.

In Australia, Négociants is a large distributor, but owing to the limitations in the United States on importing and distribution by the same firm, they are simply importers and brand representatives in the U.S. market. They represent one U.S. brand—Voss of Napa Valley.

In my interview with Danielle Winkler, Mid-Atlantic market manager with Négociants USA, she candidly admitted that newer wine shops in her region do a much better job of communicating sustainable attributes of the wine to their customers than some of the older, more established wine stores. She is encouraged, however, by the fact that in sales meetings even the large distributors are now asking questions about sustainability attributes of the wines. They finally see this aspect as a selling tool so they are getting on board and wanting to know more about the sustainability practices and accomplishments of the wines Négociants represent.

Danielle proudly indicated that, "Yalumba is the only winery (and a foreign winery at that) to ever be awarded the Climate Protection Award from the U.S. Environmental Protection Agency (they received the award in 2007). Yalumba is very seriously committed to reducing its environmental footprint and measuring their progress. For example, regarding water use, Yalumba is 1 to 1 in terms of water to wine usage whereas most wineries use 3 times as much water as the resulting volume of wine. It's hard to argue with these clear metrics," Danielle said. "Yalumba is now turning its focus to communications and telling the public about all the sustainable practices they have undertaken and accomplished."

RESTAURANTS, HOTELS, WINE BARS

One of the largest hotel and restaurant proponents of sustainable wines is Kimpton Hotels. In 2010, Kimpton committed to having at least 30 percent of all wine lists at their hotels and restaurants include eco-friendly selections. Kimpton has also created a happy-hour program that features sustainable wines. One example is the well-known (and affordable) Flip-flop wine (owned by The Wine Group, who also owns brands such as Cupcake and Franzia). They've partnered with the nonprofit Soles4Souls to donate a portion of proceeds from the sale of wine to fund the donation of shoes to children in Third World countries.

Wente Family Estates, a producer often on the list at Kimpton Hotels, is a family vineyard currently in its fifth operating generation. They have dedicated a portion of their proceeds to sponsor their "Farming for the Future" program, which is dedicated to creating sustainable soil and farmland for the future. Emily Wines is a sommelier and California-based Director of Wines for Kimpton, where she oversees the beverage selections at 50 locations. "Customers care about sustainability and they look to retailers and restaurateurs to do the research and make those wines available," she said.

Kimpton has an extensive keg wine program at their hotel restaurants. "It's something that we believe in on a couple of levels. One, for the environment: I can't count how many times I've watched a waiter open a case of wine for a banquet, empty the bottles, then throw the whole thing away—so wasteful—whereas kegs can be used over and over. The other side of it is the freshness factor. The glass of wine is as fresh from the bottom of the keg as it is from the top of the keg," Emily Wines said in an interview with *Wine Spectator Magazine*.[11]

Keg wine companies include Lioco, Au Bon Climat, Gotham in New York, and Free Flow Wines in California.

Free Flow Wines has the largest market share and the most sophisticated business model of all the keg wine companies that package wine and handle logistics for wine in steel kegs, ultimately served by the glass. Started in Sonoma County, an outgrowth of Silvertap, Free Flow began with a few boutique winery clients. Then in 2011 they began partnering with larger wineries such as Treasury Wine Estate, Constellation, Francis Ford Coppola, as well as quite a number of local, boutique wineries throughout Napa, Sonoma, Oregon, and Washington. Free Flow relocated to Napa Valley in 2013, and by 2016, they had 18 of the world's top 30 wineries using their kegs to supply their wine nationwide. And Free Flow is starting to work with a number of imports, including European and New Zealand wineries that send bulk wine to the United States to be packaged in their kegs and sent to restaurants and wine bars around the United States for wine by-the-glass programs.

In my interview with Heather Clauss, vice president of sales and marketing at Free Flow, she explained, "Of course, one of the primary reasons for doing this was sustainability, and the huge amount of waste that goes into disposal of bottles—which are very rarely recycled. The other reason was all the wasted wine at restaurants that oxidizes after a bottle is opened. Preserving wine quality for these by-the-glass programs, and also elevating the programs by allowing restaurateurs to provide better wines by the glass because when they are in kegs, there is no waste, and the wines always taste good.

"We have over 130 winery partners, over 300 SKUs, amongst those wineries, over 200 brands . . . so it has definitely taken hold and people are no longer questioning the ability or quality of wine on tap. Consumers and restaurateurs consider this wine as a premium option, as well as a very green option, so it has a lot of credibility and excitement around it."

The nature of this business is that the wineries are the primary customers, but the distributors who are selling these kegs are also key. "So, we have very close relationships with all of the major distributors throughout the country to be able to accommodate kegs," Clauss explained. "Obviously, that is a challenging feat to get them to change from a distribution system that they have always used. And then, we also need to partner with restaurateurs and larger national accounts who are interested in installing wine on tap programs so that we can properly educate them as to best practices and getting the equipment set up so they can pour wine on tap."

Marketing is handled by the winery sales team in combination with the distributors, just the same as marketing bottles of wine. The Free Flow team educates the winery teams and distributors on how to talk about wine on tap and how to persuade an account to install this system. Often, they are going into an account that does not have an existing tap, and they talk to them about the return on investment (ROI) they could see if they install taps and show them the wines that are available on tap. Sometimes new restaurant accounts already have taps installed when they acquire a space, so they are seeking a certain wine on tap.

As expected, the distributors have been the biggest hurdles. "As it relates to innovation, there are very few people [in distribution] that actually get it and embrace it and promote it. They're used to taking a case of wine and selling it and never thinking about it. Now with kegs, they have to take a deposit fee, they have to pick up empty kegs—these systems and processes can be challenging initially. Some of our long-standing distributor partners are selling a ton of kegs now. If you don't have a decent keg portfolio, you're losing out on placements, because there are so many taps going into on-premise locations. Distributors are changing their tune and realize that this is how things are going. Two years ago, they were dragging their feet," Clauss added.

The margins on wine in kegs are about the same for the distributor as wine in bottles. If anything, the suppliers are selling them at a very small discount. There's a small incentive ($0.25–0.50 discount per bottle) to use kegs. If anybody is making money on this, it's likely the retailer. Free Flow estimates that there are about 4,000 wine-on-tap programs throughout the United States, with an average of four to six taps per account. "So, that's a lot of by-the-glass programs to service. If a distributor doesn't have a product to pour on those taps, then they are losing out," she said.

In terms of logistics, Free Flow's facility is situated in South Napa Valley—right next door to where the major distributors pick up wine bottles for transport to market. They pick up kegs as well. They consolidate filled kegs with bottle products and move them to their warehouse facilities throughout the country and sell them to retailers across the United States just as they do the bottles. When the distributors deliver new kegs to an account, they pick up the empty kegs and consolidate them at their warehouses. Once they have a couple pallets of kegs, Free Flow has a return logistics partner that picks up kegs regionally from different distributors, consolidating them and bringing them back to Free Flow in Napa in truckloads, to be washed and refilled.

As of 2015, all those kegs come back to the West Coast. However, Free Flow has planned a partnership with Gotham, the country's second largest keg company in New York. As a result, Free Flow will open an East Coast facility in New Jersey in

2016, and the kegs will be cleaned and refilled there, cutting their logistical footprint and time in half and reducing the carbon footprint.

A few years ago, Free Flow completed a life cycle analysis (LCA) of steel kegs versus bottles as well as the round-trip their kegs travel. This LCA also factored in the manufacturing of their steel kegs in Germany, shipping them to California, filling them in Napa, and the numerous round-trips. Free Flow kegs are designed to last at least 30 years, but for the purpose of this study they assumed a 20-year lifespan. They determined that regardless of the back and forth trips of the kegs, in their lifetime there was still a 96 percent reduction in the carbon footprint for Free Flow kegs versus wine bottles, and then compared to plastic kegs, it was about 25–35 percent reduction in CO_2 footprint.

Not surprisingly, this trend started in California, mostly in chef-driven restaurants that really saw the value in having quality wines, and preserving wine quality for by-the-glass programs. These chefs also had a vested interest in sustainability and wanted to promote that. In many of those restaurants, they actively promoted "Wine on Tap" and stressed to their customers that this was the freshest, greenest way of drinking wine. "Quality is always perfect, temperature is always perfect. For most people these are major selling points," concluded Clauss.

Most wine bars or restaurants that I have visited that serve wine by the glass on tap do communicate the format to consumers but rarely promote the sustainability aspects. A favorite London restaurant of mine is Rex and Mariano, which serves wines by the glass only, from kegs delivered directly from European wineries. Several restaurants in the Washington, D.C., Metro area now offer wine on tap:

- *Matchbox 14th Street*—Whites, reds, prosecco on tap.
- *AIDA Bistro & Wine Bar* (Maryland)—One of the largest wine tap programs in the country.
- *Graffiato*—Many menu items and wine and beer are sourced domestically. They offer unique cocktails, domestic wine, and prosecco served straight from a tap.
- *Bar Rouge*—A bar located within Hotel Rogue, they offer white and red wine on tap.
- *Sonoma Restaurant & Wine Bar*
- *2 Amys*
- *District Kitchen*

Certified Wines in Restaurants

There are numerous restaurants in the United States and the UK that include a sizeable number of certified sustainable, organic, and biodynamic wines on their wine list. In many cases, the chef is convinced that these wines pair well with their foods that are natural, organic, "farm to table." In other cases, the restaurant owner and wine director are committed to environmental sustainability in general.

While many restaurants include sustainably produced wines on their wine list and some indicate organic certification, few go as far as requiring nearly all wines they serve to be certified sustainable. Two notable exceptions: Belmond Le Manoir aux Quat'Saisons, a restaurant with two Michelin stars in Oxford, England, and the Slanted Door, a very popular Vietnamese restaurant in San Francisco. Both set organic or biodynamic as preferences for their wine lists.

At Le Manoir aux Quat'Saisons, chef (and hotel founder) Raymond Blanc's dishes utilize the freshest, best-quality ingredients. The two-acre kitchen garden produces 90 types of vegetables and 70 varieties of herbs. The hotel's wine cellar is home to around 1,000 different wines from around the world. Around 60 percent are of French provenance. The wine list features high-quality wines that are certified organic and biodynamic wines, and the chef recently removed some New Zealand wines from their list that were not certified organic or biodynamic, even though they were otherwise certified sustainable by the NZ program.

Similarly, the Slanted Door, a Vietnamese cuisine restaurant in San Francisco's Ferry Building, includes predominately organic and biodynamic wines on its wine list. The Wine Director, Chaylee Priete, works at finding just the right wines to pair with their spicy Asian dishes. Chaylee came to Slanted Door as sommelier, having worked in food and beverage previously, because she wanted to stay just focused on wine.

Mark Ellenbogen, who wrote the initial wine list at Slanted Door, had, over the years, become more and more a staunch advocate of the biodynamic practices—in fact, so much so that his interest in biodynamics outweighed his interest in wine, which is one of the reasons he decided to move on to biodynamic farming. Chaylee continued with his wine list philosophy, changed it slightly, and expanded the list significantly. "One thing I did do—he had symbols all over the wine list to signify whether the wine was organic or biodynamically farmed. I am sure his intent was to educate the consumer—but it ended up being confusing. The server would spend more time explaining the symbols rather than talk about the whole philosophy [of the restaurant] in general."

"It's not just the wine, but we buy chicken that's really expensive—because we're buying from one farmer who's providing all of our chicken. We get only grass-fed organic beef from one producer because we're trying to say that this is the way we should be spending our money. So I took the symbols off because I wanted the whole philosophy or the whole list to be predicated on the idea that if a wine was on the list, it followed certain farming practices. Certification has become less and less of a dogmatic necessity for me. Winemakers, especially in Europe, but even now for a lot of the small winemakers here in California, are doing everything themselves, and they're not taking the time to be certified. Certification has become less of a focal point."

Chaylee buys for four additional restaurants in the Slated Door Group: Out the Door, Hard Water, South, and Green Cap Catering. The focus in all of these is natural, organic, biodynamic wine. Out the Door has a tap program of nine wines on tap. Chaylee buys about $70,000 worth of wine each month just for Slanted Door, and she changes the list once a week.

Buying with this focus requires great attention to trust in relationships with distributors and suppliers. "The relationships I have built with my brokers and importers are crucial. I've cut off a lot of relationships with brokers who assure me the wine is organic and then I find out that's not true at all. So, I buy from a very small circle of people—either direct from wineries in California that do organic or from a handful of people that I trust. Also, I end up seeing a winemaker twice a year when they come here or I go there, so you can actually talk to them in person and you can find out what their beliefs are, what their practices are."

Some in the trade, especially the big distributors, have criticized Slanted Door's list as being insular. They do not buy wine from Young's or Southern or Regal, primarily because they don't carry the organic, biodynamic, or sustainable wines to pair with the menu and fit their sustainable preferences. "The big guys in the trade are becoming more interested than they used to, because they realize there's a growing awareness of people wanting to be healthier and wanting a healthier environment. I get 300 emails a day where people are asking me to try their wines because they have this biodynamic winery or that biodynamic winery. Now it seems they all have some in their portfolio. But, I don't know how that poor biodynamic winery got into their portfolio, because they're just going to be lost in a sea of conventional wine."

Slanted Door customers seem really excited about the wine list; I certainly was when I dined there. For most diners, the sustainability aspect is an added bonus. Said Chaylee, "It can increase loyalty. I think it makes them more open to trying new things. They feel that you're taking more care, and are willing to try a new wine."

Chaylee is a bit more skeptical about certified sustainable versus certified organic or biodynamic because to her it seems sustainable wine hasn't really been established. "What does that really mean? In terms of wine, it seems like sustainable is an introductory step to the rest of the certifications." (For more information on the Slanted Door Group, visit: http://www.slanteddoorgroup.com.)

A Wine Bar Goes Green for April

An interesting example of sustainable marketing is the Earth Day promotion by Screwtop Wine Bar, which turned its entire wine list green for "Earth month of April." One the most popular wine bars in the Washington, D.C., area, Screwtop Wine Bar, featured organic, biodynamic, and sustainably farmed wines exclusively all month April 2015 in honor of Earth Day 2015.

Says Wendy Buckley, "Chief Executive Wino" at Screwtop Wine bar in her blog: "When it comes to eating, most of us want to fuel our bodies with healthy, nutritious, clean food. But what about the wine we are pairing with our meals? Do we really know what happens between the vine & the glass?

"Wine comes from grapes, which are grown using farming practices you may or may not be too keen on, or even know about. Like the use of pesticides (bug killers) and Round Up, (a weed killer) that has been linked repeatedly to health dangers, including Parkinson's, infertility, and cancers. In 2010, more than 400,000 pounds of Roundup (it's known as Glyphosate) were applied to wine grapes!"

To focus customers' attention to the issue and to show how they can make a difference for the environment, Screwtop Wine Bar decided to promote "green" wines for the entire month of April 2015, and try to show customers "that organic, sustainable, biodynamic wine tastes great!" For the entire month of April 2015, they devoted 100 percent of their wine list, wine flights, and wine club to embracing these eco-friendly philosophies.

For those Screwtop customers who wanted to learn more, they offered an informative green wine class during Earth month on the differences between organic, biodynamic, and sustainable winemaking and winegrowing. And they featured discounts as part of the promotion, offering 10 percent off the retail purchase of any eco-friendly bottle of wine from their adjacent wine retail shop and offering $10 off all bar bottles consumed on-premise.

MORE RESTAURANTS, WINE BARS, AND WINE SHOPS THAT FOCUS ON SUSTAINABLE WINES

Camino | Oakland, California

Sourcing all ingredients locally, the restaurant only serves three main dishes a night. Chef and owner Russell Moore limits spirits, wine, and beer to those that can be traced back to their source, eliminating most conventional brands.

Hearth | New York, New York

A critically acclaimed farm-to-table restaurant in New York City, serving responsibly sourced products and hard-to-find organic and biodynamic wine.

Bar Agricole | San Francisco, California

Bar Agricole embodies both the urban and the agricultural in its simple, seasonal fare, organic and biodynamic wine, and artisanal spirits.

Paul Marcus Wines | Oakland, California (Retail)

A neighborhood wine shop in Rockridge district of Oakland, California, that offers food-friendly wines and a wide selection of organic, biodynamic, and sustainable wines.

Gallagher & Graham | Washington, D.C.

This boutique liquor store carries artisanal, small-batch spirits and wine in addition to craft beer. While they offer selections from all over the world, they focus on sustainably produced, organic, and biodynamic wines.

Appellation Wine & Spirits | New York, NY

This "unconventional" wine shop in Manhattan focuses on stocking wine from small grower-producers who make organic, biodynamic, or natural wines. Or, as their website states, "we like good wine and we like wine that we believe is good for you."

Cork, A Bottle Shop | Portland, OR

This wine shop has a focus on wines that are both affordable and sustainable. They use signage throughout the store to designate products that are certified organic, biodynamic, salmon safe, LIVE certified, or otherwise indicate some sustainable method used in production or in construction of the winery.

FROM THE 2014 WINE ENTHUSIAST MAGAZINE TOP 100 BEST WINE RESTAURANTS

These restaurants focus on natural/organic/sustainable/biodynamic wine:

Hen of the Wood | Burlington, VT

It features a 100-bottle list along with 18 wines by the glass and carafe that demonstrates a completely natural focus since 2010.

Ripple | Washington, D.C.

At Ripple, small-production wineries that use sustainable, organic, and biodynamic viticulture practices are highlighted. The bartenders and sommeliers are extremely knowledgeable about these wines and the winemaking process, and eager to share information with inquisitive customers who chat with them while dining and drinking at the restaurant's bar.

Rouge Tomato | New York, NY

The program focuses on organic, biodynamic, and natural wines, with an international selection of more than 1,200 references from more than 20 countries.

Talula's Garden | Philadelphia, PA

"All of the wines on the list have been made in an environmentally conscious manner," says Joshua Rademacher, the beverage manager. "Not only is this smart farming and winemaking, but it results in wines that are more expressive of the land they've grown in. We believe that wines made with respect for the environment simply taste better, and express their sense of place more accurately."

The Blue Room | Cambridge, MA

Handcrafted, sustainable, and natural wines (particularly from small producers) are at the list's core.

The Red Hen | Washington, D.C.

The tightly edited program of about 75 bottles focuses on small, family-owned vineyards and leans toward the natural wine world, with a strong presence of Italian and Eastern European offerings along with selections from nearby Virginia.

Woodberry Kitchen | Baltimore, MD

The program is designed to reach a broad range of wine drinkers, from novices to the well informed, supporting offerings that are produced organically, biodynamically, or locally.

Miller Union | Atlanta, GA

The program aims to showcase smaller producers who use biodynamic or organic farming practices.

Longman & Eagle | Chicago, IL

The list encompasses estate-grown, organic, biodynamic, and small-production vintners (the list is approximately 50 percent biodynamic or sustainable).

AOC Wine Bar | Los Angeles, CA

The list is international, with wines from France, Italy, Spain, South America, Austria, Germany, Hungary, and Slovenia, in addition to offerings from California and Oregon. All selections are boutique in production and are farmed sustainably, organically, or biodynamically.

Ava Gene's | Portland, OR

The 375-bottle list is all Italian, with a focus on small producers that farm and make wines naturally.

WINE IN THE AIR

In the airline industry, KLM Airlines is one of the leading sustainability proponents. One part of KLM's sustainability effort is to make its entire catering supply chain environmentally responsible—from the paper products to the food and wine. In 2012, KLM conducted a marketing effort regarding sustainable wines on many of their transatlantic flights called Wineries for a Better World, serving wines from producers that care about the environment. The airline distributed a wine menu to business class passengers that described the reason they chose the wines and the actions each winery was taking to better the environment. The brochure also included tasting notes on each of the wines served, promoting the wine's quality and taste as well. What a great way to introduce sustainable wines to a captive audience!

KEY TAKEAWAYS

- If Walmart and The Sustainability Consortium, along with Systembolaget, all retail giants with powerful influence over suppliers, push wine suppliers to conform to their procurement requirements; and if Whole Foods, the most recognized brand for organic shoppers and the second largest organic food retailer in the United States, decided to fulfill its wine requirements predominantly from certified sustainable, organic, biodynamic wines in keeping with its core mission and brand, the result would be that these very different, highly influential retailers working from different perspectives and motivations could together drive suppliers and consumers to a major shift in distribution and consumption of sustainable wines in the U.S. market.
- Large distribution companies seem to be the main roadblock for small, sustainable wineries to get to market. These distributors do not carry very many (if any) organic, biodynamic, or natural wines, and when they do, they rarely promote them because they are small, get lost among the larger industrial wines, or because their smaller production means there isn't enough inventory to distribute on the scale of these distributors.
- There are an increasing number of retailers and restaurants that choose to offer exclusively (or mostly) organic, biodynamic, or sustainable wines to their customers. These small businesses are the true curators for consumer choice and preference and play a critical role in educating them on sustainable wines, often with food pairing that is "farm to table."
- New formats for wine delivery and alternative packaging are innovations that can offer taste quality, eliminate waste, and reduce carbon footprint.

CHAPTER 5 REFERENCES

1. Gaiter, D., and Brecher, J. "Navigating the Aisle to Find a Supermarket's Best Wines." *The Wall Street Journal*. 30 August 2001. Available online: http://www.wsj.com/articles/SB1030657806342560915 (Accessed 25 August 2015.)

2. Barkema, A. et al. "The New U.S. Meat Industry." *Federal Reserve Bank of Kansas City, Economic Review Second Quarter* (2001): pages 33–56. Available online: https://www.kansas cityfed.org/publicat/econrev/PDF/2q01bark.pdf (Accessed 25 August 2015.)

3. Martinez, S. *The U.S. Food Marketing System: Recent Developments 1997–2006*. USDA Economic Research Service. May 2007. Available online: http://www.ers.usda.gov/publications /err-economic-research-report/err42.aspx (Accessed 25 August 2015.)

4. Richards, T., and Patterson, P. *Competition in Fresh Produce Markets: An Empirical Analysis of Marketing Channel Performance*. United States Department of Agriculture Economic Research Service. 2003. Available online: http://naldc.nal.usda.gov/naldc/download .xhtml?id=32805&content=PDF (Accessed 25 August 2015.)

5. Rabobank International. *The Chinese Grape Wine Market: Developments, Challenges and Opportunities for Australian Wine in the World's Fastest Growing Wine Market*. Grape and Wine Research and Development Corporation. 2010. Available online: http://research .wineaustralia.com/wp-content/uploads/2012/11/RI-0901.pdf (Accessed 25 August 2015.)

6. Nielsen. *Grapes of Worth: How Supermarkets Are Becoming Local Wine Shops*. 19 February 2015. Available online: http://www.nielsen.com/us/en/insights/news/2015/grapes-of-worth -how-supermarkets-are-becoming-local-wine-shops.html (Accessed 25 August 2015.)

7. Teague, L. "Supermarket Wine: It's Come a Long Way, Baby." *Wall Street Journal*. 15 January 2015. Available online: http://www.wsj.com/articles/supermarket-wine-its-come-a -long-way-baby-1421428785 (Accessed 25 August 2015.)

8. Impact Newsletter, *April 2012*. Available online: http://www.commonwealthfoundation .org/docLib/20130517_LiquorWholesalers.pdf (Accessed 25 August 2015.)

9. Wine Institute. "New Research on Sustainability's Impact on Wine Buying Decisions." *Wine Institute*. 7 May 2013. Available online: https://www.wineinstitute.org/resources/press room/05072013 (Accessed 25 May 2015.)

10. Ibid.

11. *Wine Spectator Magazine*. 15 June 2013 Issue. Available online: http://www.winespectator .com/issue/show/date/2013-06-15 (Accessed 25 August 2015.)

CHAPTER 6

SOCIAL RESPONSIBILITY

Workers, Community, and Business Ethics

SINCE THE TURN OF THE MILLENNIUM, the global business world has been confronted with a growing number of failures in corporate governance and ethics. Trust in business and its leaders remains low. The 2015 Edelman Trust Barometer (its fifteenth annual trust and credibility survey) shows a global decline in trust since 2014, and the number of countries with trusted institutions has fallen to an all-time low among the informed public. Trust levels in business decreased in 16 of 27 countries. The majority of countries now sit below 50 percent with regard to trust in business. The food and beverage industry has a 67 percent trust level, but that trust drops off to 35 percent when it comes to the public's confidence in the industry regarding genetically modified foods. In fact, every industry sector faces an increasingly complex and challenging set of economic pressures, political uncertainties, and growing, often contradictory, stakeholder expectations.[1]

The trust issue reflects an ongoing debate over the private sector's responsibility for its economic, social, and environmental impacts. There is an emerging global consensus that since business is the engine of economic growth and international development, it can and must play an indispensable role alongside work by government, civil society, and communities to solve complex challenges such as hunger, poverty, inequality, unemployment, and climate change.

Typically, we think of CSR as making donations to good causes and helping to meet community needs. In many communities, companies make donations to cultural organizations—the visual arts, symphony, dance, galleries. In other instances, it contributes to needy causes like food banks and shelters for the homeless. All of these are quite worthy and fill a gap often left by local government. Corporate giving and volunteerism have been for many years the traditional ways that businesses have met the social needs of communities in which they operate, while branding themselves as good corporate citizens.

These remain relevant tools for an integrated CSR strategy. Yet most companies tend to think of corporate social responsibility in these generic ways instead of ways that can be more appropriate to their individual business strategies. The fact is, the prevailing traditional approaches to CSR overlook many great opportunities for companies to benefit society and themselves by strengthening the competitive context in which they operate. More progressive approaches for companies' philanthropy would be a shift toward activities that are related to their core competencies because that's where their true value lies. There are some specific areas of CSR strategy in the wine industry that can enhance community aspects of a sustainable supply chain and better manage risk. This chapter will describe many of these worthy charities and causes that winery owners and winemakers champion in their communities.

The concepts of corporate citizenship and corporate social responsibility are moving beyond the boundaries of legal compliance and glamorous philanthropy to a more central and challenging position. CSR encompasses not only what companies do with their profits, but also how they make them. It addresses how companies manage their economic, social, and environmental impacts, as well as their relationships in all key spheres of influence: the workplace, the marketplace, the supply chain, the community, and the public policy realm. Progressive companies focus on integrating CSR fully into their business strategies and planning.

Many people who aren't familiar with corporate social responsibility assume that it only involves companies making right the social wrongs that they practice, or in the case of trustworthy firms, how they are benevolent with a portion of their profits. However, the most successful companies take a more proactive approach, instilling ethical values in the workforce and contributing to causes that improve their local, national, or global community, especially in ways that also benefit the company. Companies in the world of wine are no exception, and there are many who take steps to engage in greater social responsibility.

Environmental stewardship has received much attention in the wine industry, but firms must also address social sustainability to be considered "sustainable" enterprises. Increasingly, consumers have concerns not only for how wine grapes are grown and for what happens at the winery but also for the well-being of the people whose labor helps determine the quality of the final product. Both wine producers and their customers are looking beyond environmental practices to a broader concept of overall sustainability—based on the triple bottom line approach—integrating profit, people, and the planet into the culture, strategy, and operations of a business. For the wine industry, this means growing wine grapes and making wine in ways that are environmentally sound, socially equitable, and economically viable. On the trade side, CSR is also about preventing underage drinking, promotion of drinking responsibly, and drinking with moderation.

On the production side it is (or should be) about commitment to communities and commitment to workers—taking care to provide workers a healthy environment in which to work in the vineyard and in the winery. Employee-related issues in the wine industry include workplace opportunity, human resource policies, quality of life, governance, and democratic processes. Additional social sustainability concerns include local purchases, local hiring, supporting local community events, product impacts on society, treatment of the under-privileged, and avoiding business dealings with countries or companies with unethical policies.

Research has found positive influences of such social practices on financial performance[2] and enhanced worker safety programs on economic performance.[3] In the winery environment, worker development, bonus-pay systems, seasonal worker housing, and health insurance have been tied to increased worker loyalty, productivity, and worker satisfaction.[4]

Social sustainability in agriculture and the food industry has been covered by the media and garnered public attention for decades with issues ranging from migrant worker abuses, fair pay to poor farmers who harvest crops destined for affluent markets, as well as consumer health and safety.

The rising demand for sustainable raw materials has increased the call for retailers, manufacturers, commodities traders, and producers to certify that commodities are extracted or grown according to certain standards. These myriad standards have confused consumers and farmers and, in some cases, have led to fraud and false auditing. There is also criticism among some social activists and farmers that standards and certification programs are expensive tools that fail to address the situation.

Certification requires farmers to make investments and changes that do not necessarily lead to high enough prices of the commodity to cover the costs. In the coffee trade, these certifications may foster greater transparency and social and environmental responsibility in supply chains, but do little to help farmers and harvest workers mired in poverty.

INDUSTRY COLLABORATION

The basis for social responsibility in the food and beverage sector has been articulated over time by a number of organizations that set principles for protection of farmer and worker welfare as well as environmental stewardship of farmland. Collaborations exist among agricultural companies and also partnerships between firms and mission-driven nonprofit organizations, each with the purpose of improving social status and human rights in communities. Furthermore, regional sustainability schemes for wine also contain recommendations or requirements for social responsibility and community outreach.

Sustainable Agriculture Initiative

The Sustainable Agriculture Initiative (SAI) platform is an initiative within the food and beverage industry that is focused on promoting sustainable agriculture worldwide. Over 60 members, including the largest and most recognizable global food companies such as Coca-Cola, Unilever, and McDonald's, have been working together for more than a decade to redesign the entire food value chain to make it sustainable.

Importantly, the companies now have an agreed definition of sustainable agriculture: "a productive, competitive and efficient way to produce safe agricultural products, while at the same time protecting and improving the natural environment and social/economic conditions of local communities." To facilitate sustainable sourcing, the SAI Platform has benchmarked agricultural standards and published guidelines for the industry. Members of the SAI Platform share a commitment to improve the social and economic conditions of farmers, their employees, and local communities and safeguard the health and welfare of all farmed species. This includes safe, healthy working conditions and compliance with standards of labor rights and human rights, and also providing economic benefits to local communities.

SAI is quite clear in its principles and guidance to its members. They also now have sets of principles and practices for the sustainable production of various agricultural products, ranging from coffee to dairy to fruit. As an illustrative example, in its Principles and Practices for Sustainable Fruit Production, it is quite direct in its prescriptions for safe, healthy working conditions and compliance with standards of labor rights and human rights. It also recommends that its members provide economic benefits to local communities using the following guidelines:

- Preference shall be given to local communities with regard to recruitment of permanent and temporary personnel, thus contributing to the build-up of sustainable livelihoods.
- Producers shall strive to be active members in their community, trying to contribute to its further development.
- Producers shall look to collaborate with the local community on aspects of environmental protection, health, safety, and basic professional training.
- Producers shall look to establish a continuous dialog with the local community in order to share the experience gained with the implementation of the present norms.

The SAI acknowledges that the productivity and success of farmers is closely linked to the well-being of their communities and employees. They seek to solve the problem of how to build attractive farming livelihoods and vibrant, adaptive rural communities while at the same time empowering farmers and increasing their self-reliance.

Here's the SAI approach:[5]

- Improve social relations between farmers and rural communities.
- Enhance empowerment (e.g., by providing facilities to build a strong rural social infrastructure).

- Alleviate rural communities' poverty.
- Ensure and possibly create employment.

Food Alliance

Started in 1993 as a project of Oregon State University, Washington State University, and the Washington State Department of Agriculture, the Food Alliance works at the juncture of science, business, and values to define and promote sustainability in agriculture and the food industry and to ensure safe and fair working conditions, humane treatment of animals, and careful stewardship of ecosystems.

Incorporated in 1997, it is a comprehensive system for sustainability and a scorecard for evaluation of practices. But it has a unique focus on ensuring a safe and fair workplace. Their goal is that farmers consistently implement professional, progressive human resource management practices. "In an environment where workers enjoy a range of protections and benefits, they are inclined to offer their ideas, expertise and concerns about the agricultural operation and play a key role in building a culture of efficiency, productivity and overall success. Progressive labor management strategies help agricultural employers create better jobs (full-time, part-time/seasonal and migrant) and result in true leadership when it comes to social and environmental responsibility."[6]

The Food Alliance certification program covers over 330 certified farms and ranches in Canada, Mexico, and 23 U.S. states managing over 5 million acres of range and farmland. The majority are mid-sized or smaller family-owned and -operated businesses. Food Alliance also certifies distribution centers and food processing facilities.

The Alliance has guiding principles[7] on sustainability in food and farming that form the over-arching framework of the standards and certification program. These include principles that guide environmental responsibility, and the following principles related to social responsibility:

- Farmers and food industry workers have secure and rewarding jobs that provide a sound livelihood. Employers respect workers' rights and well-being, make safety a priority, maintain a professional workplace, and provide opportunities for training and advancement.
- Animals are treated with care and respect. Living conditions provide access to natural light, fresh air, fresh water, and a healthy diet, shelter from extremes of temperature, adequate space, and the opportunity to engage in natural behaviors and have social contact with other animals. Livestock producers minimize animal fear and stress during handling, transportation, and slaughter.
- Foods are not produced using synthetic preservatives, artificial colors and flavors, genetically modified organisms (GMOs), or products derived from livestock treated with sub-therapeutic antibiotics or growth-promoting hormones.

- Food businesses are committed to continually improving management practices. Improvement goals are integrated into company culture, regularly monitored, and acknowledged when achieved. Food buyers are proactively engaged in the food system and support companies that are transparent about their improvement goals and progress.

Ethical Trade Initiative

The Ethical Trade Initiative (ETI) is an alliance of companies and organizations dedicated to promoting workers' rights around the world. ETI works across industries to ensure that all workers are free from discrimination and exploitation and enjoy safe and fair working conditions.

Ethical trade means that retailers, brands, and their suppliers take responsibility for improving the working conditions of the people who make the products they sell. Most of these workers are employed by supplier companies in countries with inadequate or unenforced workers' rights protection laws. Companies with a commitment to ethical trade adopt a code of labor practice that they expect all their suppliers to adopt and implement, covering issues such as wages, hours of work, health and safety, and the right to join free trade unions.

In 1998, the ETI completed an investigation into the rights of workers within the South African wine industry. Their discovery that many workers were living in poor housing conditions, were not being protected when working with chemicals or other hazardous materials, and were often discriminated against on the basis of gender or race led to the development of the first-ever multistakeholder monitoring initiative in a producer country: the Wine Industry Ethical Trade Association (WIETA). The WIETA was established in 2002 as a voluntary, not-for-profit organization that was dedicated to ensuring decent working conditions by monitoring members' compliance with its code of labor practice, based on the ETI code.[8]

The Business Social Compliance Initiative

The Business Social Compliance Initiative (BSCI) is a leading business-driven initiative supporting retailers, importers, and brands to improve working conditions in supplying factories and farms worldwide. Based in Brussels, Belgium, BSCI's vision is a world of free trade and sustainable global supply chains in which factories and farms are compliant with national labor laws and with ILO Conventions protecting workers' rights. The BSCI Code of Conduct, enacted on January 1, 2014, sets out the values and principles that BSCI participants work to implement with their business partners along their supply chains.

These participants source products from suppliers, many based in countries where national laws protecting workers are inadequate or poorly enforced. To address this, many companies and associations have created their own individual codes of conduct. The BSCI Code draws on important international labor standards and human rights declarations protecting workers' rights to set the highest labor protection for farm workers, among others. Each BSCI participant endorses the Code of Conduct when joining the initiative.

(Details of the BSCI code of conduct, adopted by Systembolaget and the other Nordic liquor monopolies, can be found in Chapter 5.)

Fair Trade

Fair Trade is a global trade model and certification signaling to consumers that certain products in the marketplace were produced in an ethical manner. Fair Trade is a well-known brand to consumers in many developed countries and offers them a powerful way to reduce poverty through their everyday shopping. For farmers and workers in developing countries, Fair Trade offers better prices, improved terms of trade, and the business skills necessary to produce high-quality products that can compete in the global marketplace. Through vibrant trade, farmers and workers can improve their lives and plan for their futures. Today, Fair Trade benefits more than 1.2 million farming families in 70 developing countries across Africa, Asia, and Latin America.

Globally, the Fair Trade network certifies coffee, tea, herbs, cocoa, fresh fruit and vegetables, beans and grains, flowers, nuts, oils and butters, honey, sugar and spices, wine, and apparel. In the United States, Fair Trade Certified products are available in more than 50,000 retail locations.[9]

Fair Trade principles[10] include:

- Fair prices and credit: Democratically organized farming groups, typically co-ops of smallholder farms, receive a guaranteed minimum floor price, which includes a premium (or market price if that is higher). Farming organizations are also eligible for pre-harvest credit.
- Fair labor conditions: Workers on Fair Trade farms enjoy freedom of association, safe working conditions, and sustainable wages. Forced child and slave labor are strictly prohibited.
- Democratic and transparent organizations: Fair Trade farmers and workers decide democratically how to invest Fair Trade premiums, which must be invested in community development and social improvement projects like scholarships, schools, quality improvement, and leadership training. Premiums can also be spent on business development projects like new farm equipment or reinvestment in the farm's infrastructure.

Fair Trade certifies some wine production in South Africa, Argentina, and Chile. The increase in demand for these wines can make it difficult for the wine-producing regions to safely (and responsibly) keep up with production needs. As with other Fair

Trade programs, Fair Trade Certified Wine guarantees producers a set minimum price for their grapes (which are grown sustainably without harsh chemicals) and also ensures that their workers receive a living wage and work in an environment free from harassment, child labor, or forced overtime.

Citrusdal Bergendal, a farm in the Western Cape of South Africa, is Fair Trade certified for wine and other agricultural products. They have used their Fair Trade premiums to set up their offices with new computers, upgrade a community rugby/ soccer field with irrigation and lighting, and enhance workers' housing developments.

In Argentina, Soluna Wines is Fair Trade certified by Fairtrade International and was founded solely to preserve Argentina's threatened tradition of small, family-owned vineyards. Soluna Wines is part of Fairtrasa, a for-profit social enterprise that works to empower marginalized, small-scale farmers in Latin America. Soluna involves a partnership between Bodega Furlotti (a generations-old winery in the heart of Mendoza) and Viña de la Solidaridad (an association of small-scale growers and contracted workers with family-owned vineyards).

Many of the families who work on smaller farms in Argentina live on the land as well. Difficult labor conditions, including frequently fluctuating market prices, can threaten these workers' livelihoods, causing disruptions in a vineyard's workforce. Soluna purchases grapes exclusively from the 19 small growers and contratistas (Argentinian vineyard workers) who make up Viña de la Solidaridad. By paying a fair price for the grapes (regardless of local and global commodity prices), Soluna is committed to preserving the lifestyles of small, family-owned vineyards. They also pay an additional social premium to be invested in education, health, and other social projects for the benefit of the entire community.

CSR in Wine Sustainability Certification Programs and Codes of Conduct

Social responsibility to workers and labor issues are often missing in the discussion about sustainability in wine. As discussed in previous chapters, many grape growers who pursue organic, biodynamic, LIVE, salmon safe, and fish-friendly certifications all address environmental aspects of growing practices and related environmental outcomes, with no requirements for social outcomes or impacts.

As with the regional sustainability certifications discussed previously, the industry's CSR efforts often lack specific social criteria or benchmarks. Some sustainability certification programs, such as California Sustainable Winegrowing Alliance and Sustainable Wine New Zealand, rely on wineries' compliance with national and state labor laws to "check the box" for social responsibility in their triple bottom line approach. But importantly, they also include guidance on social responsibility in their codes of conduct. Wine industry organizations that set sustainability certification guidelines should also foster social responsibility and inform and incentivize participating vineyards and wineries to adopt socially responsible initiatives.

California Sustainable Winegrowing Alliance

Section 15 of the California Sustainable Winegrowing Alliance's (CSWA) Sustainable Winegrowing Protocol regarding Neighbors and Community contains guidance for practices at the community level and beyond.

Awareness of a business's impact on the community is essential. Light, noise, and traffic, as well as potential pollution and chemical use, are common neighborly concerns, and the responsible vineyard or winery recognizes this. Engaging these stakeholders and responding to their concerns with action or clarification creates a more positive environment in which to live and conduct business.

More than taking ownership of the potential problems that could arise as a result of on-site practices, CSWA encourages its participants to donate time to their communities, whether it be in volunteering or presenting to schools, fire departments, police departments, or other community organizations. Additionally, hosting or sponsoring arts and cultural events are included as methods to engage communities.

Philanthropy is yet another way in which vineyards and wineries may demonstrate to CSWA their commitment to social responsibility. Specific examples of the causes that California wineries champion and support are detailed among best practices later in this chapter.

Argentinian Code

In creating its own sustainability protocol, Bodegas de Argentina relied on CSWA's precedent. While maintaining the vast majority of the environmental practices presented in the CSWA code, the section on social responsibility has been adapted to better fit the needs of Argentina's communities and economy.

Section 14 of the Argentinian protocol starts similarly in prioritizing response to the immediate community's concerns and requests. No matter the ability of the business, industry, or economy to reach far beyond its geography, the first consideration in both codes is neighbor relations. This creates a solid base from which to uptake further social responsibility initiatives.

The ambitions of the Argentinian code with regard to social responsibility have been appropriately adjusted to the unique needs and capabilities of their communities and industry. Thus, the focus of the section narrows to investment in the immediate community.

Traffic issues warrant their own item in the section. Vineyards and wineries are encouraged to participate in forums on the matter in their communities, respond to neighbor's concerns regarding traffic caused by business operations, and ensure that engaging with their business is easily accessible for neighbors.

Community education and health are two more items that complete the section.

Similarly, participating in community forums on these topics and assisting in building capacity in the improvement of these sectors are key points. With specific attention to health, the vineyards and wineries are encouraged to provide health-related services to their personnel and the community, including vaccinations, nutritious sustenance, and hygiene products.

New Zealand: Recognized Seasonal Employer Program

New Zealand faces a unique challenge in its labor market: 100 percent employment. The island nation simply does not have enough workers to support a robust viticulture industry, with its demand for a pool of unskilled, seasonal labor. There is an excess supply of low-skilled workers in Pacific Island countries and only limited opportunities domestically for formal employment. To stabilize the supply of labor for harvest and seasonal work in the vineyard, New Zealand created the Recognized Seasonal Employer (RSE) program. The RSE policy has deliberately focused on recruiting low-skilled and unskilled workers from rural areas where there are limited opportunities for employment.

RSE recruits workers from countries participating in the Pacific Island Forum (with the exception of Fiji) to work in New Zealand's horticultural and viticultural industries. The employer is responsible for paying for the flight to New Zealand, paying a market wage to the worker, providing basic pastoral care, and covering any costs associated with the process should an employee not return to their home country. Introduced in 2007, RSE has provided the necessary labor to foster a blossoming wine industry in New Zealand.

Workers themselves benefit from the program, citing improved English skills, greater wages, and increased ability to support their families. Despite purchasing their own return plane ticket and paying registration costs, participating in the program yields considerably higher wages for the workers than those they would collect working in their home communities. Studies show that this has translated into greater schooling for children 15–18 years old, increased durable goods purchases (small appliances, small personal vehicles), and more bank accounts being opened for families with a participating laborer.

A number of social development gains have resulted from the program, including an increased flow of remittances back to their home communities; more productive use of remittances (e.g., for entrepreneurial or investment activities, not just consumption); and work-specific training to make workers more productive and/or enabled to move into higher-paying jobs (e.g., supervisors, forklift drivers).

Community and religious leaders from the communities that send workers report increased donations and investments in communal projects. Though the labor recruitment process varies from country to country and even region-to-region, these leaders are often engaged in the worker nomination and pre-screening process. By being involved in the process, these leaders have successfully encouraged participants to invest not just for their families but also in their communities.

RSE is not without critique. Difficulties understanding registration, instances in which pastoral care has not been sufficient, and a lack of power on behalf of the

Field worker in California

Credit: Wine Institute

workers have been reported. Sending money back to Pacific Island home countries is also expensive. Greater engagement between home communities and international financial institutions could likely improve the program.

Nearly every OECD country has a migrant laborer policy, but New Zealand's serves as a model to replicate where possible.

South Africa: Wine Industry Ethical Trade Association

South Africa's Wine Industry Ethical Trade Association (WIETA) was formally established in November 2002. The association arose out of an Ethical Trade Initiative

(ETI) pilot project in the wine industry in the late 1990s. The pilot assisted the ETI, its retail corporate members, and South African partners to develop and refine inspection methodologies in monitoring their base code. It was also instrumental in bringing together private sector, labor, and civil society stakeholders in the wine industry of the Western Cape to discuss and debate issues around ethical trade.

WIETA has had considerable success in the wine industry, which led to the decision in October 2005 to extend its work down the wine supply chain and into the wider agricultural sector, while continuing to serve the needs of the wine industry.[11]

Despite the establishment of the WIETA program, conditions continued to deteriorate on some wine and fruit farms, and in 2011 Human Rights Watch released a report, *Ripe with Abuse*, that documented the terrible conditions under which many laborers within the fruit and wine industry were living and working. Denied adequate housing, proper safety equipment, and basic labor rights, the laborers are often exposed to pesticides and have no access to toilets or drinking water while working. The 96-page report is based on more than 260 interviews with farmworkers, farm owners, government officials, union officials, and academic experts.

While South African law guarantees wages, benefits, and safe working and housing conditions for workers and other farm dwellers, the laws are not consistently enforced. Additionally, some employers discourage or even prevent workers from joining unions. Even if they could join, it might not amount to much—farm worker unions in South Africa are among the most poorly organized.

As of 2011, Western Cape had about 107 inspectors responsible for inspecting over 6,000 farms. Not all farms were found to be in violation of basic human/labor rights. Some farmers take good care of their employees, going well beyond the legal standards. They give workers land to grow their own crops, pay the full cost of medical visits, provide free food to workers in the winter, or have set up trusts that benefit farmworkers. These farmers, when interviewed, said that this type of preventive care could be profitable for business.

In a press release on the Human Rights Watch website entitled, "South Africa: Farmworkers' Dismal, Dangerous Lives," Daniel Bekele, executive director of the Africa Division at Human Rights Watch, is quoted as saying, "The answer is not to boycott South African products, because that could be disastrous for farmworkers. But we are asking retailers to press their suppliers to ensure that there are decent conditions on the farms that produce the products they buy and sell to their customers."

As a result of this investigative report, in 2012, the South African wine industry expanded its WIETA program. Today, WIETA is a multistakeholder organization that actively promotes ethical trade in the wine industry value chain through training, technical assessment, and audits to assess members' compliance with its code of good practice. With over 1,100 members, their stakeholders include producers, retailers, trade unions, NGOs, and the government.

The WIETA ethical seal testifies to reasonable working conditions based on rigorous and closely monitored qualification criteria. This is believed to be a world-first among wine-producing countries.

The code contains the following important principles:[12]

- Child labor shall not be utilized.
- Employment shall be freely chosen.
- The right to a healthy and safe working environment.
- The right to freedom of association.
- The right to living wage.
- Working hours shall not be excessive.
- Harsh or inhumane treatment is prohibited.
- Unfair discrimination is prohibited.
- Regular employment shall be provided.
- Workers' housing and tenure security rights will be respected.

The code is based on the International Labor Conventions, ETI base code, and South African legislation and sets out in more detail what each of the above principles entails within the agricultural context.

Chile

In 2011, it was estimated that there were between 15 and 20 percent fewer vineyard workers in Chile than in 2009.[13] Industry experts attribute this to several factors:

- There is competition for workers with other sectors of the economy.
- Increasing mechanization.
- The 2010 earthquake created many higher-paying construction jobs.
- In some parts of the supply chain, specifically small farms, labor laws on vineyards are inconsistently enforced, including the legal requirement to provide protection from pesticide exposure to workers (while sometimes workers don't want to use protective gear, creating problems for themselves and employers).
- Workers are looking for year-round employment, not seasonal work.

As of January 1, 2013, Chile's Sustainability Code had a number of requirements that fall within a long-term vision based on the combination of environmental, social equality, and economic viability principles. Evaluations apply to each of these categories. Individual grape growers are initially evaluated against the green environmental chapter of the Code; when they become part of a larger supply chain of a certified winery, they must also be evaluated by the social equality standards.

The general goal of this project is to provide the Chilean wine-growing industry with tools and competencies that allow them to strengthen their commitment with sustainability and to integrate social responsibility into their strategic management.

Social responsibility standards of Chile's Code are unique in that these social standards are of the same priority as other standards, such as the environmental chapter. These standards in its Orange chapter include general business ethics; practice of ethical principles within the company, with suppliers, with outsourcing personnel, and within the state; community and working life quality, and commitment to human rights. There is an emphasis on implementation and monitoring.

Additionally, they must provide environmental education to their employees and vendors. As for working-life quality, vineyards and wineries being evaluated must respect diversity and provide equal entry and access to work shifts; allow workers to participate in the management of the company; maintain relationships with organized worker groups or unions; provide professional job development; maintain labor health and safety, and accommodate retirement options for workers. Wine companies must also have a commitment to the community and use their marketing and communication programs to develop trustworthy and transparent relationships with the community and consumers.

It is important to note that for the social responsibility standards, it is not the wine that is being certified but the winery and its ongoing management practices that are the subject of evaluation and certification.

Furthermore, while many social aspects of labor rights and human rights are requirements in national legislation, what the social code requires from companies is to show their procedures, strategies, and tools to demonstrate compliance with the law and ensure that social legislation is being completely fulfilled.

GOVERNMENT REGULATION: FARM WORKER HEALTH AND SAFETY IN U.S. AGRICULTURE

Issues of worker safety and fair treatment are not just limited to developing countries that have weak labor laws or lax enforcement. The report *Field of Poison: California Farmworkers & Pesticides*, published by Californians for Pesticide Reform (CPR) in 1999 and updated in 2002, documented the dangerous conditions under which farm workers toil in the production of crops and agricultural commodities. The research published in *Field of Poison* showed how long workdays, equipment injuries, physical labor, and exposure to pesticides and other chemicals make agriculture one of the most hazardous industries in which to work.

From 1991 to 1996, the California Environmental Protection Agency's Department of Pesticide Regulation reported 3,991 cases of poisoning by agricultural pesticides for an average of 665 cases per year. Pesticide exposure and the illnesses that result from it likely go underreported, as employees are reluctant to report exposure for fear of retaliation and/or termination. Both employers and employees may lack the training necessary to identify exposure or contamination, or to distinguish it from other non-exposure illness.

Most pesticide poisonings occur when workers are in the field—picking, harvesting, pruning, and so on. Grapes and soil fumigation lead in numbers of poisonings. Grapes ranked first in reported illnesses, attributed in part to frequent high-level applications of sulfur. Soil ranked second with 222 cases listed. Of those cases, 195 (97 percent) involved exposure to soil fumigants.[14]

Further exacerbating the health impacts, families of farmworkers also come into contact with pesticides in a variety of ways. Farmworkers and their families may wash their hands, outside of the house, in run-off water that contains pesticides from the surrounding fields. Pesticides can drift into their yards, homes, schools, and daycare centers when located near fields. Farmworker parents can also bring pesticides into the home on their tools, clothes, shoes, and skin and can expose their children through something as simple as a hug before they shower. The lack of washing machines in most farmworker homes means that farmworkers' clothing may not be washed as often and will not come as clean as it would if washed in a machine. In addition, workers may wash contaminated clothes with the general family laundry, rather than separating them first.[15]

The U.S. Environmental Protection Agency (EPA) estimates that 10,000–20,000 farmworkers are poisoned on the job each year due to pesticide exposure. However, accurate reporting is difficult, as there is no national surveillance system for acute pesticide illness reporting and no surveillance system for tracking chronic illness related to pesticide exposure.

An organization called Farmworker Justice (based in Washington, D.C.) seeks to empower migrant and seasonal farmworkers across the country to improve their living and working conditions, immigration status, health, occupational safety, and access to justice. Recommendations include increasing farmworker access to medical care and increasing their "right to know" about hazards associated with working with various pesticides.

California and Washington State have incident reporting systems. Since 1971, California law requires physicians to report any known or suspected illness caused by a pesticide exposure. In California, in 2009, there were a total of 916 reported cases, which were found to be possibly, probably, or definitely related to pesticides. In Washington State, the Pesticide Illness Monitoring and Prevention Program investigates about 300 pesticide-related illness cases annually.[16]

In 2012, due to a lawsuit filed by a farmworker, the California Supreme Court questioned whether the California Department of Pesticide Regulation (CDPR) complied with its legal obligation to consider alternative methods of pest control when considering the toxic fumigant methyl iodide in 2010. In approving the fumigant, CDPR shunned the findings of top scientist—including the state's own Scientific Review Committee—which has consistently said that the chemical is too dangerous to be used in agriculture. Methyl iodide causes late-term miscarriages, contaminates groundwater, and is so reliably carcinogenic that it's used to create cancer cells in laboratories.

In January 2015, the California legislature announced new strict regulations targeting chloropicrin, a pesticide injected into the ground before planting crops such as strawberries, tomatoes, and almond orchards. The state now has the strictest regulations in the country, and farmers are limited to applying the pesticide on up to 40 acres in one day, a reduction of 75 percent.[17]

Also in early 2015, California expanded liability for worker injuries on the job. At least half of the state's farmworkers are employed by farm labor contractors and not directly by farmers themselves. But a new state law that went into effect January 1, 2015, established joint employer liability in cases where an employee of a labor contractor is injured on the job. Now it is not merely the farm labor contractor liable for those injuries, but the farmer who hired the labor contractor.

Growers must communicate work expectations clearly. It isn't enough to have a poster or flier, especially since some employees may have the equivalent of a third-grade education. Compounding the challenge for employers is that the California Agricultural Labor Relations Board requires that communication must be in the language of the employee, and that includes indigent Mexican populations that do not speak either Spanish or English, but an indigenous language.

Employers are also responsible for housing conditions for farm workers. In early 2016, farm labor contractor Four Seasons Vineyard Management Inc. and winemaker Ridge Vineyards Inc. were fined a total of $42,000 for providing "deplorable" housing for farm workers by the U.S. Department of Labor. Several housing violations were found to pose a direct and imminent threat to the safety and health of workers living in a housing facility in Healdsburg, located in Sonoma County, California, on property owned and controlled by Ridge Vineyards, with substantial control of the facility by Four Seasons Vineyard Management. Both entities were held jointly liable for the housing conditions.

The Department of Labor Wage and Hour Division ruled that vineyard owners and farm labor contractors who employ and house farm workers are responsible for ensuring the safety of the housing they are providing for their employees. In addition, vineyard owners who use contractors to recruit and hire farm workers can be jointly responsible for ensuring these workers are being paid in compliance with the law and housed and transported safely. In the Ridge Vineyards case, there were numerous violations and hazardous conditions including exposed electrical wiring, fire hazards, and poor ventilation, and the housing lacked protective screens and doors, exposing the inhabitants to the elements.

The Labor Department recovered back wages due to the workers for the rent that the contractor illegally deducted from their pay.

At the national level, the U.S. EPA announced at the end of September 2015 new rules for farmworker safety. Described as "a dream come true" by United Farm Workers President Arturo Rodriguez, these new rules have been long overdue, as EPA pesticide safety standards hadn't been updated since 1992.

Significant among those changes include annual mandatory training sessions to inform farmworkers on required protections. The rules had required this training once every five years. There is also a minimum age requirement of 18 to handle pesticides. The previous rule had no age requirement.

Other revisions to the 1992 Agricultural Worker Protection Standards, include:

- Expanded training must include instructions to reduce take-home exposure from pesticides on work clothing and other safety topics.
- Expanded mandatory posting of no-entry signs for the most hazardous pesticide-treated areas until residues in these fields decline to a safe level.
- New no-entry application-exclusion zones up to 100 feet surrounding pesticide application equipment to protect workers and others from exposure to pesticide overspray.
- Mandatory record keeping to improve states' ability to follow up on pesticide violations and enforce compliance, with records of application-specific pesticide information, as well as farmworker training, must be kept for two years.
- Stricter anti-retaliation provisions.
- Changes in personal protective equipment must be tested to ensure respirators are effective, including a fit test, medical evaluation, and training.
- Specific amounts of water must be used for routine washing, emergency eye flushing, and other decontamination, including eye-wash systems for handlers at pesticide mixing/loading sites.
- No grace period for training: worker must be trained before working in an area where pesticides had been used or a restricted-entry interval (REI) has been in effect in the past 30 days.

The EPA Administrator estimated that each year more than 3,000 potentially preventable pesticide exposure incidents are reported to the agency. The new rules are intended to reduce that number. Some aspects of the new regulations are already being implemented by California, but California will need to readdress issues regarding who gets to train farmworkers.

California Seasonal Harvest

At the peak of the harvest season, California needs some 400,000 farmhands, with 70 percent of them usually undocumented immigrants, according to the California Farm Bureau Federation.

A 2012 Pew Research Center survey estimated that 6.3 percent of California's population is unauthorized immigrants, making California and Texas the second highest states in the nation after Nevada (7.6 percent). Pew also estimates that 29 percent of California's agricultural workers are unauthorized immigrants—higher than every state but New Jersey and Washington. A 2005 study by United Farmworkers showed that 75 percent of U.S. farmworkers were born in Mexico.

In 2013, many California vineyards experienced a delay in harvesting their grapes due to a shortage in workers. Increased deportations and a tougher stance on undocumented workers have made many immigrants wary of traveling throughout the state to search for work. Additionally, with a recovering economy, traditional field laborers are finding better-paying jobs in construction, landscaping, and other agricultural products.

There is some evidence of improvements in conditions for workers in California, especially in Napa Valley:[18]

- Entry-level Napa Valley farmworkers are usually hired for a minimum wage of $12/hour, substantially more than the national average—not just for agriculture, but the entire private sector. Experienced Napa Valley farmworkers and those with certificates and additional training can be paid as much as $40/hour.
- Year-round employment is a regular occurrence, as vineyards often need upkeep year-round.
- The foundation Napa Valley Grapegrowers (an organization that heralds itself as a steward of the region's land and community) provides educational opportunities for farmworkers (ranging from safety in the vineyard to English language) totaling over 215 hours to more than 2,800 farmworkers in 2014.
- The 2011 Napa Valley Wages & Benefits Survey shows that 91 percent of supervisors and 69 percent of vineyard workers are offered medical insurance plans (compared to 52 percent nationwide in the private sector) and 55 percent are offered 401k plans in Napa.

It's worth noting that the most high-paying agricultural jobs—tending vineyards in Napa and Sonoma Counties—increasingly go to workers who are legally in the United States. "What used to be a migrant population that worked their way up the state, coming here after picking strawberries, that has changed totally," said Jennifer Putnam, executive director of Napa Valley Grapegrowers. "Now we have year-round work for them. The quality that people expect in wine is predicated on knowledgeable, skilled farmworkers. This is not rote commodity agriculture that we're doing here."

Napa vineyards also need seasonal labor. "We do have labor shortages. We have 45,000 acres of grapevines that all need to be picked within a six-week timeframe," Putnam said. "Even more compact is the pruning, which all needs to be done in January and February."[19]

Napa is the only county in the United States where growers assess themselves in order to fund farmworker-housing centers, where individuals benefit from lodging, meals, laundry, and recreational amenities.

Harvest in Sonoma
Credit: Wine Institute

TAKING THE NEXT STEP: STRATEGIC PHILANTHROPY AND CREATING SHARED VALUE

Understanding the needs of workers and communities, the wine industry must take steps to address them. Successful businesses now recognize that philanthropy is a key component of corporate citizenship and overall business strategy. In 2015, U.S. corporations donated more than $18 billion to nonprofits—and billions more if the value of employee volunteerism is included.

Yet too often, corporate philanthropy is random and uncoordinated. To be truly effective, it must be strategic. Strategic philanthropy is a unique and powerful way to combine company-marketing goals with the desire to increase the well-being of mankind. It is a positioning that usually connects a company with a not-for-profit organization or cause. In this way, while the company is being helpful and working for the common good in its community, the business is receiving parallel benefits. These benefits include exposure, lead generation, employee retention, and increases in performance and productivity. They can even include benefits to the bottom line.

Strategic philanthropy can be useful in market differentiation and distinguishing a business from some competitors who are stuck in old "business as usual" paradigms, thinking that the purpose of business is merely to sell things and make money. Authentic strategic philanthropy is based upon the advantages of a much more empowering and abundance-filled set of beliefs: that the purpose of business is to understand and meet many groups' needs, including the owner(s), employees, consumers, community, and even the natural environment. The high-level purpose of business is to create and distribute excellent products and services, in a manner that generates profits and abundance for everyone involved.

To create a strategic philanthropy program, or to make an existing program more strategic, a business must take this approach:

Understand the positive impact of profitability.

Align all of the resources.

Develop a comprehensive strategy.

Create Shared Value.

Next it must create an action plan to:

Set a clear mission and goals.

Narrow the focus and manage for impact.

Communicate with stakeholders.

Engage in strategic partnerships and plan for them to evolve over time.

Design cause marketing campaigns.

Understand the positive impact of profitability.

Donations can make a difference to the recipient and also contribute positively to an entity's bottom line. Internally, such efforts enhance employee recruitment, retention, productivity, and engagement—thereby reducing a company's cost of operations.

Externally, strategic corporate philanthropy improves customer attraction and loyalty, reputation, brand awareness, risk management, and overall community image with stakeholders. These benefits can increase sales and support a company's social license to operate. Social license can be defined as the community's approval of a specific project, expansion, or business plan. It can be interpreted as the trust by neighbors that the enterprise will conduct its business in a socially and environmentally responsible way and will do no harm to the best interests of the community. Having a social license to operate paves the way for regulatory approvals, permits, waivers, or other political consent needed by a business. In the case of wineries, this can mean a waiver to access water tables, approval to convert existing land to a vineyard, or resentment at the rapid growth of vineyards and wineries.

In fact, it is more accurate to describe the social license as the approval of a "network of stakeholders" rather than the community more generally. Key external stakeholders include customers, neighbors, activists, suppliers, regulators, investors, public shareholders, lenders, media, and community leaders.

Align all of the resources.

Businesses have tremendous resources to contribute to good causes. Too often, however, these efforts are random and uncoordinated. Aligning all of a company's resources—including human and intellectual capital, products, skills, and volunteerism, as well as financial capacity—in support of carefully chosen nonprofit partners promotes deeper stakeholder engagement. In addition, aligning philanthropic strategy with a company's products and operations creates synergy between philanthropy and business objectives.

Examples include health care company support of wellness, disease prevention, and cure; manufacturing company support of environmental issues; technology company support of STEM education—science, technology, engineering, and math; food production company support of hunger-related initiatives; and resource extraction company support for creating small enterprises in different sectors to create local economic growth, so positive commercial activity still exists even after the mines are closed or when the harvest is done. An illustrative example is the Mercy Corps Community Health and Advancement Initiative (CHAI) project in India that has helped thousands of youth from tea gardens with scholarships, technical skills trainings, and apprenticeships—like working in a local beauty parlor or as a paramedic. Engaging with community groups and nonprofits can help identify what are the most important needs that a winery can help address.

Develop a comprehensive strategy.

Companies devote much time and talent to developing strategies for business success. Philanthropic strategy has rarely enjoyed the same rigorous analysis. Community citizenship should be considered a key part of annual planning. Philanthropic values and plans should be elevated in importance and incorporated into every aspect of the business—to create a culture that empowers and engages all stakeholders in corporate philanthropy. In today's highly competitive environment, corporate philanthropy must be more than random acts of kindness. It must be treated as a critical element of business success—helping companies achieve the highly valued triple bottom line of people, planet, and profit.

Recent studies have shown that many companies are discovering they can have a real, lasting impact on important social and environmental causes, while also creating significant value for employees, business units, and reputation—benefits that go beyond the traditional goals of corporate giving. Starbucks, for instance, is committed to increasing access to education and training in the communities that produce its coffee, tea, and cocoa. Chevron made the elimination of mother-to-child transmission of HIV a priority in Angola, Nigeria, and South Africa, where the virus affects employees and communities in which the company operates. And Pfizer's Global Health Fellows program offers employees three- to six-month assignments to help address a range of global health issues in partnership with development organizations in over 40 countries around the world. The program has given Pfizer a better understanding of global health concerns and has allowed employees to use their skills to directly help those in need.[20]

Activities such as these are important tools for increasing employee engagement and commitment. They can also promote learning, as employees gain new skills at the same time that they transfer capabilities to the nonprofits they work with. Importantly, they create important stakeholder relationships in markets that are critical to existing business operations and future growth.

Of course, most wine companies are not global, like these corporate examples, and their sphere of influence is usually local. However, the process of determining what philanthropic and social efforts align best with the business is pretty much the same for small and large enterprises.

Slow growth, budget constraints, and a focus on getting more value from tight resources create pressures for business managers and of course affect charitable giving. CSR and company foundation managers must figure out how to do more with less and achieve a greater return on their social investments.

Create shared value.

To respond to competing pressure from investors, governments, and activists, innovative businesses approach their giving strategically by improving the business climate and infrastructure in the places where they operate. This approach is called corporate shared value (CSV), originally proposed by Michael Porter of Harvard University Business School, and Mark Kramer of the social impact advisory firm FSG. Companies could bring business and society back together if they redefined their purpose as creating "shared value"—generating economic value in a way that *also* produces value for society by addressing its challenges.

A shared value approach reconnects company success with social progress and views social responsibility not as damage control or a PR campaign but as an opportunity for value creation for the company and the community. CSV is a powerful concept that can prompt companies to think differently about their approach to social and environmental issues. It is a way to grow economies, marketplaces, companies, and communities in the long-term interest of businesses and all their stakeholders.

An example of shared value: Starbucks redesigned its coffee procurement system into C.A.F.E. Practices described in Chapter 1 and also created regional agronomy offices called Farmer Support Centers in Costa Rica, Ethiopia, and Rwanda. In these centers, knowledgeable agronomists work intensively with small farmers on practices to improve productivity, quality, and environmental conservation of water, soil, and animal species. This was done in partnership with a number of expert NGOs and also the U.S. Agency for International Development. The company pays farmers, co-ops, and mill owners a premium for better beans and also works with the Fair Trade organization to ensure co-ops invest a portion of the premium in community projects. Even if some of the coffee is sold to another roaster, the overall economy improves. Higher yields and better quality have increased the growers' incomes, while the environmental impact of farms has been reduced and a continuing supply of high-quality coffee is ensured. Over time, these coffee farmers and farm workers have earned the resources to keep their children in school, build better homes, and fund health clinics through their co-ops. Shared value was created.

Unilever provides good examples of CSV. The Unilever Sustainable Living Plan intends to double the size of its business while reducing its environmental footprint and increasing its positive social impact—with a focus on deforestation and climate change; water, sanitation, and hygiene; and sustainable agriculture and smallholder farmers. The company approaches these issues as a moral duty and a business opportunity. In 2012, Unilever reported that it reached 224 million people with programs to reduce diarrheal disease through hand washing with soap; provide safe drinking water; promote oral health, and improve young people's self-esteem. Unilever's brand Lifebuoy soap reached 71 million people in 16 countries in 2012—five times as many people as in 2010. It is also one of Unilever's fastest-growing brands and achieved double-digit growth over 2010–2012.

Another Unilever example of CSV, and also integrating sustainability into the brand proposition, is dry shampoos such as TRESemmé and Dove that don't require hot water. This small change results in 90 percent fewer greenhouse gas emissions compared to washing hair in heated water. With Flora/Becel margarines, using technological innovation, the biggest of its kind for 60 years, Unilever has been able to reduce saturated fats by around 25 percent and calories by 20 percent, contributing to healthier consumers and a healthier bottom line.

CSV involves a commitment to creating inclusive economies that expand opportunities for more broadly shared prosperity, especially for those communities facing the greatest barriers to advancing their well-being. Agricultural firms, guided by the SAI recommendations, should seek to solve the problem of how to build vibrant, adaptive rural communities while at the same time empowering farmers and workers, increasing their self-reliance.

The wine industry could make strategic investments in their communities, to better integrate social justice in its business strategy and improve social conditions in rural communities. This can be accomplished not simply by making annual donations to schools and clinics, as important as those efforts are, but also enhancing empowerment (e.g., by providing facilities to build a strong rural social infrastructure) to alleviate rural communities' poverty and to ensure creation of quality employment.

For example, in U.S. wine regions, the industry could enhance the inclusion of Mexican-American workers in the economic growth, through education, training, and partnering with government to provide small business loans. For decades, these individuals were hired as guest workers and migrant labor, tending the vines upon which Napa and Sonoma Valleys' international reputation rests; planting rootstocks, picking ripened fruit, and fermenting the juice into wine. No longer migrant labor, many are now residents, yet they remain underrepresented in winery tasting rooms, as managers, or as business owners supplying products and services to this lucrative industry.

Another good example is the South Africa wine industry, which has not integrated indigenous workers into the industry, continuing its discrimination in worker housing and compensation, failing to create opportunities for black-owned wineries and winemakers. Of the 350 exhibitors at the 2015 Cape Wine exhibition, only 1 was a black-owned winery.

Successful wineries could take this "shared value" approach and create strategic partnerships that help to prepare workers for leadership and entrepreneurship. Investing in suppliers and creating economic revitalization and development should be goals of supplier diversity in U.S. wine regions and black economic empowerment in South Africa.

Once the company is clear on its approach, it can set an action plan:

Set a Clear Mission and Goals.

What is the company trying to achieve with its giving program? Are there particular issues that connect to the core business or resonate with employees, business leaders, and stakeholders? Making deliberate choices about what activities or causes the company will and will not contribute to is important. What's important here is to align the internal management team on the priorities and ensure that they see the company's charitable giving as a strategic lever rather than a pot of money for pet projects that are beyond the company's strategic focus.

Narrow your focus and manage for impact.

Many companies dilute their efforts by managing a highly fragmented portfolio with many small grants devoted to a wide range of causes. To have a greater impact, consider giving more money to a small number of causes that align with the company's business, and build expertise over time in those key areas. This focused approach is also a more effective way to build a positive association with the company's brand and helps to measure impact and results over time. For instance, Ken Wright Cellars in Oregon has become nearly synonymous with ¡Salud!, a project to provide health care for seasonal workers and their families.

Communicate with stakeholders.

Key internal and external stakeholders are too often unaware of a company's commitment to community. Developing real two-way communication avenues will create a feedback loop that informs all participants about what works and what does not. This means actually having a social engagement team member or community relations staff person who interacts with the community on a regular basis through one-on-one conversations, town hall meetings, round tables, and grievance mechanisms. Depending on the size of the business and potential ongoing impact on community interests, it could mean establishing a formal community advisory panel to share upcoming business plans in advance.

The growing importance of corporate social responsibility has made businesses realize the need for an effective communications strategy. Such a strategy helps raise awareness of the social impact of the company's giving program, and sharing the success of corporate-giving efforts helps establish the company's commitment locally or globally. It is therefore critical to share the value of these efforts with employees, the community, and other key stakeholders.

Engage in strategic partnerships and plan for the relationships to evolve over time.

Businesses can improve their social and environmental performance and find new market opportunities through partnerships with nongovernmental organizations—or NGOs. As the name implies, NGOs are groups that are not directly affiliated with a government and that work for social or environmental purposes. NGOs are usually nonprofit organizations, but there are as many different types of them as there are social causes. Some are academic and research-oriented, like the African Wildlife Foundation; whereas others focus more on direct service, like Save the Children; and still others devote their resources to advocacy work, like Greenpeace. NGOs that work in partnership with companies are typically human rights and labor rights groups, environmental groups, religious organizations, women's organizations, community development associations, children's organizations, and sociological research institutes.

NGOs also vary widely in their geographical scope and management structure. Some are like multinational corporations in that they have their headquarters in one country but branches or operations in a number of countries. These international or regional NGOs are usually rather sophisticated, somewhat bureaucratic, tend to have stronger management systems, and often have a network of affiliations with other NGOs; examples are Oxfam or CARE.

Other NGOs are locally based with a local or countrywide focus. These NGOs have varying degrees of sophistication, ranging from grassroots-level organizations to more formal, professional institutions. They are likely to have more direct contact with workers and communities than do their international counterparts.

Strategic partnerships are key to successful sustainability and social responsibility programs. These partnerships with nonprofit groups and with government entities who are knowledgeable about community needs and experts in such areas as poverty alleviation, human rights, and fair treatment of workers can assist wine companies in fulfilling their social goals while creating more vibrant rural communities.

Several of the case studies in this chapter highlight the important work being done in partnership with nonprofit groups that have the knowledge of the local community, the needs of intended beneficiaries, and also the expertise of how such programs can best be executed, expertise that the winery often does not have.

The primary motivation for a business to enter such a partnership is to enhance its brand, reputation, and credibility. On the other hand, NGOs enter partnerships primarily to access funds. Long-term stability and impact is the second most important motivation for both parties; therefore, each has an incentive to build long-term relationships. NGOs and companies can often accomplish more of their mutual social and environmental goals together than they could alone.

Businesses must get to know potential partners and make sure that expectations are aligned, before deciding which nonprofit partner is the best suited. Starbucks partnered with Conservation International to help train coffee farmers on its preferred sustainability growing techniques in Central America; with Save the Children for its educational programs for indigenous children in coffee growing communities in Guatemala; and with the African Wildlife Foundation for its farmer training programs in Kenya. The Nature Conservancy and General Mills have worked together for decades to protect lands and waters in the company's home state of Minnesota. This has helped them shape a global water footprint strategy for General Mills.

The South African wine industry partnered with the World Wildlife Fund to create the Biodiversity and Wine Initiative (BWI), in the Cape wine lands, which has promoted changes in farming practices that reduce impact on biodiversity of the Cape Floral Kingdom, one of "hottest hotspots" in the world, with over 7,000 plant species found nowhere else. One-third of the wine industry now has environmental management plans in place, together with training to deliver on these guidelines, and these wineries are certified as BWI Champions. In all these examples, the nonprofit organizations help design and execute the programs.

Partnerships with groups that only involve monetary donations from the company to the NGO should not be one-sided in its benefits. The corporate funder should receive adequate recognition for their donations and have opportunities to connect employees directly with the community projects. The NGO partner should help promote the important role the company plays in fulfilling its mission.

Business-NGO partnerships are complex and challenging. But they can benefit both the company and NGO participants while accomplishing an important and worthy cause. To give new partnerships the best chance of succeeding, approach relationships carefully, structure them thoughtfully, and seek ongoing, sustainable support and development as they evolve. Environmental conditions, interests, and positions will change. Social justice issues can be solved and human needs met. In some instances, these changes may mean that the partnership has run its course and served its purpose, which is great.

Design cause marketing campaigns.

Aside from outright donations, companies can often be strategic through cause marketing. Cause marketing is now the norm, and customers who visit a company's website and see their advertising want to know that the firm shares their desire to make the world a better place by supporting an important cause. As described in earlier chapters, the number of consumers who say they would switch from one brand to another, if the other brand were associated with a good cause, has climbed dramatically in recent years.

Cause marketing is an ideal way to create a strong connection between entrepreneurship and giving. The challenge is to make the socially responsible efforts a winning proposition for the NGO partner, the community, and the business. Here are five important steps:

- Cause marketing works best when a company's management and employees feel great about the help they are providing to a nonprofit group. They will work hard to make a difference when they truly believe in the cause.
- A company should choose a cause that relates to their business or products. For example, it is understandable why large wine and spirits distributors choose to sponsor projects urging responsible consumption of alcohol and prevention of drinking under the influence. A good example is South Africa's Backsberg Estate Cellars that marketed a special wine series to raise funds for worker housing.
- Contribute time and sweat equity. For many types of businesses, cause marketing involves donating products or services and not simply writing a check. This can help form even stronger consumer associations between the product and the good works. I recommend to clients that in addition to making grants to an organization they have senior managers volunteer to serve on the board of a local nonprofit, providing management, financial, and marketing expertise that can be more valuable as the funds the company donates.
- Work with the nonprofit to define how it will help the business increase its visibility, brand, or company awareness. If the organization has a newsletter or other communications with its constituents, do joint promotions, special offers to its members. Use the organization's logo and name in the marketing campaigns,

and permit the NGO to use the company logo and name in its press releases, on the organization's website, and in other materials.

Success in cause marketing often means motivating an audience to take action, such as making a donation or participating in an event. Using a dedicated marketing campaign, a company can reach and persuade the target group while also raising awareness for the business and its commitment to social responsibility. Consumer products companies have successfully raised millions of dollars for disaster relief while selling a related product to customers who might not otherwise know how or where to donate to relief efforts.

WINERY CSR BEST PRACTICES AND ILLUSTRATIVE CASE STUDIES

Talley Vineyard's Fund for Vineyard and Farm Workers, California (https://www.talleyvineyards.com/)

California's Talley Vineyards established an endowment in 2004, the Fund for Vineyard and Farm Workers, with the goal of amassing a $1M fund, the interest of which will fund (in perpetuity) grants to nonprofit organizations that assist San Luis Obispo County agricultural workers and their families. Their Mano Tinta series is specially designated for the fund, and local grape growers and winemakers are invited to produce their own specially designated wine as cause marketing for the endowment's sake. Mano Tinta, "Red Hand," is a wine dedicated to the pride and commitment of farm workers to their craft. All of the grapes, materials, and services used to make this wine are donated and all profits from the sales of Mano Tinta benefit the Fund.

The recipients of these funds are nonprofits dedicated to local charity work including education, reading programs, literacy, after school programs, and housing for migrant and seasonal labor. Using the product of their region and engaging with fellow wine businesses for the benefit of their community is the model of Talley Vineyards.

Lumos Wine Company, Oregon (http://www.lumoswine.com)

The Lumos Wine Company of Corvallis and McMinville, Oregon, is one of the first wineries to address sustainability holistically, with audits of the vineyards and the winery for social as well as environmental issues.

With this step, the Lumos Wine Company has shown its concern not just for how grapes are grown or the environment, but also for the well-being of the people whose hands help determine the quality of the final product.

"We're interested in looking at the whole system," said Dai Crisp, co-owner of Lumos and vineyard manager. "Sustainability is critical for the people and the land. Businesses are about the people involved and if you take care of your people they are invested in what you are doing. And if you manage the land sustainably you can minimize exposure to chemicals for the people and the fruit. That is why we use natural materials and a whole systems approach in the vineyard. We farm in a way that cycles the nutrients back into the ground and that has an impact on fruit quality. That's important because wine is food.

"I've managed our vineyards according to organic principles for many years," said Dai during our conversation in McMinville, Oregon, during the International Pinot Noir Celebration in July 2015. "Labor isn't a part of most of the other certification programs out there. You can't make wine without people in the vineyard. Many people view farm labor as unskilled. That just isn't the case. Our crew is a highly skilled workforce that is in the vineyard from December to October in every kind of weather."

RdV Vineyards, Virginia
(http://www.rdvvineyards.com/)

RdV Vineyards in Delaplane, Virginia, has "put the state of Virginia on the global wine map," according to wine critic Jancis Robinson. Founder and General Manager Rutger de Vink is a former U.S. Marine who spent 2001 working the harvest at nearby Linden Vineyards with renowned winemaker Jim Law. Today, RdV works with wine consultants based in Bordeaux to ensure the production of world-class wine.

Rutger's philosophy guides RdV's labor and community practices. From the beginning he was very adamant about having no seasonal workers/labor. "We have a full-time vineyard team of 4 workers. They work year round and have been here with us since the beginning. Most of them are now going on 8 years," said Josh Grainer, winemaker. In my interview with him, he stressed, "It's the right thing to do. And, quite frankly, it's also good business in the sense that these guys know these plants and all the winemaking processes intimately and care for them. It's a lot easier for someone like me—so I don't have to train individuals every year," Grainer said.

RdV's vineyard crewmembers are all from Mexico—Florencia and Puebla, Mexico. "We try to do the harvest all ourselves. If there is inclement weather bearing down on us, we will bring in part-time labor. It would certainly be cheaper to not employ a team of farmers throughout the dearth of winter. But we have the ability to do so, and it's something that Rutger feels is important, as do I, so we do it."

Another aspect of RdV's social responsibility is being a part of the community and the winery's charitable commitments to Hope for the Warriors and Navy Seals.

As a result, a lot of individuals coming back from combat spend a lot of time at the winery, including helping out with harvest. RdV did a special bottling in 2010 called Exurgo, and all of the proceeds from this wine went to Hope for the Warriors. "We don't do a very good job of advertising all this," Grainer said. "Indirectly, if folks visit us they get the feel for the family and community aspect of the vineyard."

Domaine Chandon, Argentina
(http://www.chandon.com/)

Domaine Chandon in Argentina has always prioritized their workforce for the development of their own personal growth. One of the first foreign investors in Argentina, the French champagne house Chandon, realized the region's great potential for sparkling wines after a visit to the region in the 1950s. As one of the most important sparkling wine labels in the world, their investment attracted other investors, and they are credited with creating a boom of foreign interest in the region.[21]

The winery has also collaborated with its neighbors on projects that produce a better quality of life. Bodegas Chandon believes that any company carrying out CSR should also consider other aspects such as job discrimination, appropriate building conditions, good wages, training opportunities and job growth, good working atmosphere, respect, ownership, and valuation.

Bodegas Chandon has been very successful in its priority program, "Education in Harvest." The harvest workers had been accustomed to taking their children to the vineyard at harvest time, which exposed them to a variety of risks and accidents. Since 2006, Bodegas Chandon has been going beyond the legal framework related to child labor and has implemented a recreational education program for children of pickers at harvest time. This happens during the month of February, when the children are not attending school. Up to 100 children between the ages of 1 and 15 are moved from their rural homes to the nursery garden and sports center of Tupungato, where they participate in sports and recreational activities. They also receive breakfast, lunch, and medical checks.

This program has been carried out in cooperation with the municipal government in Tupungato, the Ministry of Sport and Recreation, and the Ministry of Social Development of Mendoza. From the year 2010, "Education in Harvest" prompted the creation of the Provincial Program, "Good Harvest," that replicates similar experiences in various areas of Mendoza where others also benefit.

The program's positive impact led other companies to join, including Bodega Catena Zapata, Canale Group (Alco) Shirley Hinojosa, and Don Antonio Vineyards (Pulenta Brothers).

No doubt, this program strengthens the employment relationship of the harvesters, the moms and dads who can work in a concentrated way, knowing that their children are cared for and safe; and so the workers return to Chandon each year.

Backsberg Estate, South Africa
(http://backsberg.co.za/)

Individual wineries have used their product designs to create special wine series that benefit chosen causes. These "wines for a cause" have seen great success, engaging the consumer as a stakeholder in the sustainability cause by making the good identifiable and person-based.

In 1998, for example, South Africa's Backsberg Estate Cellars introduced a special wine series titled Freedom Road. A cause-marketing initiative, Freedom Road aimed to raise funds for housing construction projects so that laborers of Backsberg would own their own property without being encumbered by significant debt and lessening reliance on employer housing that is common in South Africa.

The South African government was a key player in this effort, providing housing subsidies for first-time homeowners. The workers themselves were responsible for maintaining their 14 hectares of land and the building itself. Backsberg created and marketed Freedom Road, financing the initiative for its laborers. The collaborative nature of the effort is evident, but the winery itself was the facilitator of the process, making it all possible.

PROMINENT CHARITIES AND GOOD WORKS IN THE UNITED STATES

Regional Partnerships

At the regional level, organizations are engaging with social responsibility in a number of exciting ways. Bonded by their geography, participating vineyards and wineries are joining together for greater social involvement, too.

Napa Auction
(http://auctionnapavalley.org/)

Since its first year in 1981, the annual Napa Auction has raised and donated $120M on behalf of philanthropic causes in its local community. Organized by Napa Valley Vintners, the auction seeks donations on behalf of local wineries. The packages include Napa Valley wine, as well as luxurious themed trips and planned vacations around the world. In 2013 alone the auction generated $18.7M with 49 lots donated by Napa's wineries.

In 2013, these donations went to a variety of local charities and initiatives with a wide array of purposes. Contributions include $3M to health care providers and access; $1.8M to education, $1M to mental and emotional health and wellness, $600K to family services, and $500K to geriatric care. In addition to these umbrella donations, $1M was set aside to aid in closing the achievement gap in Napa County schools. Another $2.5M was marked for creating the Wine Trail, as an effort to promote healthy living and highlight the natural beauty of California wine country.

In June of 2015, Auction Napa Valley brought in over $15.8 million in proceeds for local charities. David Pearson, 2015 honorary Auction Napa Valley chair and CEO of Opus One, recalls a recent example of how this money can be put to good use:

"Just a day after the South Napa Earthquake last August, an immediate cash infusion of just a few thousand dollars to the American Canyon Family Resource Center provided essential food and emergency supplies to a multitude of families in dire need. Imagine what we can continue to provide for our community with this year's Auction Napa Valley's proceeds."

In addition to the clear good that comes from philanthropic giving, such an event organized at a regional level raises the profile of all of Napa Valley's wine, branding them as wines for causes, products that do good. This positive image translates relatively simply into marketing and consumer recognition.

Must! Charities
(http://www.mustcharities.org/)

Another great example of regional partnerships making a difference in the wine industry is Must! Charities in San Luis Obispo's North County of California. Must! works to empower local health, education, and social service organizations to make significant changes in the lives of children in the area. Given the proximity to the Paso Robles and Santa Lucia Highlands AVAs, many of those in need are children of seasonal workers. Must! works with organizations like The Boys and Girls Club to ensure that these children have a safe place to go after school and have mentors in the community to lean on.

Must! Charities is dedicated to improving quality of life through empowering local organizations to make lives better for the families that are often a part of the larger wine industry (seasonal workers, etc.). Recent projects include a partnership with the Big Brothers Big Sisters of San Luis Obispo County to partner young children with adult mentors in the community and working with The Food Bank Coalition's Children's Program to take meals to every eligible child in the north county.

Central Coast Wine Classic Foundation
(http://www.centralcoastwineclassic.org/foundation.php)

The Central Coast Wine Classic Foundation was created in 2004 to sustain 501(c) 3 foundations in San Luis Obispo County and Santa Barbara County whose missions are in the Healing, Performing and Studio Arts. From 2004 through 2014, the Foundation has granted over $2,500,000 to 125 such nonprofits.

WINERIES

Philanthropic giving is a tradition of many individual wineries and, as noted, is included in the sustainability codes of various industry organizations. Individual wineries also sponsor cause marketing efforts, creating a special wine series or brand to raise funds for a variety of social needs and to benefit chosen causes.

Murphy Goode
(http://murphygoodewinery.com/wine/homefront-red)

Through the sales of their Operation Homefront Red, Murphy Goode Winery supports Operation Homefront, an organization that provides emergency and financial assistance to the families of service members and wounded warriors.

Ehler's Estate
(http://www.ehlersestate.com/)

In 1985, French entrepreneur and philanthropist Jean Leducq began acquiring small parcels of vineyard land in Napa Valley's acclaimed St. Helena appellation—parcels that would eventually become Ehler's Estate. In 2002, Jean Leducq passed away from heart disease, leaving the winery in trust to the nonprofit Leducq Foundation that he and his wife had founded in 1996. One hundred percent of the profits from the sale of Ehler's Estate wines are returned to the Leducq Foundation, which awards over $30 million annually to directly support international cardiovascular research. Additionally, they produce a Cabernet Sauvignon with the name "One Twenty Over Eighty"—a nod to the ideal blood pressure (120/80) and to the heritage and main philanthropic cause of the estate.

Staglin Family Vineyards
(http://www.staglinfamily.com)

Staglin Family Vineyards in the Rutherford area of Napa Valley created the Salus wine label to support the International Mental Health Research Organization (IMHRO). IMHRO funds research to find better treatments and cures for schizophrenia, bipolar disorder, and depression. "Great wines for great causes" has been the winery's motto. The Staglin Family has donated and raised more than $800 million to support charities, including their main cause, the Music Festival for Brain Health, which brings together generous chefs, wineries, top-billed musicians, and scientists to raise significant funds and awareness for the cause of brain health.

Ken Wright Cellars
(http://www.kenwrightcellars.com/history.shtml)

¡Salud!, a program sponsored by winemaker Ken Wright, is a joint venture between the Oregon wine industry and Tuality Hospital, and provides health care for the seasonal workers and their families who are so integral to the industry. An annual event in November benefiting ¡Salud! showcases the Valley's top 42 pinot noir producers who auction just five cases of wine from the best barrel in their cellar. With over $6 million raised to date, ¡Salud! has had a profoundly positive health impact on thousands of seasonal workers and their families.

OTHER CHARITIES

Heart's Delight Wine Tasting and Auction
(http://www.heartsdelightwineauction.org/)

This four-day wine event brings top winemakers and culinary minds to Washington, D.C., to benefit the American Heart Association. The event began in 1999 in memory of Bruce Bassin of MacArthur Beverages, a wine and spirits destination in Washington, D.C. With demonstrations, tastings, and live and silent auctions, the 2014 event brought in over $1 million for the American Heart Association.

Heart Ball
(http://www.dcheartball.com/)

Also benefiting the American Heart Association is the Heart Ball—a black-tie event at the Mandarin Oriental in Washington, D.C., featuring spectacular live and silent auctions, seated dinner, inspirational stories of survival, live music, and dancing.

ONEHOPE
(http://www.onehopewine.com/about-us)

ONEHOPE is a social enterprise that integrates causes into products and services to make a greater social impact. Their cornerstone products are the ONEHOPE wines, and through a partnership with Robert Mondavi and produced in partnership with Rob Mondavi, Jr., their portfolio makes an impact with every bottle sold by donating half of the profits to partner causes, including organizations working toward breast cancer prevention and treatment, pediatric AIDS prevention and treatment, autism research and treatment, U.S. forest preservation and protection, and ending childhood hunger.

Benefit Wines
(http://www.benefitwines.com/)

Benefit Wines is an online wine retailer that specializes in creating wines for various charity organizations. Consumers can purchase wines for causes they support, with 100 percent of proceeds benefiting that charity. They've donated over $1.9 million since 2007.

Destin Charity Wine Auction Foundation
(http://www.dcwaf.org/)

The Destin Charity Wine Auction Foundation (DCWAF) connects wine enthusiasts to raise money to benefit children in need in Northwest Florida. Founded in 2005, DCWAF has donated more than $8 Million to Northwest Florida charities that support children afflicted by health issues and abuse.

The Grape Foundation
(http://www.thegrapefoundation.com/faq-s/)

The Grape Foundation receives wine and valuable gifts from all and any persons in the wine industry. They then auction off these gifts to benefit various children's charities.

Shoe Shine Wine
(http://shoeshinewine.com/about-us/)

Located in Berkeley, California, Shoe Shine Wine's goal is to help sustain and redefine California's own petite syrah varietal. Additionally, they are committed to and support a national Living Wage campaign.

Wine Sisterhood
(http://winesisterhood.com/)

Wine Sisterhood is an online community where women can join the conversation about wine, food, travel, style, and entertaining. They have a line of wines, one of which, also called Wine Sisterhood, benefits foundations that support women and families in need.

CSR in Wine Retail and Responsible Consumption of Alcohol

In its original sense, the term corporate social responsibility (CSR) is defined as a moral and stakeholder obligation, emanating from a notion that business is responsible to society in general and thus corporations should be answerable to those who directly or indirectly affect or are affected by a firm's activity. Despite these impressive good works by wineries just presented, the overall value of the alcohol industry's sustainability and social justice accomplishments remain questionable to some stakeholders. For example, public health advocates note the fundamental contradictions between the alcohol industry's claims of responsibility and their continuing promotion of alcoholic products.

CSR has become an integral element of the alcohol industry's self-representation and image. With renewed public awareness of the serious injuries that can be caused by alcohol consumption and the prospect of adverse implications on profits, a growing number of alcohol corporations are adopting CSR strategies in an attempt to portray themselves as good corporate citizens.

As alcohol manufacturers and national distributors develop their own unique CSR programs, these invariably include or involve some sort of sponsorship activities related to drinking responsibly, public awareness talks or dialogs, education programs, networking events, and partnerships with government as well as voluntary codes of practice for marketing and advertising.

Several support the World Health Organization's goal of reducing alcohol-related harm, have set specific goals in this regard, and have adopted programs to tackle misuse of alcohol and communicate about consuming alcohol responsibly. They support community empowerment and local projects. They make statements regarding good governance and ethics in society. And, they set measurable targets in all these areas to track their progress and report to stakeholders on their CSR priorities.

In the United States, organizations like Mothers Against Drunk Driving (MADD) and the Foundation for Advancing Alcohol Responsibility campaign against drunk driving promote responsible consumption and moderation. As a result of their successful organization efforts, these groups have become quite influential with local and state governments. The Foundation, established in 1991, is enhanced by the collective power (and reach) of their corporate members: Bacardi USA, Brown-Forman, Bean Suntory, Constellation Brands, Diageo, Edrington, Hood River Distillers, and Pernod Ricard USA.

Demand for Low-Alcohol Wines in Australia

In Australia, one of the big social responsibility issues within the wine industry is the link between high-alcohol wines and drunk driving. With many Australian wines topping out at 15–16 percent alcohol by volume, one glass can often put a driver over the legal limit for safely driving home. DrinkWise, an Australian nonprofit dedicated to creating a healthier and safer drinking culture in Australia, was established in 2005 by the alcohol industry. Their aim is to educate consumers (especially young consumers) on the dangers of binge drinking and to teach them to "drink properly."

As public service announcements and health warnings surrounding the dangers of drunk driving and over-consumption of alcohol increase, it appears that some consumers would prefer lower-alcohol wines so that they can consume a glass of wine without the associated risks. A 2013 study by the International Journal of Wine Research was the first of its kind to define the market opportunity for lower-alcohol wines in Australia. A survey of over 850 adults who drink wine regularly defined low-alcohol wine as containing 3–8 percent alcohol. The majority of respondents who would be interested in low-alcohol wines were women who typically drink wine with food. However, the study also revealed preferences for the taste of high-alcohol wine versus low-alcohol wine. So, the challenge lies in creating better-tasting (e.g., less sweet) low-alcohol wines, as there is a moderate segment of Australian consumers that would be interested in such a product.[22]

Consumers also want to manage their alcohol intake more easily because of increasingly tougher standards for drunk driving. In Australia and the European Union, the blood alcohol content (BAC) limit has been reduced from 0.08 to 0.05.

BUSINESS ETHICS

A responsible company isn't simply a good and generous philanthropist; it should also be an ethical company and conduct its business according to certain practices of honesty, trustworthiness, and integrity. Simply put, ethics involves learning what is right or wrong, and then doing the right thing—but "the right thing" is not nearly as straightforward as conveyed in a great deal of business ethics literature.

As recently as a decade ago, many companies viewed business ethics only in terms of administrative compliance with legal standards and adherence to internal rules and regulations. Today the situation is different. Attention to business ethics is on the rise across the world, and many companies realize that in order to succeed, they must earn the respect, confidence, and trust of their customers. The concept has come to mean various things to various people, but generally it's coming to know what is right or wrong in the workplace and marketplace, and doing what's right in regard to effects of products/services and in relationships with stakeholders.

Like never before, corporations are being asked, encouraged, and prodded to improve their business practices to emphasize legal and ethical behavior. Of course, businesspersons should absolutely comply with the law but should also observe laid down principles of morality and values in their dealings. Ethical values cover all aspects of business, including business strategies, treatment of employees, and treatment of suppliers as well as sales and accounting practices. Companies, professional firms, financial institutions, and individuals alike are being held increasingly accountable for their actions as demand grows for higher standards of corporate social responsibility and business behavior.

In some industries, ethics refers to a prescribed or accepted code of conduct. The Electronics Industry, for example, has formed the Electronics Industry Citizenship Coalition (EICC) and adopted the EICC Code of Conduct, which is a set of standards on social, environmental, and ethical issues in the electronics industry supply chain. Members are assessed on the various provisions of the code. Ethical issues are sometimes considered a set of moral values that should be addressed while carrying out business. Business ethics can also include critical issues of institutional governance and anti-corruption, with an expectation that firms will desist from taking part in corrupt practices such as selling low-standard goods or bribing government officials.

Wine is an area where trust particularly matters. Ethics in the wine industry can include manipulation and use of additives during wine production; nonpayments by and to producers involving importers, distributors, service providers, and marketing agencies; truth in advertising; customer service; nondelivery by merchants; honest communication by wine critics; ethical advertising; and counterfeiting. I've also been amazed when importers and brand agents recount instances where they have heard distributors lie to retailers and restaurant managers alleging that the wine they are selling is sustainably produced or grown according to organic methods (without the certification, of course) when in fact this is totally untrue. At least they recognize that retailers and restaurant sommeliers want sustainable wines. Hopefully, they are just misinformed and uneducated about what that means exactly, and not deliberately misleading the retailer.

Honesty in Communications

The Ethics of Wine Writing

Along with America's growing fascination with and increasing purchases of wine comes an opportunity for newspapers and wine specialty publications to provide an important service. Consumers typically turn to wine columns in newspapers or magazines to untangle some of the confusion caused by the myriad varietals and blends, foreign classification systems, and vintages. Yet these wine columnists and writers aren't always providing unbiased recommendations along with their education.

One of the most prized and time-honored tenets of American journalism is objectivity. When I studied journalism in college, one of the repeatedly stressed lessons of good news reporting was how critical it is to remain neutral. On their first day in a newsroom journalists are taught the importance of removing conflicts of interest and avoiding even the appearance of impropriety. The journalistic principle is a simple one: Don't accept anything from people you cover. But in fact, some wine writers do not see themselves as journalists at all, which conveniently enables them to sidestep the traditional tenets of ethical reporting.

Famed wine critic Robert Parker wrote, "The role of the [wine] critic is to render judgments that are reliable." For Parker, that means paying his own way—both in real life (he pays for over 60 percent of the wine he tastes and has not accepted gratuitous airline tickets or accommodations) and online (*The Wine Advocate* and eRobert-Parker.com are 100 percent subscriber funded and supported). This eliminates the need to "please" advertisers or "return the favor" by writing a good review, which unfortunately can be the way of the wine advertising world.

In an article on her website entitled, "The Ethics of Wine Writing," Jancis Robinson shares similar challenges in her work as one of the world's most heralded wine critics. She writes, "AXA Millésimes, for example, have been in the habit of sending out to wine writers a very handsome wooden carry case of examples of six of their wines (which include such landmarks as Pauillac second growth Ch Pichon Longueville). When I suggested to Christian Seely of AXA Millésimes that this might be construed as improper, he replied that this response plunged him into gloom. 'Has the world really become so politically correct?' seemed to be his gist. 'I want you to see how these wines are at a more mature stage (typically four or five years old) than when you taste them en primeur.' I pointed out that I did have quite a few examples of his wines in my cellar already but he sounded so glum and his feelings so hurt that I cancelled my cancellation, so to speak—although I still feel rather guilty about it. There seemed to be no way of solving this dilemma to our mutual satisfaction."[23]

Robinson also makes it a point to pay for her own accommodations while traveling and not to accept invitations to events outside the wine industry with wine industry folks. Additionally, her husband is a restaurant critic, so she steers clear from advising restaurants on their wine lists.

While it's clear that not every wine critic willingly or unwillingly abides by the stringent standards that many of the world's top wine critics abide by, the growing media attention given to these standards may serve to influence ethical standards for wine critics the world over.

Ethics in Marketing

WineTrust: UK is a British online retailer dedicated to sharing with their customers a constantly refreshed selection of 100 of the best wines, for their price, from all over the world. The managing director and founder, John Valentine, says that WineTrust was born out of the need for transparency in the wine retail industry, because existing retailers often mislead their customers when selling wine.

Valentine felt consumers were being shortchanged, often buying poor-quality wines at inflated prices simply because consumers had no real way of discerning value (quality for the price) at the point of purchase, especially online.

With many online shops inflating their prices to provide a "discount" on limited stocks of wine that may not be available for purchase elsewhere in the UK, customers aren't able to efficiently price compare or make an informed decision.

In contrast, WineTrust has a team of experts that meets at least 10 times a year to review its list and to agree what new wines to add and which wines to remove, while committing to a fresh and honest approach to wine selection and retailing. They strive to have a selection representative of the classic types available from across the world of wine, as well as some interesting wines that most would not usually stock.

The Wine Institute: Advertising/Marketing Standards

Applicable to the over 800 member wineries of the Wine Institute in California, Advertising Standards (and newly added Digital Marketing Standards) were put in place to ensure that members advertise their products in a responsible way to a legal audience. With many terms and conditions shaping the type of advertisement that is appropriate, the Wine Institute shows that it is proud of their members' wines and is committed to ensuring their wines are promoted responsibly to those adults who choose to consume them.

Some examples of guidelines include:

- Wine advertising shall encourage the responsible consumption of wine and shall be adult-oriented and socially responsible.
- Advertising of wine has traditionally depicted persons enjoying their lives and illustrating the role of wine in a mature lifestyle. Any attempt to suggest that wine directly contributes to success or achievement is unacceptable.
- Any advertisement that has particular appeal to persons below the legal drinking age is unacceptable, even if it also appeals to adults.
- Wine advertising shall in no way suggest that wine be used in connection with operating motorized vehicles such as automobiles, motorcycles, boats, snow-mobiles, or airplanes or any activities that require a high degree of alertness or physical coordination.
- A distinguishing and unique feature of wine is that it is traditionally served with meals or immediately before or following a meal. Therefore, wine advertising when appropriate should include food.

Counterfeiting and Fraud: Rudy Kurniawan

Probably the most well-known example of unethical behavior in the wine industry is the case of Rudy Kurniawan's counterfeiting trial and its implications for the wine industry, as well as some of the technological solutions that have been developed to deal with counterfeiting.

Kurniawan, an Indonesian wine collector, came onto the international wine scene in the early 2000s. He was known for his passion for vintage Burgundies and his ability to "sniff out a fake" bottle. He also made the rounds in private wine auctions, both buying bottles for and selling bottles from his collection.

His reputation was tarnished in 2008 when 22 lots of wine (supposedly from Burgundy producer Domaine Ponsot) that Kurniawan had consigned to an Acker, Merrill, and Condit auction were withdrawn from the auction. The wines' authenticity was called into question by a collector at the auction, which prompted other collectors to question authenticity of the wines they had purchased from Kurniawan's "cellar." In 2012, the FBI searched his home and found boxes of materials (hundreds of bottles, corks, labels, seals, etc.) that looked like the raw materials for making rare wine. Kurniawan used his sophisticated palate to mix low-cost wines to mimic the tastes, smells, and experience of drinking a rare wine. He then poured the blended wines into bottles and labeled and sealed them. In 2013, a federal jury pronounced him guilty of fraud for selling more than $1.3 million of counterfeited wines, and in 2014 he was sentenced to 10 years in prison.

What are the implications of the Rudy Kurniawan case? Unfortunately, the world's most sought-after wines are also the wines most likely to be counterfeited, which has led to a drop in market value. It has also created a need for technology that can help deter customers from purchasing fake wine.

In 2014, INSIDE Secure (a company that provides embedded security and protection for mobile devices) and Selinko (an object identification and traceability company) joined forces to produce CapSeal—a chip that can be embedded where the cork meets the bottle to ensure authenticity of a wine. A tamper-proof capsule with an embedded chip connected to an antenna is inserted on the neck of the bottle, just above the cork. Resellers, agents, and consumers can check whether the capsule on the bottle has been tampered with and the cork has been removed. To prevent anyone from refilling a bottle, the tag is mechanically deactivated when removing the capsule from the bottle. This would block someone from refilling an empty wine bottle from a prestigious producer with less-expensive wine and re-corking it for sale. The technology is made to work with bottles of wine that have already been sealed—so there is no need for a producer to rebottle wine.

Other forms of technology, like detecting the gamma rays in a bottle of wine, are being used to "sniff out" fraudulent wines. Still other "inspectors" use more traditional forensic tools—magnifying glasses, razor blades, blue lights—to search for clues as to the authenticity of a bottle.

Kurniawan's crime has certainly weakened the bond of trust between buyers and sellers of old and rare vintages. The provenance trail is even more critical now for any traded fine wine. As the wine has gotten more expensive, more people have taken interest in copying it, and wine fraud is rampant, yet the auction houses and retail sellers that claim to be experts aren't doing the kind of due diligence that's required.[24]

KEY TAKEAWAYS

- The rising demand for sustainable raw materials has increased the call for retailers, manufacturers, commodities traders, and producers to certify that commodities are extracted or grown according to certain standards, including fair treatment of workers and reducing exposure to unsafe and unhealthy conditions.
- Issues of worker safety and fair treatment are not just limited to developing countries that have weak labor laws or lax enforcement. Even in the United States regulators are slow to enact changes and improvements to rules regarding proper use of pesticides and adequate protections for workers.

- Employee-related issues in the wine industry can lead to business success. Good social practices can have a positive influence on financial performance, and enhanced worker safety programs can improve economic performance.
- CSR has become an integral element of the alcohol industry's self-representation and image, although most efforts are focused on preventing underage drinking, drinking responsibly, and in moderation.
- At the regional level, organizations are engaging with social responsibility in a number of exciting ways. Bonded by their geography, participating vineyards and wineries are also joining together for greater social involvement, addressing community needs and concerns.
- Truth in advertising has taken on an entirely new meaning in the wine world. From authentic sustainable or organic designations, to more details about a vintage and how a given wine rates among its competition, consumers need accurate and honest information to be able to make informed purchase decisions.
- Growers, marketers, distributors, and in-store sales staff must all recognize that ethics and trust are critical to the wine industry's reputation and individual wineries' brands.

CHAPTER 6 REFERENCES

1. Edelman. *2015 Edelman Trust Barometer: Trust and Innovation*. Available online: http://www.edelman.com/2015-edelman-trust-barometer-2/trust-and-innovation-edelman-trust-barometer/ (Accessed 26 August 2015.)
2. Waddock, S., and Graves, S. "The Corporate Social Performance-Financial Performance Link." *Strategic Management Journal* Volume 18. Issue 4 (1997): pages 303–319. Available online:
3. http://onlinelibrary.wiley.com/doi/10.1002/(SICI)1097-0266(199704)18:4%3C303::AID-SMJ869%3E3.0.CO;2-G/abstract (Accessed 26 August 2015.)
4. Brown, K. "Workplace Safety: A Call for Research." *Journal of Operations Management* Volume 14. Issue 2 (1996): pages 157–171. Available online: http://www.researchgate.net/publication/256523835_Workplace_safety_A_call_for_research (Accessed 26 August 2015.)
5. Thach, L. "Social Sustainability in the Wine Community." *Wine Business Monthly.* July 2002. Available online: http://www.winebusiness.com/wbm/?go=getArticleSignIn&dataId=17442 (Accessed 26 August 2015.)
6. Sustainable Agriculture Initiative Platform. Social Objectives. Available online: http://www.saiplatform.org/sustainable-agriculture/social (Accessed 26 August 2015.)
7. Food Alliance. *Sustainability for Food and Agriculture*. Available online http://foodalliance.org/ (Accessed 26 August 2015.)
8. Food Alliance. *Guiding Principles.* Available online: http://foodalliance.org/about/excellence (Accessed 26 August 2015.)
9. Ethical Trading Initiative. *South African Wine Project*. Available online: http://www.ethicaltrade.org/in-action/programmes/south-africa-wine-project (Accessed 26 August 2015.)

10. Fair Trade USA. Available online: http://fairtradeusa.org/ (Accessed 26 August 2015.)

11. Ibid.

12. Wine and Agricultural Ethical Trade Association. Available online: http://www.wieta.org .za/ (Accessed 26 August 2015.)

13. Wine and Agricultural Ethical Trade Association. *WIETA Code.* Available online: http:// www.wieta.org.za/wieta_code.php (Accessed 26 August 2015.)

14. MercoPress. *Chilean Vineyards Face Shortage of Field Workers; Most Migrate to Construction.* 18 February 2011. Available online: http://en.mercopress.com/2011/02/18/chilean -vineyards-face-shortage-of-field-workers-most-migrate-to-construction (Accessed 26 August 2015.)

15. Reeves, M. et al. *Fields of Poison: California Farmworkers and Pesticides.* Available online: http://www.slideshare.net/Z3P/x3a73?utm_source=slideshow02&utm_medium=ssemail &utm_campaign=share_slideshow (Accessed 26 August 2015.)

16. Farmworker Justice. *Environmental Health.* Available online: http://www.farmworkerjustice .org/content/environmental-health (Accessed 26 August 2015.)

17. Beyond Pesticides. *Judge Questions California Approval of Methyl Iodide.* 20 January 2012. Available online: http://www.beyondpesticides.org/dailynewsblog/?p=6665 (Accessed 26 August 2015.)

18. Smith, S. *California Unveils Strictest Rules on Pesticide.* Phys.org. Available online: http:// phys.org/news/2015-01-california-unveils-strict-pesticide.html (Accessed online 26 August 2015.)

19. Wine Business. *Busting Myths About Napa Valley's Farmworkers.* 18 June 2014. Available online: http://www.winebusiness.com/blog/?go=getBlogEntry&dataId=134548 (Accessed 26 August 2015.)

20. Gray, B. "Vineyard Needs Prompt Action Over Illegal Workers." *Wine Searcher.* Available online: http://www.wine-searcher.com/m/2015/07/vineyard-needs-prompt-action-over -illegal-workers (Accessed 26 August 2015.)

21. BCG Perspectives, Boston Consulting Group, "Rethinking Corporate Philanthropy," by Max Silverstein, Priya Chandran, and Sarah Cairns-Smith, May 9, 2013.

22. Lucero, A. "CSR in Bodega Chandon. Committed to Sustainable Development." *Wines of Argentina.* Available online: http://blog.winesofargentina.com/la-rse-en-bodega-chandon- apostando-al-desarrollo-sustentable/ (Accessed 26 August 2015.)

23. Saliba, A. et al. "Consumer Demand for Low Alcohol Wine in an Australian Sample" *International Journal of Wine Research* Volume 2013. Issue 5 (2013); pages 1–8. Available online: http://www.dovepress.com/consumer-demand-for-low-alcohol-wine-in-an-australian -sample-peer-reviewed-article-IJWR (Accessed 26 August 2015.)

24. Robinson, J. *The Ethics of Wine Writing.* Available online: http://www.jancisrobinson.com /about/ethics-of-wine-writing (Accessed 26 August 2015.)

25. Decanter Staff. *Has Rudy Kurniawan Damaged Trust in the Fine Wine Market?* 9 September 2014. Available online: http://www.decanter.com/people-and-places/wine-articles/587467 (Accessed 26 August 2015.)

CHAPTER 7

MEASURING SUSTAINABILITY AND CARBON EMISSIONS

Life Cycle Analysis and the Wine Value Chain

As consumers have grown more socially and environmentally conscious, especially as it concerns products that they buy, many industries have begun to consider their carbon footprint, or the impact that an industry's emissions have on the environment and the climate. Furthermore, companies look for ways to measure their overall environmental impact, with energy consumption impacts being a critical element. Wine is no exception; in the last few years, many wine companies and the industry more generally have wondered: what exactly is the carbon footprint of the wine industry? What are the carbon-intensive parts of wine's life cycle? And how are leading wine companies reducing their footprint? This chapter will endeavor to answer these questions. Additionally, it will provide some case studies of impact measurement in the wine industry, as well as explore some of the best practices in decreasing the greenhouse gas (GHG) emissions of the business.

Many of the books and academic papers written about sustainability in the wine industry involve some kind of tracking of the carbon impact of a bottle of wine. Yet it is actually very difficult to track every kilogram of carbon emitted from the growing of grapes to the disposal of a wine bottle. This kind of complete, systematic tracking of a product's environmental impacts is known as life cycle analysis (LCA).

Life cycle analysis (also known as life cycle assessment) is one environmental management tool that the wine industry could utilize to manage and improve its environmental performance. LCA assesses the environmental burdens of a product throughout its life cycle, from the extraction of raw materials, through to the manufacture, distribution and use, and on to end-of-life disposal. LCA can assist in identifying opportunities to improve the environmental performance of products at various points in their life cycle. It is used in a range of industries and is widely recognized as one of the most sophisticated and comprehensive environmental assessment methods available.

LCAs not only quantify metrics like the carbon footprint of a product but also take into account materials used, from minerals to lumber to water and everything in between. As the name implies, LCAs try to account for every stage of the life cycle of the product, which is sometimes referred to as "cradle to grave" analysis. A life cycle analysis typically extends from the extraction and processing of raw materials, through to product manufacture, distribution, consumption, and product end-of-life and is widely regarded as one of the leading tools available to assess the environmental impact of a product.

Environmental impact analyses typically fall under three overarching categories: 1) impacts on human health, 2) the natural environment, and 3) resource depletion. Covering the whole product life cycle in the analysis helps ensure that environmental improvements do not result in a shifting of burdens—either to other life cycle stages, from one geographic area to another, or from one environmental medium to another.

While this chapter will mainly focus on the carbon impact of the wine industry, LCAs more broadly have been productive for wineries around the world in analyzing their overall environmental footprint. For example, Yalumba, Australia's oldest family-owned winery, used LCA to reduce its use of energy, water, and packaging. Yalumba has made its own operations more sustainable by setting aside over 135 acres of land for conservation and carbon emission offsets. In addition, it runs an energy-efficient winery that also includes a wastewater management program.

However, improving a company's sustainability goes far beyond improving its own operations, and LCAs help companies do just that. By engaging with its stakeholders, who include its suppliers, its distributors, and its customers, Yalumba was able to identify other areas in its wine's life cycle where they could reduce impact. For instance, Yalumba has reduced its solid waste by ensuring that 98 percent of its packaging either comes from recycled materials or is in itself recyclable. These kinds of improvements require communication with suppliers (in this case, the packaging suppliers) as well as communications with consumers so that consumers know how to most sustainably dispose of packaging. In other words, LCAs help companies in any echelon of a value chain understand the full "cradle-to-grave" cycle of the product in order to assess areas for improvement.

Certain phases of a product's life cycle may contribute disproportionately to the total sum of its environmental impacts and may vary depending on the specific impacts of interest. Life cycle "hot spots" (i.e., the parts of the life cycle with the most environmental impact) differ among various production systems. Farming is often cited as the most important life cycle stage for certain crops. The agricultural production stage is responsible for a relatively large share of the environmental impacts of fruit and vegetables, driven in particular by the use of pesticides and fertilizers. In addition to crop production, the manufacture of packaging is typically a very important life cycle phase for products packaged in glass, such as beer and wine.

This chapter strives to use an LCA framework to quantify the carbon impact of the wine industry. Though accounting for many of the subtleties of the industry can be difficult, walking through each stage of the process does bring to light where the most carbon-intensive stages of the life cycle are.

LIFE CYCLE ENVIRONMENTAL IMPACTS OF WINE

The winemaking process involves a number of quite different processes that contribute to climate change, which will in turn directly affect the industry itself, such as through changes in precipitation, occurrence of droughts, and higher temperatures. Given that many wine grape varieties can only be grown across a fairly narrow range of climates for optimum quality and production, the wine industry is therefore at a greater potential risk from climate change than many other broad-based crops. Viticulture (grape growing), viniculture (making wine), manufacturing glass bottles, various transportation links, refrigeration, and recycling of glass bottles are processes within wine's life cycle that necessitate the transformation of materials and energy and thus result in emissions that contribute to various environmental impacts. Formalized life cycle assessments of wine, as well as other analyses that have employed similar thinking and approach, provide insight into the relative importance of each of these phases as well as the nature of the associated environmental impacts. In each of the following discussions the functional unit was one 750ml bottle of wine.

CALCULATING CARBON FOOTPRINTS

LCA can be used to measure the life cycle GHG emissions of a product or service, a process also known as carbon foot printing.

Conducting a carbon audit for an industry can be a daunting task when we see how many effects we need to take into account to quantify it. Stakeholders and auditors often wonder how broad the considerations of a carbon footprint calculation should be. If they were calculating the carbon impact of a specific company, they would quantify on-site electricity use, for example, but what about the emissions of their suppliers? In other words, just how much carbon is each stage in the production line responsible for?

To help answer this question, the World Resources Institute (WRI) delegated three "scopes" of consideration for GHG emissions to help auditors organize and prioritize GHG emissions tracking. We can think of them as concentric circles of impact. Scope 1 includes direct GHG emissions, which are emissions from items controlled by or operated by the company in question. This scope would include onsite electricity and heating, chemical and physical processes, the fossil fuel use of operating equipment like tractors or forklifts, and emissions from leaks and spills. Scope 2 emissions widen the circle of influence, including the production of electricity from facilities not owned by the company. Scope 3 emissions, indirect GHG emissions, are often referred to as "embodied carbon." These include emissions of non-company equipment that creates a sellable wine product. This category includes transport activities, non-Scope 2 electricity, extraction and production of purchased materials (like bottles or wine barrels), and impacts from waste disposal. [1]

As can be seen from the scopes method, using a company as the locus of carbon footprint calculation can make it difficult to draw the line of where one's carbon emissions end. In this chapter, we will quantify the carbon impact of the wine industry as a whole so as to explore the carbon impacts of as many echelons of production as possible. The scopes method, however, does help the auditor have a framework to think about where emissions might come from at each stage in wine's life cycle.

There exist many carbon calculators and calculation frameworks that have been specified, by the International Organization for Standardization (ISO) standards 14044 and 14040, relevant to conducting a corporate LCA. The International Organization of Vine and Wine (OIV) has developed a carbon calculator specifically for viticulture and viniculture: General Principles of the OIV Greenhouse Gas Accounting Protocol for the Vine and Wine Sector (GHGAP) that is adaptable to each country's situation.

The OIV GHGAP includes enterprise level calculations and also product level calculations. The principles are very specific about what should be identified and measured, and what is excluded at the enterprise level and the product level.

To help wineries in the development of emission policies and business goals, the OIV GHGAP has defined three Scopes:

Scope 1—Direct Greenhouse Gas Emissions

Direct Greenhouse Gas emissions, or Scope 1 emissions, occur from items directly controlled by and owned by the company. This "control" means that the company has the power to directly influence the GHG emissions of the activity.

For the vine and wine industry, typical examples of Scope 1 emissions include the following:

- onsite fuel use (e.g., tractors, forklifts, etc.)
- onsite waste disposal (anaerobic digestion or incineration)
- gas recharge of cooling systems (refrigeration, air conditioners etc.)
- CO_2 used in the winemaking process (dry ice, blanket tanks, pipe flushing's etc.)
- emissions related to the production of purchased grapes or must when, by contract, the winery directly controls the production system of the purchased grapes or must
- emissions of N_2O and CH_4 resulting from the nitrogen fertilization of the soil

The majority of the Scope 1 carbon footprint is typically fuel use.

Scope 2—Purchased Power Utility

Many companies are heavily reliant on electrical power. The emissions that occur from the production of electricity in facilities not owned by the company are categorized as Scope 2 emissions. They are regarded as indirect emissions because they occur in equipment owned by another company, generally a power station. Scope 2 also includes emissions generated from purchased steam or heat, but this has not been considered as important for the vine and wine industry.

Purchased electricity is separated from other indirect GHG emissions as electricity generation is considered to significantly contribute to global warming. For many organizations, purchased electricity is the largest component of GHG emissions and a necessary component of GHG management strategies.

Scope 3—Indirect Greenhouse Gas Emissions

For the vine and wine industry, emissions categorized as Scope 3 are emissions that occur as a consequence of producing a finished saleable viniculture and viticulture product, emitted from equipment or plant owned and controlled by another company, but on which the enterprise retains an indirect control.

By definition, the classification of Scope 3 is dependent upon the operational boundary or ownership. For example, if a vineyard owns a harvester and uses it to harvest grapes, then the emissions generated from the harvester engine will be classified as Scope 1. If the vineyard does not own a harvester and instead utilizes a harvesting contractor, rents or leases it, then the emissions from the contract harvester will be classified as Scope 3.

Scope 3, for instance, comprises emissions from activities that are part of the core process of the enterprise but have been outsourced to other companies.[2]

The basic production chain of wine includes grape growing, winemaking, packaging and distribution, consumer use, and waste disposal, as pictured in the preceding graph. This chapter will explore the source of carbon impacts at each of these stages, as well as describe best practices in the industry for carbon reduction and make suggestions for further improvements.

In terms of life cycle stages for the wine industry, most studies begin at the grape growing stage, and continue through to the winemaking, packaging, and distribution to consumer stages (while others start with soil cultivation and planting of root stocks and extend the life cycle through to the end of life stage, i.e., consumption/use of the product and packaging).[3]

Many assessments include the manufacture of agrichemicals in the analysis while the manufacture and distribution of winemaking additives (such as bentonite, enzymes, and yeasts) tend to be excluded from analysis. The commonly stated reason for this exclusion is a lack of available data.[4]

In general, most studies identify either packaging or distribution to consumer as the life cycle stages of wine with the greatest environmental impact. These two

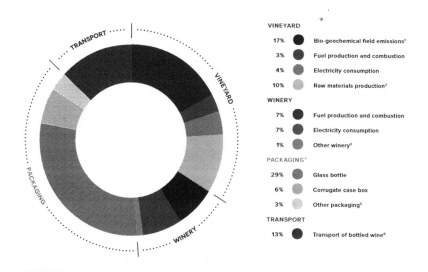

VINEYARD

17% ● Bio-geochemical field emissions[1]

3% ● Fuel production and combustion

4% ● Electricity consumption

10% ○ Raw materials production[2]

WINERY

7% ● Fuel production and combustion

7% ● Electricity consumption

1% ● Other winery[3]

PACKAGING[4]

29% ● Glass bottle

6% ● Corrugate case box

3% ○ Other packaging[5]

TRANSPORT

13% ● Transport of bottled wine[6]

[1] Footprint associated with greenhouse gas emissions that are a result of natural bio-geochemical processes and impacted by local climate, soil conditions, and management practices like the application of nitrogen fertilizers.
[2] Footprint associated with the manufacture and shipment of materials used at a vineyard such as fertilizers and pesticides.
[3] Footprint associated with the transport of grapes from vineyard to winery, raw material production, refrigerant losses, and manufacturing waste treatment.
[4] Footprint associated with the manufacture and shipment of materials used for packaging wine.
[5] Footprint associated with the natural cork closure with aluminum foil and treatment of waste at packaging manufacture.
[6] Footprint associated with fuel production and combustion in trucks and trains based on typical distances for the industry when shipping in the United States to retail facilities.

Caption: Relative impacts for the carbon footprint of packaged wine, cradle-to-retail gate. Credit: CSWA

Kruger, Barry. *A Logistics System for the RSA Wine Industry.* Available online: http://www.wineland.co.za/technical/a-logistics-system-for-the-rsa-wine-industry (Accessed 18 August 2015.)

stages are linked, as the impact from transportation is largely related to the type of packaging used, as will be discussed later in the chapter. This is because heavier glass bottles require more energy to transport than either shipping in bulk, or using plastic or lightweight bottles. The impacts of packaging are largely related to production of the glass bottle, which makes a significant contribution to energy consumption and global warming potential (GWP).

Many of the calculations detailed in this chapter will reference carbon emissions in grams or kilograms of CO_2 released. While these emissions calculations might seem arbitrary and difficult to contextualize, the more GHG-intensive parts of the process will reveal themselves as emissions are quantified at each stage. To help give these numbers some meaning, consider the following benchmark. Estimates of the amount of CO_2 released from burning a gallon of gasoline range from 8.88kg, or 8,8887g per gallon to 10.5kg, or 10,500g, per gallon.[5]

Agricultural Stages of Production

During the process of growing grapes, a fair amount of carbon is released due to fossil fuel consumption of agricultural machinery. Tractor use and irrigation both use significant amounts of fuel, a carbon expense that probably makes up the largest chunk of GHG emissions in the vineyard. Compared to other crops, grapes require higher fuel intensity. One study estimates that growing 1 ton of grapes requires 34 gallons of fuel, as compared to about 6 gallons required per ton of corn.[6] For every gallon of fuel used, between 8.88 kg and 10.5 kg of CO_2 are released into the atmosphere.[7] This calculation translates to about half a gallon of fuel used in the agricultural stage to create a case of wine, producing up to 5.25 kg of CO_2 released per case of wine.

Because of the natural focus on fossil fuels in the vineyard, one might easily overlook one of the other culprits of emissions in the field: fertilizers and tillage. The grape growing stage is also significant, largely due to the manufacture and application of agrichemicals. The application of nitrogen and phosphorus fertilizers also makes notable contributions to energy production and acidification potential.[8]

Nitrogen fertilizers are almost always used in conventional agriculture, and they produce another greenhouse gas called nitrous oxide, which is extraordinarily potent. In fact, several estimates have found that nitrous oxide has 300 times the greenhouse gas potential as carbon dioxide.[9] In addition, the tillage of soil releases a fair amount of CO_2 that otherwise would have been sequestered in the soil. While often in agricultural production the release of methane also needs to be taken into account, methane emissions seem to be negligible for grape production.[10] (There may be some amount of methane released in biodynamic vineyards that have their own cows on site for manure and other preparations, but that is probably not significant enough for discussion here.) In any case, understanding the carbon changes that occur during production demonstrates the importance of conducting a comprehensive LCA. If we only calculated carbon emissions from, say, once the grapes were already harvested, many of the carbon impacts of wine production would be ignored.

One of the most common suggestions for cutting net carbon emissions in the agricultural phases of production involves carbon sequestration. Since plants take in CO_2 to undergo photosynthesis, more plants theoretically means more carbon taken out of the air. Some recommend cover cropping. Adding different plants such as grasses or other native species in between rows of vines gives more plant mass to take in CO_2. Cover cropping has other benefits as well, such as preventing soil erosion and absorbing excess water.

Using biomass for sequestration, though, can have its drawbacks. More plants might imply greater use of fertilizers, which, as mentioned, can have a *more* damaging GHG effect than carbon dioxide.[11] Furthermore, using cover crops particularly involves tillage, which as discussed, can release a not insignificant amount of carbon as well. Though not a GHG concern, more biomass also requires more water, which in water-thirsty California, for example, may not be worth the trade-off. In short, the biological variables to calculate whether carbon sequestration is ultimately carbon-negative can be trickier than they look at first blush. It appears that, if biomass is going to be used as a sequestration method, it is best done through the use of more "permanent" vine structures, such as roots and cordons, which require more carbon intake than just vines and leaves.[12]

Using biomass or biogas as energy does not have to require growing plants exclusively for that use, however. Backsberg Estate in South Africa has installed a biomass boiler, which runs on waste wood chips. Thus, Backsberg not only uses a lower-carbon fuel for this boiler, which is connected to a heat exchange chiller that creates refrigeration, but also reduces its waste by using excess plant matter as fuel. Backsberg's plant waste-to-energy system shows that biomass is often an efficient way to reduce carbon impacts in agricultural industries since plant waste matter is a guaranteed by-product.[13]

Cover cropping can also be a useful tool if native species are used that will grow well on their own and thus won't require use of fertilizers and pesticides. Even so, the California Sustainable Winegrowing Alliance (CSWA) study "California Vineyard Greenhouse Gas Emissions" recommends further research be done about carbon sequestration at the agricultural level of the wine industry. It seems that in certain locations and when handled well, cover cropping can be both a useful vineyard tool and a way to sequester carbon.

One area of contention is the question of whether carbon sequestered from the vines should be counted as an environmental credit. However, at this point in time it is generally accepted that the amount of carbon sequestered by the vines is approximately the same as the carbon released during fermentation, and the exclusion of sequestration and fermentation is commonly seen in wine LCA studies.[14]

It is very difficult to estimate the carbon footprint of the agricultural stages of wine production since agricultural practices vary so widely. Fossil fuel use in the vineyard contributes heavily to emissions in some places, but in others, growers have managed to cut fossil fuel use tremendously. For example, Yealands Estate in Marlborough, New Zealand, uses Babydoll sheep, an endangered breed of miniature sheep that cannot reach the grapevines, to graze between rows of vines. Yealands thus cuts down on the use of mowing and tractor machinery, avoiding a great deal of fossil fuel use. In other words, agricultural practices *can* be carbon-intensive in the wine industry, but only because of the ways humans choose to mechanize agriculture. Growing grapes should not be inherently a carbon-intensive process; rather, it should actually be carbon-negative. In any case, many wineries have found ways to make their emissions in the vineyard negligible. Cutting down on the use of fossil fuels by avoiding machinery in the field can slash carbon emissions associated with each bottle of wine.

The Winery

Wineries face several energy efficiency challenges similar to many other production facilities. They consume electricity and fuel for various operational reasons like most buildings, and wineries also use energy for actual harvesting, refrigeration, and other

Yealands Estate, Marlborough, New Zealand

Credit: SWNZ

production needs. Wine production is an energy-intensive business, as the wine needs to be warmed (prior to fermentation and bottling) and cooled (for storage and stabilization).

In the winery, the fermentation process naturally has its carbon footprint as well. Fermentation of grapes involves chemical reactions between the natural glucose in the grapes and yeast that exists on the grapes and the yeast that winemakers add. The chemical products that result are alcohol, of course, but also carbon dioxide. Fermentation of a case of wine creates about 8.4kg of CO_2. This is a notable amount considering that the estimated fossil fuel use in the vineyard contributes about 5.25kg of CO_2 per case on average.

However, it is important to understand the chemical processes at play in winemaking in order to understand that the winemaking process essentially involves the release of some carbon dioxide. These emissions are unavoidable since they are integral to the chemical reactions that produce alcohol. Reducing fossil fuel use in the field may be doable, but reducing CO_2 by-products from wine fermentation is not really possible. As such, wineries choose to *offset* these emissions with renewable energy credits (RECs) or carbon sequestration. Wineries take this unavoidable CO_2 into consideration in their carbon "budget," understanding that other areas in their operations will allow them to ultimately offset that carbon.

There are several opportunities for wineries to reduce energy consumption. There are numerous examples of wineries that have installed solar panels and green roofs to be more energy efficient and reduce energy consumption. A few are LEED certified: Stoller Family Estate, located in Oregon's Dundee Hills area, became the first Gold LEED-certified winery in the nation back in 2006. HALL Wines was the first winery in California to receive LEED Gold Certification for its Napa Valley St. Helena winery. In Virginia, LEED Platinum certification was awarded to the Cooper Vineyards in Louisa, Virginia, for its newly built tasting room, and the first for a winery on the East Coast of the United States.

LEED is an internationally recognized certification system that measures how well a building or community performs across all the metrics that matter most: energy savings, water efficiency, CO2 emissions reduction, improved indoor environmental quality, and stewardship of resources and sensitivity to their impacts. Developed by the U.S. Green Building Council (USGBC), LEED provides building owners and operators a concise framework for identifying and implementing practical and measurable green building design, construction, operations, and maintenance solutions. It certifies several levels of environmental accomplishment in buildings from LEED Silver to Gold to Platinum.

Case studies at the end of this chapter describe several best practices in energy reduction.

THE SURPRISING EFFECTS OF WINE PACKAGING

When people consider the carbon impact of the wine industry, they often think of the carbon footprint of transport and maybe also of agriculture. What many don't think of more immediately is the surprisingly large carbon impact of wine's packaging. While glass is the primary packaging material for wine, we also have to consider the carbon impact of corks, paper, and oak wine barrels, as well as other materials.

Glass or Plastic?

Some estimates find that glass alone takes up half the carbon load of the wine industry.[15] Glass is not only heavy and thus carbon-intensive to transport, but it also requires significant energy to produce in the first place. Objectively, we package wine strangely: in the average 750 ml bottle, only 40 percent of the volume of the final product is actually wine, and the rest is glass.[16] However, glass has been a great packaging material for the wine industry for a reason. Seventy percent of a glass bottle is made from silicon dioxide, which is not only cheap but is readily and abundantly available around the world. Despite what one may think, glass bottles actually hold up relatively well during transport, and so very few bottles reach their destination broken or spilled. Glass has also become the standard for wine products and gives the consumer the sense that the product is more expensive than wines in plastic bottles or in boxes.

Plastic bottles offer a few benefits as a wine container. First of all, plastic is, of course, a great deal lighter than glass bottles, with (empty) plastic wine bottles weighing in around 0.10 pound and glass bottles weighing about 1 pound. Therefore, plastic bottles are less carbon-intensive to ship. Secondly, PET is shatterproof; fewer plastic bottles are damaged during shipping than glass bottles. Yealands Estate in New Zealand has contended that its Peter Yealands wine has 54 percent less carbon footprint than a standard wine since it is packaged in a 100 percent recyclable PET which is 89 percent lighter than standard glass bottles.

In a study by Allied Development Corporation, PET had lower GHG emissions to produce at 732.5 lbs./1,000 units versus 1,395.8 lbs./1,000 units for the glass bottle (90 percent more than the PET bottle). PET had lower energy consumption to produce at 7,132 MJ/1,000 units versus 12,480 MJ/1,000 units for the glass bottle (75 percent more than the PET bottle).

PET is an environmentally responsible packaging choice for wine. PET offers shape benefits and similar line speed efficiencies compared to glass. Increased recycle rates, and the inclusion of PCR (post-consumer recyclate) content into new bottles would help lower PET's current environmental footprint. PET does provide increased package robustness versus the glass bottle as well. Depending upon spoilage rates due to package failure, this can be a significant cost.

PET Benefits:
- Significant weight savings over glass (shipping cost advantages).
- Shape Flexibility—can assume traditional bottle shapes.
- Rapid ramp-up time to set up preform-blowing production cells.
- Robustness of PET package versus glass.
- No major retooling requirements to run PET on glass-filling lines.[17]

Comparing the Total Environmental Impact of Wine Packages in North America

As a study by the UK-based Wrap.org demonstrates, there are many facets that go into the carbon impact of both glass and plastic wine bottles.[18] The carbon impact of course depends heavily on the weight of the bottle, percentage of recycled content, and how far the bottle is ultimately going to be transported. It is thus impossible to say decisively whether glass or plastic bottles are preferable in all cases; they certainly each have their benefits. Nevertheless, a few improvements can certainly be made in the wine industry to reduce the carbon footprint of bottle packaging.

First, location of the bottler can have a major impact on the ultimate carbon calculation for wine. Since the weight of the bottles accounts for much of the carbon footprint during transit from places like California and Australia to markets like the East Coast of the United States and to Europe, best practices include efficient bulk shipping. In other words, instead of sending wines to markets already bottled, wineries can send wine in larger shipping containers and then have the wine bottled closer to where it will ultimately be sold.[19] Some companies, like Sonoma's Laurel Glen, send wine in bulk in 23,500-liter stainless steel tanks from places like Argentina and then bottle it in California. Other companies use large plastic sacks, much like the bags on the inside of boxed wine, except much larger, called Flexitanks. For example, one study estimated that shipping wine in bulk instead of pre-bottled from Australia to European markets shaves about 164 grams of CO_2 off the footprint of each bottle, or 1968 grams of CO_2 per case of wine.[20] For reference, recall the factoid that burning a gallon of gasoline releases about 8,887 grams of CO_2, or 8.88 kg of CO_2.[21]

Second, the ultimate carbon impact is affected by the amount of recycled content in the bottle. Recycling not only reduces the amount of waste produced from a product at the end of its useful life; using recycled material in manufacturing a bottle also generally cuts down on the energy required, compared to making a product from completely virgin materials.

Glass is a fabulous material to recycle because it can be used repeatedly without its material being degraded over time; it's one of the few materials that is endlessly recyclable. PET, on the other hand, tends to degrade over time. Glass pieces that are used to make new glass products are called *cullet*, and the use of cullet saves huge amounts of energy when creating new bottles. Just how much energy is a bit hard to say: recycling of bottles depends on the amount of recycled content and the rate of recycling in the area of interest. The Wrap.org study estimates European rates of recycled glass content to be around 81 percent.[22] In the United States, 90 percent of recycled glass is used to make new containers of some sort.[23] The Glass Packaging Institute estimates that every 10 percent recycled glass content cuts down on the energy requirements of production by 2 to 3 percent, because cullet does not need to be heated to quite as high a temperature as virgin sand to be made into glass.[24]

Third, the weight of the bottle affects the energy required both to make the bottle and to transport it to retailers. Glass bottles can range in weight drastically from 300 grams to 500 grams in weight. Not surprising, heavier glass bottles are more energy-intensive to create as well as to transport. About 80 grams of CO_2 are not emitted when a 365-gram bottle is produced as compared to a 496-gram bottle.[25]

PET is less cooperative in the recycling process, not least because it tends to be recycled at a lower rate than glass and tends to degrade in the recycling process. PET is simply not viable to be made with large amounts of recycled content, partly because it is harder to recycle and also because rates of recycling for plastic are relatively low. Studies show that when the average 81 percent recycled content glass bottle is compared with the average 0 percent recycled content plastic bottle, the carbon impacts of manufacture were almost identical. In other words, the fact that the PET bottle was one-seventh of the weight of the glass bottle did not decrease the carbon impact significantly because PET is much more carbon-intensive to create than glass.[26]

It should also be noted that in terms of other greenhouse gases, such as methane and nitrous oxides (collectively referred to as NOx), PET is more climate-threatening than glass. If CO_2 equivalents for these GHGs were to be added to the calculations already considered, the total for PET would increase about 14 percent, while the total for glass would increase about 10 percent.[27]

While these calculations can certainly be daunting, the takeaway from these studies is this: the carbon impact of lightweight glass with a high-recycled content is about the same as the carbon impact of an average PET bottle. In other words, using PET as an ultra-lightweight bottle does not drastically change the carbon impact of a bottle, especially considering the relatively high recycling rates for glass and the low ones for PET. Thus, best practices for wineries looking to decrease their carbon footprint would include light weighting their glass bottles, as it will not only save on energy to produce the bottles but also to transport them. Light weighting bottles still allows the company to use glass, which as said before gives the product a more "expensive" look than plastic, which customers tend to like.

Contrary to what one might think, lightweight bottles hold up just as well during transportation and against damaging UV light as standard bottles, according to another Wrap.org publication.[28]

Boxed Wine: Not Just for the Cheap Stuff

The biggest hurdle for changing wine packaging is in consumer perception. As other alternatives to wine bottles have come onto the market, such as boxed wine or wine in cartons, American customers tend to be uncomfortable with the idea; they often assume that boxed wine means cheaper, lower-quality wine. Unfortunately, decades of pretty mediocre bag-in-box (BiB) wine has solidified that impression in consumers' minds, but the ecological and economical benefits of BiB packaging have begun to change the tides of the industry.

Boxed wine would mean much more carbon-efficient wine. Tyler Colman, author, wine educator, wine writer, and award-winning blogger, explained in a 2008 *New York Times* op-ed that "switching to wine in a box for the 97 percent of wines that are made to be consumed within a year would reduce greenhouse gas emissions by about two million tons, or the equivalent of retiring 400,000 cars." This change makes the other carbon impacts discussed so far in this chapter seem completely insignificant. The packaging-to-wine ratio would be greatly reduced, as would the weight of the packaging itself. Furthermore, it would be beneficial to the customer: wine can keep up to four weeks in an opened box, while it remains good for only a few days in an opened bottle. Packaging wine in boxes or cartons could also give wine companies a competitive advantage, as it would cut costs so significantly that companies could sell wine at a lower price.

But what of consumer perception? While the switch to boxes has certainly not happened in a big way in the United States, many mainstream and good-quality wine companies are choosing to package some—and sometimes even all—of their wines in boxes. They have designed stylish packaging that oftentimes explains the ecological benefit to customers. Wine companies have also been able to sell the BiB idea to customers by explaining that the wine, once opened, will last much longer (sometimes more than 40 days). The bag in the box does not allow extra air inside, unlike an opened bottle. Thus, BiB is particularly helpful to restaurants that often serve wine by the glass instead of by the bottle.

Don't let the Franzia image fool you: most boxed wines now, especially high-quality wines, are being sold in attractive, mid-sized boxes of about 3 liters, or about four bottles' worth, which often costs upwards of $25. But customers certainly get more wine for their dollar, since $25 for 3 liters comes out to only about $6 a bottle. Black Box Wines, for example, has built their brand on the slogan of "Award-Winning Wines at 40% Less." With chic black boxes and plenty of communications to the consumer about the quality and eco-friendliness of the wine and box, Black Box has managed to break its way into the market at an impressive profit margin. And with a fraction of the carbon emissions that wine bottled in glass or PET has, it's hard for the eco-conscious consumer to turn their nose up at BiB.

Bag-in-box wines are a global success. But in Sweden they probably beat all records. Bag-in-box wines account for 57 percent of the total amount of wine sold in Sweden, and they must maintain a high level of quality to meet the requirements of the discerning Swedish wine consumer. In Sweden, the bag-in-box format is primarily a packaging alternative for good-quality wine. Using the bag-in-box format to sell simpler, low-quality wines, as has been the case previously in the U.S. market, doesn't work.

Box wines make up half or more of the volume of wine sales in Australia, Sweden, and Norway, and a good 20 percent in the UK and also France. In the United States, the category accounts for about 18 percent of wine sales volume.[29]

One thing is certain: wine companies need to communicate the benefits of their chosen packaging options clearly, which will help American customers overcome any uneasiness about lightweight bottles, PET, and even boxed wines.

Oak, Iron, and Cork

Wooden wine barrels are typically made of French oak, which from the outset sounds as if it perpetuates deforestation. A 2007 report published by the American Association of Wine Economists, however, claims that the net carbon impact of using French oak is actually negative; the sourcing of old trees makes room for the planting of young trees in these properly managed forests. Younger trees grow quickly and take in large amounts of carbon.[30]

Wine makers use barrels for different amounts of time depending on several factors. The purpose of using oak in the first place is to add tannins and flavor from the oak to the wine, and so different vintners use different "recipes" for what kind of oak they use and how long they let the wine age in the barrel. Eventually, barrels lose their oaky potency, but the barrels are so valuable in and of themselves that they are often sold to next-tier wineries after first use for higher-priced wines.

Extreme care goes into the management of these forests, whether it is French or American oak, since the barrel business, such as the cooperage (barrel maker) Seguin Moreau based in Cognac, can only be sustainable (in the business sense of the word) when the forests are managed environmentally sustainably. An equal level of care goes into creating the wine barrels for cooperages since the barrels can have such a large effect on the wine profile. Recognizing the commitment of their winery customers who desire reductions in carbon emissions, Seguin Moreau has, since 2010, created *CarbonNeutral* barrels with a net zero carbon footprint.

Another potentially carbon-intensive aspect of the barrel can be the iron rings that help to secure the barrel staves. Some customers request 8 to 10 iron rings around

Barrels being "toasted."

Credit: Wine Institute

Initial stages of barrel production.

Credit: Wine Institute

the barrel. This is really only aesthetic; 5 to 6 rings would be sufficient for stabilizing the barrel. According to Seguin Moreau, the construction of barrels with fewer iron rings creates an opportunity to be more sustainable and reduce GHG emissions. Fewer rings require less iron—less iron ore means less energy used to mine the iron and less energy to produce the iron rings. Seguin Moreau has been encouraging wineries to add fewer iron rings. This relationship between suppliers like cooperages and wine companies further demonstrates some of the benefits of conducting an LCA, examining every aspect of the life cycle of the product to pinpoint areas at each stage of the value chain to improve.

Cork use is another good example of the negligible carbon effect achieved by carefully managed forests. While the cork is only a tiny part of the finished wine product, it can be a contentious issue: half of the world's cork comes from Portugal, where it has to be harvested carefully from valuable Montado trees in order to be a sustainable product. Montado trees are important habitats for hundreds of species in Portugal and thus need careful management.

The actual cork substance comes from the bark of this tree, which can be harvested from a single tree about every nine years and leave the rest of the tree healthy and living. Cork is a renewable resource; every year farmers go to a different part of their land to harvest, only returning to the same tree every nine years. Farmers remove bark from the same trees used by their grandfathers. The intricate process takes only a few cuts before the harvesters peel the bark away like sharpening a pencil.

If corks were causing major deforestation, they would have a much larger carbon footprint, but Montado forests have been carefully managed such that the carbon impact is negligible. The largest GHG emissions from cork use—some 78 percent—come from their transport from places like Portugal. Some companies have turned to plastic or aluminum bottle stoppers instead of corks based on cost, but real corks have actually been found to have the least overall environmental impact, particularly carbon footprint.[31]

Transporting Wine Around the World

Sending wine from the best winegrowing regions in the world—from New Zealand and Australia to Europe and the United States—requires expensive and carbon-intensive transportation methods. However, there are some clear distinctions about which methods of transportation are more environmentally friendly than others, and so it is easy to outline best practices for wine companies in reducing their footprint.

Firstly, there is a distinct hierarchy of transit types based on carbon emissions. Sending wine by air cargo is easily the most carbon-intensive way to ship wine, though some companies focus on sending custom cases of wine to customers that must be shipped overnight in order to be under strictest temperature control. The carbon impact of these transit types can be measured in CO2 per transport unit, as in CO2 per ton-mile. Air cargo clocks in at a whopping 570 grams of CO2 emitted per tonne-km.

The use of trucks and trains, used of course for the inland transit of wine, slices that by more than half. Trucks emit about 252 grams of CO2 per tonne-km (368 grams of CO2 per ton-mile), while trains only emit about 200 grams per tonne-km (292 grams of CO2 per ton-mile).[32] While trucks are the more common transit system for wine moving inland, rail transport provides a relatively clean alternative for getting wine from, say, California to the East Coast. Yet rail lines are in declining use for third-party logistics providers, such as FedEx or UPS, which are two major transporters of wine from company to consumer.[33]

By far the best shipping method, however, is just that: shipping. Sending wines by boat, while the slowest shipping method, is by far the least carbon intensive. For refrigerated boats, carbon impacts clock in around 67.1 grams of CO2 per tonne-kilometer (98 grams of CO2 per ton-mile). For unrefrigerated boats, this number falls to about 52.1 grams per tonne-kilometer (76 grams of CO2 per ton-mile).[34]

These somewhat surprising calculations demonstrate that economy of scale matters: the carbon impact has more to do with the method used for shipping rather than the pure number of miles traveled. In a report by author Tyler Colman and sustainability metrics specialist Pablo Päster, "Red, White and 'Green': The Cost of Carbon in the Global Wine Trade," they ask the reader to imagine, to this end, there is essentially a line that runs down the middle of Ohio. For states west of this imaginary line, it is most carbon-efficient to purchase West Coast wine, but east of Ohio, it is generally more carbon-efficient to purchase wine from France that was transported by ship to New Jersey and then trucked west to Chicago. This finding certainly seems unexpected considering that we often think of purchasing more "local" products as being better for the climate.

Interestingly, many studies that walk through the carbon emissions at each stage of wine's life cycle find that the most carbon-intensive part of the journey is the trip in the consumer's car. While the distance is relatively short, usually the consumer has one to six bottles of wine in the car, instead of a strategically packed truck full of cases like in previous steps of the shipping process. The result is a high CO2-to-bottle ratio in comparison with other steps of the shipping process.[35]

Furthermore, the number of points in the transportation chain can add or decrease emissions substantially. Oftentimes, third-party logistics (3PL) companies will go out of their way on the road in order to consolidate shipments at a warehouse, which usually makes the overall carbon-to-bottle ratio decrease from the added efficiency of the truck packing.[36] This finding suggests that, at least for the sake of carbon emissions, it is better for smaller wineries to use 3PL companies or a distributor to deliver wines instead of trying to transport small shipments themselves. 3PL providers make their business off of packing trains and trucks efficiently, and so the carbon impact for wine decreases with use of these companies.

In the transportation stage especially, it is worth exploring the possible impact of energy use from refrigeration. Wine should preferably be cool but not *cold*, and so energy costs for refrigeration at about 13 degrees Celsius are relatively insubstantial compared to the fuel needs for actual transit.[37] Many companies have decreased energy use from refrigeration by using temperature-regulated packaging, as well.[38] Examples of temperature-regulated packaging include gel packs, insulated shipping containers, and "ice" blankets. Compared to the carbon differences between air, truck, and boat, the emissions variances therefore between refrigerated and unrefrigerated transit methods are negligible.[39]

So What? Putting the Wine Industry in Context

Does the wine industry's footprint matter in the grand scheme of things, especially compared with some of our world's much more damaging industries? The answer, like many in this chapter, is both yes and no. The Colman-Päster report estimates that the global GHG emissions from wine production and distribution in 2001 was 5,336,600 tons, which represents about 0.08 per cent of global GHG emissions. Yes, this proportion feels insignificant, but those emissions are "equivalent to the fossil fuel combustion of roughly 1,000,000 passenger vehicles over a year." This is a benchmark for the industry; wineries should work toward emission reductions and move the needle.

To review, wine companies can integrate carbon reductions in their sustainability strategies, for themselves and influencing other players in their supply chain, in the following ways:

- Agricultural Stages
  - Sequestering carbon in the agricultural processes by using cover crops and planting trees.
  - Taking advantage of natural ecosystem services, like native plants and leaving land undeveloped, to reduce needs for fertilizers.
  - Using legumes integrated into vineyards to provide nitrogen into soil and so reduce the need for as heavy a load of nitrogen fertilizers responsible for creating nitrogen oxide (heavy GHG).
  - Reducing tillage to only what is necessary.
  - Reducing the use of engines that require fossil fuels to only what is necessary.
- Winery operations
  - Using energy-efficient lighting within winery buildings.
  - Assessing refrigeration needs and reduce to what is needed.
  - Purchasing renewable energy onsite to power facilities or buying renewable energy credits (RECs) to offset carbon that cannot be avoided.
- Bottling
  - Considering shipping wines in large containers and packaging closer to the final destination.

- Ensuring the use of partially recycled glass or plastic bottles.
- Consider selling some wines in boxes and advertising its high quality and other benefits to consumers.
- Light weighting glass bottles as much as possible.
- Using cork closures and avoiding metal or faux-cork closures.
- Distribution
  - Avoiding distribution by air unless absolutely necessary.
  - Taking advantage of the carbon efficiency of third-party logistics carriers.
  - Shipping in large tanks and with lightweight shipping packaging if possible.

CASE STUDIES: WHAT ARE LEADING WINERIES DOING?

As detailed previously in this book, wine is a uniquely positioned product for sustainability improvements, as it is one of the few agricultural products that consumers take an active interest in, regarding wine's origin, production, and story. The following case studies demonstrate that sustainability initiatives, in particular energy efficiency and renewable energy projects, can ultimately be profitable for the winery's bottom line. However, what they also demonstrate is that customers are increasingly more attracted to brands that take environmental sustainability into account and make the consumer feel more environmentally responsible when they purchase that company's product. Many of these companies have found that as they have received positive press for their sustainability initiatives, their sales increase as eco-conscious customers flock to their wines. When customers can be involved in what they feel is a positive story of sustainable winemaking, wine companies' profits benefit.

In other words, the wine industry seems to *want* to change, and it seems to stand to *benefit* from lowering its carbon emissions. Consumers have become excited about the industry's embracing carbon reductions and are beginning to select their brands this way. The wine industry might represent a small proportion of the world's carbon emissions, but these are emissions that can be reduced, powered with renewable energy, or offset with renewable energy credits.

A good deal of the preceding analysis might make greenhouse gas reduction seem difficult. In all fairness, many stages of wine's life cycle are difficult for wine companies to control. Many might not have a say about how their 3PL providers handle their carbon emissions, or what the embodied carbon of their packaging is, and even less control over how their consumers choose carbon-efficient wines and dispose of them in the best way possible. The case studies below show how some of the world's wineries are taking action on each of those energy choices to reduce their footprint and describe how some of the leaders in the wine industry are experiencing success in their carbon-reduction initiatives.

Jackson Family Wines (California, U.S.)

In 1974, Jess Jackson and his first wife, Jane Kendall Wadlow Jackson, converted a pear and walnut orchard in Lakeport, California, to a vineyard and began creating their own wine in 1982. What was then the Kendall-Jackson Wine Estates now exists under the company Jackson Family Wines (JFW), a company with wineries in six countries. Now with almost 35,000 acres of vineyards worldwide, JFW has managed to grow substantially while pursuing its passion for handcrafted fine wines that are produced sustainably. Although JFW owns labels all around the world, it continues to be a family-owned company and is Certified California Sustainable Winegrowing (CCSW). In 2013, JFW pledged $4 million to the University of California, Davis, to create the Jess S. Jackson Sustainable Winery Building in order to further viticulture studies in California.

The family makes it a priority to take a "generational approach" to growing, harvesting, and producing wine, to ensure that the land remains healthy for future generations. They have made particular effort in the three-pronged strategy of reducing energy, producing onsite energy, and REC purchases. In 2008, the company took on a comprehensive energy audit of all of its operations. From then, JFW "began to measure energy as a key performance indicator directly tied to the bottom line."[40] Understanding its energy usage as being tied to potential cost savings proved beneficial for both the company's profits and for the climate.

Starting in 2008, JFW began massive energy reductions within its operations. They began with lighting retrofits and then moved to HVAC renovations. With many retrofits throughout its wineries since 2008, JFW has reduced its energy consumption by 5.3 million kWh every year, the equivalent of taking about 3,850 cars off the road. This also resulted in a total greenhouse gas emission reduction of 51 percent company-wide, and perhaps even more excitingly, savings of $15 million for JFW.

JFW turned these savings into even more emission reductions by investing part of their savings into 7 MW worth of onsite solar installations on nine of its California wineries. This onsite production has further saved JFW $30,000 and 700,000 kWh worth of electricity purchases each year. The solar installations help power JFW's lighting, cooling, and hot water production at these facilities. As a result, about 60 percent of JFW's total electricity use is produced on its own sites.

Not content to stop there, JFW plans to invest these savings in a Tesla energy storage battery and put solar panels on all of its winery facilities. The company installed its first fleet of batteries at La Crema winery. The batteries store energy produced by the solar panels so that it can be used when the sun isn't shining. The batteries also help manage costs by predicting usage patterns based on previous years and minimizing load spikes, which keeps utility prices low and predictable. By the end of 2015, JFW expects to be the largest solar producer in the wine industry with 6.5 megawatts providing about 30 percent of its current energy needs. The company has a goal to produce 50 percent of its energy needs from solar power by 2020. Over the 8 years since JFW began purchasing solar panels, the price of panels has dropped by 80 percent, while utility costs have gone up 3 to 5 percent per year.

JFW has saved over $15 million by setting up sustainability programs that include energy efficiency improvements. Money aside, the firm has conserved a noteworthy 5,300 megawatts of energy per year since 2008 by making energy efficiency a key performance indicator (KPI). That's an impressive 51 percent reduction in greenhouse gas emissions organization-wide!

By the end of 2015, JFW became the largest solar energy producer in the wine industry with 6.5 megawatts providing about 30 percent of its current energy needs. The company has a goal to produce 50 percent of its energy needs from solar power by 2020.

For the electricity that it cannot yet produce onsite, JFW has purchased renewable energy certificates (tradable, non-tangible energy commodities that represent proof that 1 megawatt hour of electricity was generated from a renewable energy source; also called RECs) since 2009 to cover 100 percent of the company's GHG emissions. Even better, it has also purchased RECs to cover 100 percent of the emissions from its employees' homes, for a net total of 130 percent of JFW's emissions offset by RECs.

Mission Estate (New Zealand)

The "birthplace of New Zealand wine," Mission Estate traces its roots back to 1838, when a group of French missionaries established a Catholic mission in northern New Zealand. Mission Estate Winery was then founded in 1851 using traditional French winemaking techniques. Today, Mission balances its French traditional roots with the use of innovative wine practices and technologies. Mission emphasizes sustainability across not only all of its vineyards using precision viticulture techniques but also holds its suppliers to a similar standard of environmental consciousness. With several vineyards throughout Hawke's Bay as well as a location in Marlborough, Mission uses its precision viticulture and organic agriculture techniques to treat the land properly in each location while harvesting unique tastes from each area.

Mission Estate, certified sustainable by Sustainable Wines New Zealand (SWNZ), combines old world winemaking techniques with cutting edge technology.

Mission Estate has made sustainability a benchmark in their own operations in a way that both reduces greenhouse gases but also is meant to help their bottom line. Measuring their performance based on kilowatt-hours (kWh) used per liter of juice produced, they have reduced their energy use to 5 times lower than the national average and 20 times lower than that of the highest energy consuming winery.

Though Mission Estate built a new bottling and warehouse facility in 2005, their overall energy use barely increased thanks to several energy efficiency and renewable energy projects. Mission's energy use is as follows:

Lighting: 32 percent of total energy use

Bottling: 9 percent of total energy use

Vintage: 31 percent of total energy use

Cold stabilization: 5 percent

Other (mostly refrigeration): 23 percent

Mission has decreased its energy use through efficient refrigeration techniques. For example, in their brine system, insulated tanks have reduced the need for temperature regulation. Further, in their barrel storeroom, they only bring the temperature down to 15 degrees (the lower range of cool) once a week. It takes a full week for the barrels to return to 18 degrees C (the high range of recommended cooling temperature), and so they simply return the temperature down once per week and thus do not sacrifice the quality of the cooling process. While different wineries have various methods and temperatures at which they cool their wines, the point is that many companies are finding ways to reduce refrigeration energy use.

Backsberg Wine Estate (South Africa)

Located in the foothills of the Simonsberg Mountains just outside Paarl, Backsberg Wine Estate emphasizes a wine culture of "drinkability" to a wide range of wine drinkers. Backsberg produces an array of wines from its Black Label Range to its Fortified and Sweet Wines all the way to its brandy. With an emphasis on "an overall umbrella of Care," Backsberg aims to embody "care of our land, our product and the people who work for us—and care of the environment in which we find ourselves." Although this philosophy appears through its selection of wine, Backsberg added a range of wine called Tread Lightly. These wines, including a chenin blanc, a sauvignon blanc, and a merlot, are bottled in 1-liter PET bottles to reduce their environmental impact.

Backsberg Wine was the first winery in South Africa to bottle certified wine in PET, and it is the world's third-ever carbon-neutral winery (and the first in South Africa). Backsberg Wine Estate has found ways not only to reduce its carbon emissions but also offset the ones it can't reduce.

Backsberg's carbon emission reductions have come in a variety of forms, from growing biomass to use for a less carbon-intensive fuel, to using methane from burning waste to heat water. Michael Back, current owner of the Estate, has admitted proudly that these measures have saved Backsberg quite a bit of money in electricity bills. They have also achieved carbon reductions through the light weighting of many of their wine bottles. Some bottles they use simply have less glass, while for another series of wines called Tread Lightly, they have switched to ultra-light PET plastic bottles. This change has, according to Michael Back, also saved the company money in shipping costs since they export a large portion of their wines out of South Africa.

Backsberg took carbon consciousness further than many other wineries by endeavoring to become carbon-neutral. First, they worked with the firm Promethium to conduct an extensive audit of their operations' energy use. Promethium is one of several groups that help businesses and governments conduct carbon audits and then find energy reduction strategies. They also help institutions use the Carbon Disclosure Project to publish their footprint and improve it.

The Back family partnered with the South African nonprofit Food and Trees for Africa. With the help of the organization, Backsberg plants hundreds of trees throughout the nearby city of Klapmuts, where many of their employees live. They plant an equivalent number of trees that take in as much carbon dioxide as the company emits in order to offset their emissions in a natural way. Furthermore, the trees provide other benefits to Klapmuts, like lowering energy costs when planted near people's homes, since trees provide shade and insulation.

Michael Back's son, Simon, has explained that the positive press that has come from the carbon neutral certification has increased the company's sales, and customers' awareness of the effects of carbon emissions has only grown since. The combination of cost savings from carbon reductions and the good reputation Backsberg has earned through carbon neutrality has only made Backsberg Wine Estate more profitable.

KEY TAKEAWAYS

Many businesses are guilty of "greenwashing": claiming vague phrases like "natural" or "green" for their products. Life cycle analyses and carbon footprint calculations allow businesses not only to substantiate these phrases (and hopefully use even more precise language!), but also to do the following:

- Identify energy- and emission-intensive processes.
- Identify opportunities for energy and emission reductions, which can lead to reduced operational costs or carbon credits.
- Prepare for compliance with regulation.
- Enhance brand image and market advantage.
- Demonstrate continuous improvement on climate change to stakeholders.[41]

Tyler Colman (also known as Dr. Vino to readers of Wine Spectator) and Pablo Päster recommend that wine producers can minimize the carbon impact in the winery and the vineyard in the following ways:

- Cutting down forest or converting highly productive farmland to vineyard should be avoided, but converting overgrazed land may have a positive impact on restoring some biological productivity to a parcel.
- Minimize agrichemical use.

- Improve irrigation to maximize water efficiency.
- Use imported oak barrels longer, switch to local oak barrels, use oak chips, or, most sustainable of all, use no oak.
- Improve the efficiency of winery operations and use renewable energy and biofuels.
- Procure recycled-content bottles, manufactured regionally or consider non-glass packaging options.
- Reduce shipping distance and select the most efficient mode possible, which means not shipping by air.
- Once all economically feasible carbon emissions mitigation measures have been put in place, purchase verified carbon offsets for all remaining activities.[42]

CHAPTER 7 REFERENCES

1. International Wine Carbon Calculator Protocol, Version 1.2. Available online: http://www.wineinstitute.org/files/International%20Wine%20Carbon%20Calculator%20Protocol%20V1.2.pdf (Accessed on 18 August 2015.)
2. International Organization of Wine and Vine (OIV), *Resolution OIV-CST 431-2011: General Principles of the OIV Greenhouse Gas Accounting Protocol for the Vine and Wine Sector.* Available online: http://www.corkqc.com/S-mat/OIV-CST431-2011.pdf (Accessed on 18 August 2015.)
3. Aranda, et al. "Economic and Environmental Analysis of the Wine Bottle Production in Spain by Means of Life Cycle Assessment." *International Journal of Agricultural Resources, Governance and Ecology* Vol. 4. Issue 2 (2005): pages 178–191.
4. Ibid.
5. United States Environmental Protection Agency, *Clean Energy.* Available online: http://www.epa.gov/cleanenergy/energy-resources/refs.html (Accessed 18 August 2015).
6. Colman, T., and Päster, P. *Red, White and "Green": The Cost of Carbon in the Global Wine Trade.* Available online: http://www.wine-economics.org/dt_catalog/working-paper-no-9/ (Accessed 18 August 2015.)
7. Carlisle et al. *California Vineyard Greenhouse Gas Emissions: Assessment of the Available Literature and Determination of Research Needs.* California Sustainable Winegrowing Alliance. Available online: http://www.sustainablewinegrowing.org/docs/CSWA%20GHG%20Report_Final.pdf. (Accessed on 18 August 2015.)
8. Aranda, et al, "Economic and Environmental Analysis of the Wine Bottle Production in Spain by Means of Life Cycle Assessment."
9. United States Environmental Protection Agency, *Overview of Greenhouse Gases.* Available online: http://epa.gov/climatechange/ghgemissions/gases/n2o.html (Accessed on 18 August 2015.)
10. Carlisle et al. *California Vineyard Greenhouse Gas Emissions: Assessment of the Available Literature and Determination of Research Needs.* California Sustainable Winegrowing Alliance. Available online: http://www.sustainablewinegrowing.org/docs/CSWA%20GHG%20Report_Final.pdf. (Accessed on 18 August 2015.)
11. Ibid.

12. Ibid.

13. Ridley, A. *Michael Back Wins Green Lifetime Achievement Award 2015.* 22 April 2015. Available online: http://backsberg.co.za/2015/04/22/michael-back-wins-green-lifetime-achievement-award-2015/ (Accessed on 18 August 2015.)

14. Notarnicola et al. *Life Cycle Analysis of Wine Production.* Woodhead Publishing and CRC Press, Cambridge-England (2003), pp. 306–326.

15. Dugan, Barry. *Wine's Large Glass Carbon Footprint and How to Shrink It.* Available online: www.winebusiness.com/wbm/?go=getArticleSignIn&dataId=94993 (Accessed 18 August 2015.)

16. Cholette, S., and Venkat, K. "The Energy and Carbon Intensity of Wine Distribution: A Study of Logistical Options for Delivering Wine to Consumers." *The Journal of Cleaner Production* Volume 17, Issue 16 (2009): pages 1401–1413. Available online: http://www.sciencedirect.com/science/article/pii/S0959652609001838 (Accessed 18 August 2015.)

17. Case study: *Wine Packaging Performance in North America—Quantifying Environmental Impacts of Wine Packaging,* Allied Development Corporation and Husky IMS Ltd., Ontario, 2009. Available online: http://www.factsonpet.com/Articles/Case%20Study%20Wine-NA_FINAL.pdf (Accessed 18 August 2015.)

18. Wrap.org, *The Carbon Impact of Bottling Australian Wine in the UK.* Available online: http://www.wrap.org.uk/content/report-carbon-impact-bottling-australian-wine-uk-pet-and-glass-bottles (Accessed 18 August 2015.)

19. Colman, T., and Päster, P. *Red, White and "Green."*

20. Wrap.org, *The Carbon Impact of Bottling Australian Wine in the UK.*

21. U.S. Environmental Protection Agency, *Clean Energy.* Available online: http://www.epa.gov/cleanenergy/energy-resources/refs.html (Accessed 18 August 2015.)

22. Wrap.org, *The Carbon Impact of Bottling Australian Wine in the UK.*

23. U.S. Environmental Protection Agency, *Common Wastes and Materials: Glass.* Available online: http://www.epa.gov/osw/conserve/materials/glass.htmL (Accessed 18 August 2015.)

24. Glass Packaging Institute, *Glass Recycling Facts.* Available online: http://www.gpi.org/recycling/glass-recycling-facts (Accessed 18 August 2015.)

25. Wrap.org, *The Carbon Impact of Bottling Australian Wine in the UK.*

26. Ibid.

27. Ibid.

28. Ibid.

29. Patterson, T. *How Good Is That Wine Bag, Really?* Available online: http://www.winesandvines.com/sections/printout_article.cfm?article=column&content=73697%20 (Accessed 18 August 2015.)

30. Colman, T., and Päster, P. *Red, White and "Green."*

31. Amorim, Price Waterhouse Coopers. *Evaluation of the Environmental Impacts of Cork Stoppers versus Aluminum and Plastic Closures.* Available online: http://www.amorimcork.com/media/cms_page_media/228/Amorim_LCA_Final_Report.pdf (Accessed 18 August 2015.)

32. Colman, T., and Päster, P. *Red, White and "Green."*

33. Cholette, S., and Venkat, K., "The Energy and Carbon Intensity of Wine Distribution."

34. Colman, T., and Päster, P. *Red, White and "Green."*

35. Cholette, S., and Venkat, K., "The Energy and Carbon Intensity of Wine Distribution."

36. Ibid.

37. Ibid.

38. Ibid.

39. Ibid.

40. Jackson Family Wines, *The Sustainability Story at Jackson Family Wines.* Available online: http://www.jacksonfamilywines.com/sites/default/files/jfw_sustainabilitycasestudy.pdf (Accessed 18 August 2015.)

41. Promethium Carbon, *Service Offerings.* Available online: http://promethium.co.za/service -offerings/#page/carbon-footprint (Accessed 18 August 2015.)

42. Colman, T., and Päster, P. *Red, White and "Green."*

CHAPTER 8

CONCLUSION

Greener Wines and a Better World

WHERE WE ARE

Wine has been part of our culture from the beginning. As we adjust to the reality of our lives in a networked, global space, we carry with us the things and ideas that will work in that reality. As is evidenced in the previous pages of this book, there is no across-the-board understanding of how to best affect this in the wine world. Grower to grower, manufacturer to manufacturer, practices vary. Not all have adopted best practices, but most are attempting to.

Factors from the wider world of business have affected how producers distribute, and consumers access, the end product. Consolidation in retail has created giant retail operations that can have tremendous impact on wine producers. These mega-retailers have influenced sustainability standards for many of the products they stock, either through their own purchasing practices or in tandem with industry organizations like the Sustainability Consortium.

Beyond standards for sustainably grown commodities, raw material, and packaging, there is a need for accountability regarding social responsibility. Consumers are expressing increased interest in the social aspects associated with production: child labor, fair trade, the rural economy, and the conservation of cultural heritage. Ethics in the marketplace, worker health, safety, and compensation are among the criteria used to define the broader vista of corporate social responsibility. Engagement with the immediate community is also a priority for individual wineries and for the industry as a whole.

The language of greening has become commonplace in marketing and across business sectors. Growers and subsequent producers in the supply chain are feeling the benefits of sustainability. Making those benefits apparent to consumers has been a long and not entirely successful project. Efforts to communicate more clearly, create labels, and categories have in some places run ahead of initiatives to implement fully sustainable practice. When this happens, producers run the risk of "greenwashing" and harming the business, its reputation, and their products. Thus, the key to a successful green marketing strategy is seeing that actual implementation precedes communication about it.

The term sustainability has been used for some decades, while there remains considerable confusion regarding its meaning. Yet it is one of the most popular buzzwords in today's food world. Along with this come efforts to reconcile what consumers say they want with their actual buying habits.

Furthermore, the marketplace remains confused by the terminology of sustainability and believes sustainable wines might be of lesser quality than conventionally produced wines. Sustainability means balancing the needs of humanity with the needs of the living earth. It's meeting today's demands without compromising what's essential for tomorrow. Understanding this can lead to many answers but it is, essentially, a comprehensive philosophy.

International organizations and governments have commenced working on various aspects of sustainability, addressing the issues holistically. Their efforts, as well as the efforts of the industry at individual, national, or regional levels do not yet benefit from a high level of coordination. However, a common denominator is emerging: the majority of the sustainability approaches around the world, generated by industry or by organizations, recognize the importance of environmental, social, and economic aspects. On the other hand, it is also apparent that most solutions up to now have only been concerned with environmental aspects.

This diversity of approaches and interests hamper the ability of the wine sector to pool resources and knowledge to implement and promote the best solutions for the sustainability of the value chain. Lack of harmonization in approaches and priorities make the communication between various parties difficult, and, more importantly, it makes communication with policy makers and society, including wine consumers, more difficult.

Innovation in wine production that leads to the conservation of natural resources and biodiversity, and to the mitigation of climate change, can generate growth opportunities for the winegrowing sector. This ranges from the creation of new products, the development of new markets for products and services (e.g., tourism, recreational services), to actions that provide public goods (water quality, carbon sequestration, biodiversity preservation, landscape management, etc.). But to make this real in the wine world, some things must be addressed. The vineyard sector must clearly identify the economic, social, and environmental gains that can be made from the adoption of sustainable practices in order to provide winegrowers with the incentive to invest time, effort, and resources in innovative solutions and sustainability measures. The challenge to achieve sustainable competitive advantage is to balance an economically viable wine sector with environmental performance that makes a positive impact on society.

To support this process, consumers and society in general are demanding action from various industries to become more sustainable. Such demands cover the entire wine value chain, from primary production to processing, packaging, distribution, and consumption.

Sustainable wine production will not only comply with consumer demands but will also contribute to positively raising the industry's profile. Ideally, sustainable wine brands will also enhance a wine's competitive advantage on the international market.

The global wine industry must clearly articulate its aim to make a positive contribution to social, environmental, and economic well-being at the local, domestic, and international levels. Social aspects and economics of sustainability should be given equal consideration with environmental issues. Stakeholder collaboration and consultation, as distinct from competition and self-interest, is essential. Hence, training and education along with existing knowledge must be implemented and disseminated on a large scale (and new technical solutions provided to end users in a timely manner) to ensure that all players in the wine value chain have the tools to become sustainable. Likewise, consumer education is important because sustainability approaches need to be recognized, valued, and rewarded in the marketplace.

Sustainability cannot be achieved by addressing only some aspects or stages in the life cycle of a product. An integrated approach is essential to manage all the pressures and benefits from the providers of goods and services all the way to the wine consumer.

Although consumer demand for sustainability is a powerful incentive for the sector, there is a dichotomy between consumer demands and consumer action. Despite the growing interest of consumers in the availability of sustainably produced food and drink, there is slow growth in the quantity of sustainably certified food products entering the market. Some claim this is caused by difficulties in the distribution chain. But much of it is due to the fact that although there has been change in consumer attitude, this is not yet reflected in consumer behavior. For example, most consumers still tend to make purchase decisions on product price and brand rather than on aspects of sustainability.

So while there has been an overall positive change in consumer attitude toward sustainable farming and food production in general, there is also a lack of clear communication and interaction with consumers to bring actual changes in their purchasing behavior. Except for organic, sustainable agriculture and food production remains an unclear concept, and consumers do not always believe the sustainability claims made by producers. Furthermore, all the research on the topic bears out the premise that taste and quality are absolute prerequisites for consumers who purchase sustainably produced wines (as with all wine purchases).

In terms of wine specifically, the marketplace remains confused by the terminology of sustainability and believes these wines might be of lesser quality than conventionally produced wines. Essentially consumers have not valued these initiatives by purchasing sustainably produced wines in the way they have adopted Fair Trade, shade grown, and organic certification in other agricultural and consumer products. It is therefore critical for the industry to be more transparent and to undertake smart communication strategies, encourage cooperation across wine regions, and avoid proliferation of sustainability labels. The wine industry's goal should be to enlighten and educate, so consumers and critics alike will understand Certified Sustainable and the distinctions between the various farming and winemaking systems and will be able to cut through the marketing myths.

Could the wine industry also benefit from a simpler measurement and rating system that would be easier for consumers to understand? Perhaps we should adopt a new approach to wine certification and marketing and provide shoppers with an at-a-glance "Good," "Better," or "Best" rating for sustainable farming practices —an easier methodology for communicating sustainability in wine to the marketplace and to connect sustainable credentials with a quality offering. This might be accomplished by establishing a new, simple, universal global rating system for sustainability that will also be linked to quality wine ratings and help consumers make informed buying decisions. The goal of such a rating system would be to ensure and communicate a sustainability quotient in wine for consumers as well as offer an appealing wine that consumers will want to buy and drink with their friends and family.

The sustainability movement reflects an awakening of society to a growing heartfelt need—a need to care about others as well as ourselves and to care about future generations as well as our own. Likewise, those who pursue the goals of sustainability care about their impact on the planet and are motivated to do their part as individuals and companies to preserve the natural environment for future generations and for their businesses.

SUSTAINABILITY CHALLENGES

In order to be considered fully sustainable, the farming industry will need to address several challenges. The most serious of these challenges include the clearing of forest for new farmland, which makes up the largest source of man-made greenhouse gases (since 1960, an estimated one-third of the world's farmable land has been lost through erosion and other degradation) and the estimated 5.2 billion pounds of pesticides used worldwide each year. With adequate water and water quality also major issues in many parts of the developing world, such as Africa and India, the fact that agriculture uses 70 percent of the world's accessible fresh water becomes another major challenge.

Agricultural businesses must be resilient. They must adapt and grow to survive, to maintain their livelihoods, and be responsible to their stakeholders and the planet. A fully sustainable farming system is capable of maintaining its productivity and useful function indefinitely. Such systems must be resource conserving, socially supportive, commercially competitive, and environmentally sound. Over the past decades, farming methods and strategies have diversified, and practices that were once considered novel have become mainstream.

Specifically, a farm achieves sustainability goals when it can reduce inputs; use ecological pest and weed management strategies; cycle nutrients back into the soil for fertility and health; strengthen rural and urban communities; produce viable farm income; promote social values; and bring the consumer back to agriculture.

Climate change is the most vexing environmental issue of our time. The wine industry, through vineyard management and winery operations, contributes to climate change through equipment and fuel use, energy consumption, and emissions. Furthermore, global warming has already affected how and where wine grapes can be grown, now and in the future.

The growing general awareness of our carbon footprint has influenced the dialog on sustainability. As described in Chapter 7, individual wine companies have tested and adopted technologies for heat capture and resource reuse to offset energy used in their manufacturing processes. However, the wine industry's water footprint is also very significant—possibly more substantial than its carbon footprint. Drought and water crises point to the need for grape growers and viticulturists, in California especially, to adapt to dwindling water resources, comply with new rules and regulations for water usage, and negotiate water rights with residents who demand their rightful share of precious water tables.

Pesticide management is critical for maintaining soil balance, and for the health of workers and surrounding communities. Agricultural businesses, including wine producers, have a unique opportunity to contribute to the health of their immediate environment when they adopt processes that are less chemical-intensive.

Building standards that are used in other industries can also benefit wineries. Ecological and environmental sustainability can be baked into the winery's workflow in the construction phase, as builders commit to the use of eco-friendly building materials, alternative energy systems, and other standards that result in buildings with reduced carbon footprints. Other green building practices include LEED certification; green roofs; natural lighting and venting; building orientation/insulation; alternative energy such as geothermal, solar, and wind; CO_2 capture; rainwater collection; and water and materials recycling.

In many ways, the global dialog over sustainability is shaped by the acknowledgment that the business of winemaking is a large global business with the U.S. market acting as a central player, both in terms of production and consumption. In fact, three American corporations—Gallo, Constellation, and the Wine Group—which own over 300 wine brands between them, accounted for more than 52 percent of U.S. wine sales in 2014. Clearly this dispels the myth of the mom-and-pop winemaker and points out the major impact the industry can have on a sustainable future.

CHANGING WITH THE WORLD

There's more to a glass of wine than crushed grapes. Wine is a complex product. Science and society have their say about the finished product as surely as the sun and soil affect the vine, the fruit, and the wine. Each generation of vintners, winemakers, and consumers has helped create the ideal of consistently great wines. Its status as a social medium gives the wine industry a unique position for carrying the message about responsible agriculture and about businesses that succeed with a strategy that assumes responsibility for the total means of production. Wine is the most ordinary daily foodstuff, while at the same time being at the center of most of society's important and solemn occasions. It's only fitting then that as we learn to adopt practices that will better care for the land, wine could lead the way.

Wineries have always had to balance today's profits with tomorrow's viability. As the industry develops practices to preserve and replenish land, water, and other resources, the values embodied in the word *terroir* take on even greater meaning. It's easy to get the impression that green practices and standards can only have a negative impact on the bottom line. But the balance of environmental and business imperatives is at the heart of sustainable agriculture and greatly affects the bottom line through consumer awareness and decisions.

THE TRIPLE BOTTOM LINE

The wine industry is embracing sustainability in a tactical sense, using cover crops in the vineyard, lighter bottles, and other measures that create a less ecologically impactful product. But a larger strategy to fully develop the triple bottom line of financial operability, social responsibility, and environmental stewardship is still a work in progress. It is that complete picture of the vineyard's health—physical, financial, and human—that indicates the true long-term viability of a winery.

Looking at regional and national sustainability programs, it is clear there are certain best practices and standards that can be applied to any winery. At the same time, there are particularities of climate and terrain that shape each region's approach to sustainability. Wineries in the so-called "New World" tend to be on the leading edge of progress, and winemakers in Europe are learning from them. Organic and biodynamic farming have long been part of European agriculture and many wineries, but sustainability is more comprehensive and responsible for a greater range of inputs. This includes carbon impact, emissions, biodiversity, packaging, and the social needs of a winery's workers and the communities that surround it.

ORGANIC AND BIODYNAMIC VITICULTURE

As discussed in Chapter 2, the term organic is somewhat limiting. While it means that a producer is not using chemical products in the vineyards, that doesn't necessarily extend to fewer additives in the winery and it says nothing about social practices.

If you go back a decade, organic wines were a trade-off—flavor and quality had to be sacrificed for the ecological behavior of the producer. The jury is still out on whether earth-friendly practices yield better tasting wine. It is certainly possible to make both good and bad wine with organic grapes. There are an estimated 1,500–2,000 organic wine producers globally, and most of them come from the leading organic winegrowing nations Italy, France, and Spain. Vineyards are managed without the use of systemic fungicides, insecticides, herbicides, or synthetic fertilizers. And while regulations for organic certification vary in every country, any sprays or treatments used must comply with that area's organic guidelines. Biodynamic wine has been described as organic mixed in with homeopathy and mysticism and is certified by Demeter, a third-party organization. Like organic, no chemical pesticides or fertilizers are permitted. The only treatments allowed are the slew of required hand-made compost preparations, such as manure buried in cow horns over the winter, yarrow flowers wrapped in stag's bladder, and animal skulls filled with oak bark. Contemporary biodynamic practice does attempt to address the harmful effects of chemical additives—but biodynamics is after something much larger than restricting chemicals. It is an all-encompassing agricultural, philosophical, ethical, and spiritual system, focused on cultivating health rather than treating symptoms.

Many winemakers shun the mystical, "voodoo" aspect of biodynamics, but the proof is in the results. A number of hard-nosed engineering-type vintners and farmers have been persuaded to try some of the biodynamic techniques and then, noticing the improvement in their crops and wines, have become die-hard proselytizers. This increases dramatically every year. The "biodynamic effect" on the taste and quality of wine is said to add life and a suppleness not found in a non-biodynamic wine.

Although some wine enthusiasts will tell you that drinking natural wine is the best way to understand the true characteristics of the grapes, these growing methods can be a double-edged sword. When biodynamic and other "natural" vineyards encounter less than ideal growing seasons for example, those deficiencies will show up in the wine, though this would be true of any vineyard. When they have perfect growing seasons, however, the unique character of the grapes can really shine.

In some regions it's not practical for grape growers to go organic. For these reasons, some of these wine regions have created sustainability standards that incorporate more comprehensive means of stewardship. This includes reclaiming wetlands, protecting biodiversity, and reducing the carbon footprint, as well as stewardship of social justice, such as child labor, fair trade, employee safety and health, the rural economy, and the conservation of cultural heritage. At the same time, economic sustainability is the *sine-qua-non* condition to realize all the other objectives.

CERTIFIED SUSTAINABLE

Sustainable viticulture practice is probably the best of the three methodologies—organic, biodynamic, and certified sustainable—utilizing the least amount of intervention possible while managing in a way that sustains the long-term health of the vineyards as well as the economic viability of the operation. Combined with softer, less intrusive, winemaking practices, sustainable viticulture gives us the best shot at producing great wine over the long haul. A Certified Sustainable framework is the ideal approach for the wine industry, one that takes account of all the material and social inputs that contribute to the finished product, and includes a process in which a third party provides validation that a grower or farming operation is in compliance with a defined set of mandatory standards or practices. Certified Sustainable wine is the pragmatic approach to being "green" in a balanced way and examines social and economic sustainability of the entire business rather than focusing solely on the farming operation. Wine is made in a manner that minimizes its impact on the environment but maintains the right to use both manmade and natural treatments to control pests as necessary. In most instances sustainability follows a triple bottom line approach, with certification requirements that are broader than pesticide use management but includes biodiversity, water usage, energy, and social responsibility.

Sustainable approaches do not encourage or promote extensive pesticide use. The reality is that integrated pest management is critical for maintaining soil balance and for the health of workers and surrounding communities. Overuse of these chemicals is being reexamined and avoided in many locations. A growing number of lawsuits in France have begun to uncover the serious risks faced by those exposed to dangerous

Yealands Estate, Marlborough, New Zealand

chemicals who work in nonorganic vineyards. After 23 years of U.S. farms operating under outdated safety standards, the U.S. EPA announced new rules for pesticide use in agriculture in September 2015. These new rules are designed to protect farm workers and their families.

A BETTER FUTURE

The trend toward earth-friendly wines is undeniable. Though all agriculture before the Industrial Revolution was in some sense "organic," that is to say farmers used no chemicals, all the current designations are to some extent a response to gathering ecological crises.

Nowadays, with a growing conservation consciousness, most wineries and producers—even those with no formal certification—are working harder to do the right thing by reducing their carbon footprint or energy usage, protecting the natural environment, treating their employees and community with care, and implementing sensible business practices that safeguard the present and the future. Others profiled in this book are complying with seals of approval from third-party certifying organizations.

The reality of a globally active, socially, and environmentally conscious winery might not automatically square with what we imagine as a bucolic, inherently "natural" product, but winemakers who have gotten out in front in this are creating exciting products and programs for the public. As we continue to build an understanding of human impacts on the broader world, the wine industry, perhaps more than any other, can be a bellwether of an environmentally friendly, sustainable future.

AUTHOR BIOGRAPHY

S ANDRA E. TAYLOR is an internationally recognized expert on environmental sustainability, social responsibility, and sustainable agriculture. She specializes in sustainability in food and beverage industries, and consumer products companies. Taylor spent many years as an executive with global corporations, where she directed corporate responsibility strategies and programs, and she understands uniquely the connection between authentic sustainability and brand equity. Currently she is president and CEO of Sustainable Business International LLC, a consulting business she launched in 2008 to assist companies at various stages of sustainability and CSR practice.

Previously, Taylor was senior vice president of corporate responsibility (CR) at Starbucks Coffee Company in Seattle, where she led the strategic development and direction of all global CR programs, including the creation of environmentally responsible standards for sustainable production and ethical procurement of coffee, tea, and cocoa; the reduction of the environmental impact of Starbucks retail operations; and the publication of the company's award-winning CR annual report.

Additionally, Taylor has held several senior leadership positions in public affairs, international trade policy and corporate citizenship worldwide at top-tier organizations, including Eastman Kodak Company and ICI Americas Inc. (the North American arm of London-based Imperial Chemical Industries Plc.). Early in her career, she served as a legislative counsel for international trade policy in the U.S. Senate, and was a U.S. Foreign Service Officer. She speaks French. Taylor received a BA in French from Colorado Women's College and JD from Boston University School of Law.

Taylor's expertise provides innovative approaches to supply chain sustainability, strategic philanthropy, and partnerships for social investments. She has studied wine extensively for many years and completed the French Wine Scholars course in 2010. Taylor is also a recent graduate of the Ecole de Management de Bordeaux (BEM)— Kedge Business School in France, where she earned a Wine MBA.

She is a public speaker on wine and a member of the prestigious Magnum Club, based in Europe, a limited-membership, global network of leading women in the world of wine dedicated to creating a platform for finding solutions to questions of importance in the wine industry, as well as to support and inspire women in the industry.

A wine collector and wine educator, Taylor is also the founder of Fine Wine Divas of Washington, D.C., an adventure in learning for women wine enthusiasts who wish to know how to identify and express their own tastes and sensations in fine wine and learn about terroir, varietals, and the heritage and philosophies of wineries around the world.

Taylor resides in Washington, D.C.

ACKNOWLEDGEMENTS

I WISH TO THANK Savannah Brown Schuerman, my executive assistant and marketing manager at Sustainable Business International and fellow wine enthusiast, who tirelessly arranged multiple interviews, planned my travel to wine regions and researched many aspects of this book. She proved herself to be an excellent fact checker. My long time friend and great literate Susan Lynner was my first editor reviewing early drafts of each chapter for structure, and clarity as an educated wine consumer, a member of my Fine Wine Divas club, an avid reader and writer herself. I promised her some good vintages of Barolo!

In addition I had the help of two very bright smart and hardworking interns from Georgetown University – Seamus Guérin whose Spanish language skills helped me navigate through materials on Chile and Argentina's wine sustainability programs and who also conducted in-depth research on social responsibility in the wine industry. Caroline James, an avid champion of GHG reductions, conducted in-depth research for the chapter on climate change and life cycle analysis. Some sections of this chapter resulted from her early drafts. My Magnum Club colleague Erica Landin, a Swedish journalist who writes about wine, food and sustainability conducted interviews at Systembolaget, the Swedish wine retail monopoly and provided a draft of the section in the chapter on the wine trade, which describes in great detail how the monopoly buys wine and influences sustainability at origin of production and also collaborates on the buying practices of other Scandinavian retailers.

Many thanks to all those who work in vineyards, wineries, industry associations, in retail and importing who graciously offered their time for interviews, referrals to others they thought I should speak with and insights based on their experience. I am especially grateful to Hal Hinkle of Sei Querce Vineyards in Geyserville, California, who was a sounding board and advisor early in the process of developing the book concept; to Allison Jordan, Executive Director, California Sustainable Winegrowing Alliance (CSWA); Karissa Kruse, President of the Sonoma County Winegrowers; Chris Serra and Abby Cullinan of LIVE in Oregon; Philip Manson, Sustainable Wine New Zealand (SWNZ); and Patricio Parra of Wines of Chile, for time spent with me and for organizing opportunities for orientation and interaction with producers in their regions. This was most valuable!

And while I traipsed around the world visiting wineries and retailers, my dear sister, Avis Taylor-Ikeji took care of my precious dogs Augie and Bella.

Finally I am grateful to the Rockefeller Foundation for granting me a month long residency at its amazing Bellagio Center on Lake Como in Italy, a beautiful setting and motivating atmosphere for research, writing and creativity. There in the company of impressive writers, academics, environmentalists and experts on planetary health and human rights advocates, I shaped my recommendations for how to educate and motivate consumers and meet their expectations of accountability from the wine industry. My ultimate goal is to make sustainability an attribute for purchase decisions and a key element of customer loyalty, to support the efforts of growers and winemakers who are committed to sustainable production.